A Handbook of Hardy Fruits More Commonly Grown in Great Britain, Volume 1

Edward Ashdown Bunyard

A HANDBOOK OF HARDY FRUITS
MORE COMMONLY GROWN
IN GREAT BRITAIN

FURTHER VOLUMES
IN PREPARATION

—

STONE FRUITS—

Cherries, Plums, Peaches and Nectarines

BUSH FRUITS—

Currants, Raspberries, Nuts, &c.

A HANDBOOK OF
HARDY FRUITS

MORE COMMONLY GROWN IN
GREAT BRITAIN

APPLES AND PEARS

BY

EDWARD A. BUNYARD, F.L.S.

LONDON
JOHN MURRAY, ALBEMARLE STREET
1920

PREFACE.

THE present work is designed to fill the place formerly occupied by Dr. Hogg's Fruit Manual which has now been out of print for some time, and as it is more than thirty years since the last edition appeared, there are a large number of fruits which have not yet been described save in the weekly gardening Journals. In preparing the present handbook, the author has endeavoured to provide information in a popular form without any loss of accuracy, and the references given to the coloured plates in the standard Pomologies will facilitate a study of the fuller descriptions in these works.

The present volume will shortly be followed by a similar one on Stone Fruits, Peaches, Nectarines, Plums and Cherries, and completed by one containing the smaller fruits, Gooseberries, Raspberries, Currants, Nuts, etc. It was thought well to publish the Apples and Pears at once rather than wait another year or eighteen months before presenting the complete volume.

There are, of course, a large number of varieties not included in the work, but the Author has thought it unwise to include other than those which are more generally cultivated. In Pears, for instance, the list might easily have been quadrupled but without any corresponding advantage to the general reader.

5

The Author will be glad to receive from any readers any historical facts respecting fruits and also any old varieties which he has not included so that they may appear in a second edition should such be needed.

He has to thank a large number of friends, too many to mention individually, for their help in sending him grafts of various kinds and in many other ways.

E. A. BUNYARD.

Allington,
Maidstone.
September, 1920.

INTRODUCTION.

THE descriptions will be easily followed, but the following points require explanation. Following the name will be found a reference where possible to a coloured plate of the variety described. Thus Adams Pearmain is illustrated in the *Herefordshire Pomona*, Vol. I., plate 14, abbreviated as *Her. Pom.* I., 14, the volume being given in Roman, and the number of the plate in Arabic figures. For a complete list of the works referred to, see below. Next follows the name in French where it is different, abbreviation F., and in German, abbreviation G. Next follow the synonyms in brackets. The season, use and size of fruit is then given, the latter being in inches, the breadth always coming first, height second. A word of caution must be given as to the very deceptive appearance of many fruits. Thus Adams Pearmain is in appearance conical but the measurements of height and breadth are identical. It must also be noted that these dimensions are only given from average specimens and are chiefly of value in denoting the relation between height and width.

The descriptions of fruits follow the accepted methods, but those of leaves need some explanation. These always refer to the spur leaf, not that of the shoot.

7

I have chosen this as on many older trees it is often difficult to find a young shoot. After the size has been given the pose is next considered. This is a very valuable aid to recognition which has hardly received the attention it demands. The leaf may be *flat* or the edges may be folded upwards (*upfolded*) giving a V shape, it may be curved upwards as a spoon, *upcupped*, or the reverse, *downcupped*, The edge of the leaf may also be *curved* or *undulating*, or if much so, *twisted*, thus an upfolded leaf may also have its edges curved. The small teeth or serrations of the leaf may be either *serrate* or with sharp angular teeth like a saw, or they may be rounded without a point. These are *crenate*. An intermediate type occurs which is called *curved serrate*. In this the tooth is pointed, but the edges are curved and not straight as the serrate toothing.

This all refers to the pose taken by the leaf blade and its edges. The leaf further be held on its petiole in an erect position, *held up*, or if horizontally it is *outheld*. If the petiole is weak, the whole leaf hangs down it will be *down-hanging* or *lax*.

After the origin a general note is given of the value of the fruit in my experience. It will, of course, often be that a variety which is unsatisfactory with me may do well on another soil.

TABLE OF THE
WORKS REFERRED TO.

ABBREVIATION :

Arbor. Belge.   " Bulletin d'Arboriculture Belge."

Bivort.   " Album de Pomologie." A. Bivort, 4 Vols., 1847-51.

Decaisne.   " Le Jardin Fruitier." J. Decaisne, 1858-75.

Deutsh. Obstb.   " Deutsche Obstcabinet." L. E. Langethal, 1855-8.

Fl. and Pom.   " The Florist and Pomologist."

G. Mag.   " Gardener's Magazine."

Garden.   " The Garden " in publication.

Gard. Chron.   " The Gardener's Chronicle " in publication.

Her. Pom.   " Herefordshire Pomona " by Hogg and Bull, 2 Vols. London and Hereford, 1876-1885.

Ill. Hort.   " Illustration Horticole."

Journ. Pom.   " The Journal of Pomology," a periodical in publication.

Lanche.   " Deutsche Pomolgie, 6 Vols., 1882-3.

ABBREVIATION :

Lind. Pom. Brit.	" Pomologia Britannica." J. Lindley 3 Vols., 1828-30.
Ned. Boom.	" Nederlandsche Boomgard." Otto-lander and others. 2 Vols., 1868.
New York.	" The Apples of New York." S. A. Beach, 2 Vols., 1905.
Rev. Hort.	" Revue Horticole." A periodical in publication.
Ronalds.	" Pyrus Malus Brentfordiensis " by Hugh Ronalds, London, 1831.
Svensk. Pom.	" Svensk Pomona " by Olaf Eneröth, 1864-66.
Trans. R.H.S.	" The Transactions of the Royal Horticultural Society, 1815-35."
Verger.	" Le Verger." Alphonse Mas., 8 Vols., 1865-74.

KEY TO APPLES DESCRIBED
IN THIS WORK.

It is extremely difficult if not impossible to formulate a key or classification to apples. The differences of colour, size, flavour, which result from varying external conditions are perhaps greater in fruits than any other garden plants.

I have, however, attempted to make a key to the varieties described in the following pages in the hope that it will be of some service to the pomological student. Even a faulty classification is better than none and this attempt must be regarded only as a ladder which can be discarded when it has served its purpose. The arrangement of the key is purposely made as simple as possible and is based first on the external appearance and secondly on season and form.

Each variety is placed as nearly as possible in the middle of its season, thus a winter apple in season from November to February will be found in December. In shape the following rules have guided the grouping. Flat apples are those which are wider than high, round are those which are apparently equal in both dimensions. Conical are those which are higher than wide and which taper more or less to the eye; oblong those which are higher than broad but with an inclination to flatness at eye and stem. Oval fruits are those which taper equally to eye and stem, but are higher than broad. Intermediate forms are placed as far as possible in an intermediate position. In using the key the greatest reliance must be placed upon season next upon form.

Apples which are round and even in shape in transverse section, such as Stirling Castle, are marked with an asterisk.

There are certain apples of which the ground colour turns quite white when fully ripe, *e.g.*, Lord Grosvenor in the Codlins and Emperor Alexander in the striped group, these are marked with a dagger. Large fruits are printed in the large type, and medium in medium, and small in italics.

Other special marks will be found in the different tables. Thus if a flat green apple is found, of which the cross section is round, *e.g.*, Ecklinville Seedling and the season is not known, it will only be necessary to glance down the column headed " Flat " and pick out those marked with the asterisk. Similarly if the apple turns white it will only be necessary to refer to those marked with the dagger.

Table I.—Lord Derby Group.—This contains the green skinned apples which are not striped and only rarely flushed of which Lord Derby may be considered a type. In this come the Codlins and large cooking apples, which are as a rule green when on the tree. They are all such as would be classed as cooking apples. There are, however, a few which turn white on the tree such as Lord Grosvenor, Domino, Venus Pippin. These are marked with a dagger to show this typical character, as described above.

Table II.—Lanes Group.—This contains those smooth skinned apples which will also in most cases be classed as " cookers " but which are distinctly striped, the typical representative being Lanes Prince Albert. A few here are a little sweet and are specially designated by //.

Table III.—Peasgood Group.—This contains the smooth skinned striped apples which are nearly all of sufficient sweetness to be classed as dessert. In cases where doubt might exist as to this quality, they are also placed in Table II.

All these have the stripes distinctly marked and not obscured by any extent of flush.

Table IV.—Golden Noble Group.—This contains those apples which have a markedly golden skin, such as Golden Noble and Golden Spire, and are occasionally flushed, *but not striped*. A few of these turn white when fully ripe and are so marked.

Table V.—Baumann Group.—This contains those fruits which have a dark brown red flush covering nearly the whole of the fruit and which are rarely striped, or if so, the stripes are not prominent as in Class III., but are largely obscured by the overlying flush. This may be called the Baumann group.

In this group, flavour is not a special distinction, but a few are notable for this and are so indicated. They are distinguished from Class VI. by the absence of Russet.

Table VI.—Cox's Group.—This contains the Reinettes and includes a very large proportion of the best flavoured fruits. The characteristic is a mixture of red and russet as in Cox's Orange Pippin and Blenheim Orange, coupled with a good or fairly good flavour. No acid cooking varieties will be found in this group.

Table VII.—Russet Group.—This contains the russet varieties which have no red flush or striping. The Russet may be golden as in Egremont Russet, gray as in White Nonpareil, or dark brown as in Golden Knob.

I.—LORD DERBY GROUP.

SMOOTH GREEN SOUR APPLES.

* Round and even.
† Turns white.

	FLAT.	ROUND.	CONICAL.	OBLONG.	OVAL.
AUG.	Juneating.*		Early Julian. White Transparent.† Emneth Early. Lord Suffield.†	Sugar Loaf.	
SEPT.	Stirling Castle.*	Norfolk Dumpling.	GRENADIER. GOLD MEDAL. Lord Grosvenor.† James Welch.	Domino.† Venus Pippin.*	
OCT.	Ecklinville Seedling.*	New Hawthornden.	Antonowka.†	POTTS' SEEDLING. CHAS. EYRE.* TRANSPARENT DE CRONCELS.†	
NOV.	BYFORD WONDER. Nelson's Glory.	WITHINGTON FILL- BASKET.	White Melrose.† Schoolmaster. WARNER'S KING.	DUTCH CODLIN.† LORD DERBY	
DEC.			Dr. Hogg.	OATSHEAD.	HAMBLING'S SEEDLING.
JAN.	Paul's Winter Hawthornden.*		Nelson Codlin. TOWER OF GLAMIS.	GLORIA MUNDI. ENCORE. BUFF COAT. ALFRISTON. EDWARD VII.*	
FEB.	Betty Geeson.*	Small's Admirable.			
MAR.	Murfitt's Seedling. French Crab.*		Rhode Island Greening. Gooseberry. London Pippin. Winter Majetin. CALVILLE DES FEMMES.	Hormead Pearmain.* Gospatrick.	Lemon Pippin.

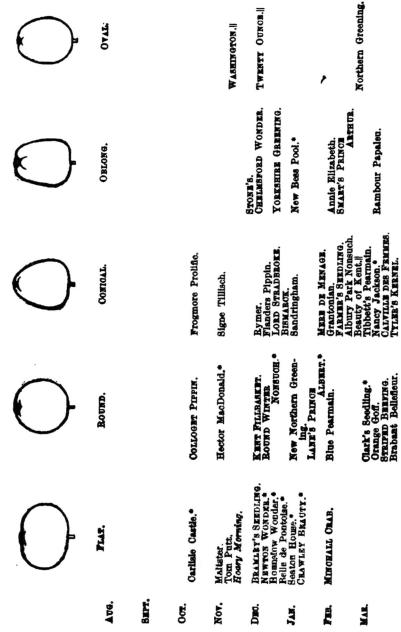

STRIPED-SMOOTH SOUR.

‖ Sweet.	FLAT.	ROUND.	CONICAL.	OBLONG.	OVAL.
Aug.					Washington.‖
Sept.					Twenty Ounce.‖
Oct.	Carlisle Castle.*	Colloget Pippin.	Frogmore Prolific.		
Nov.	Maltster. Tom Putt, *Hoary Morning.*	Hector MacDonald.*	Signe Tillisch.		
Dec.	Bramley's Seedling. Newton Wonder.* Homsnow Wonder.◊ Belle de Pontoise.* Seaton House.* Crawley Beauty.*	Kent Fillbasket. Round Winter Nonsuch.*	Rymer. Flanders Pippin. Lord Stradbroke. Bismarck. Sandringham.	Stom's. Chelmsford Wonder. Yorkshire Greening.	
Jan.		New Northern Greening. Lane's Prince Albert.		New Bees Pool.*	
Feb.	Minshall Crab.	Blue Pearmain.	Mere de Menage. Grankonian. Farmer's Seedling. Albury Park Nonsuch. Beauty of Kent.‖ Tibbett's Pearmain. Nancy Jackson.* Calville des Femmes. Tyler's Kernel.	Annie Elizabeth. Smart's Prince Arthur.	
Mar.		Clark's Seedling.* Orange Goff. Striped Beufing. Brabant Bellefleur.		Bambour Papalen.	Northern Greening.

III.—PEASGOODS GROUP.

STRIPED SMOOTH SWEET.

* Round.

† Turn White.

Shapes: **FLAT.** · **ROUND.** · **CONICAL.** · **OBLONG.** · **OVAL.**

	FLAT.	ROUND.	CONICAL.	OBLONG.	OVAL.
AUG.	Irish Peach, Beauty of Bath *†, Reynolds Peach, Maidstone Favourite *†		Red Juneating, Gladstone, Cardinal †, Feltham Beauty, Langley Pippin.	BELLO BOROODAWELL †, Lady Sudeley, Hitchin Pippin *	Benoni *, Kerry Pippin *
SEPT.	Thorle *, Lord Lennox, Nonsuch *	Duchess of Oldenburgh *†, Hunt's Early, Miller's Seedling †, Beauty of Bedford, Autumn Rouge.	James Grieve.	William's Favourite.	
OCT.	Devonshire Queen, PEASGOODS, Coronation *, THE QUEEN †	Mackintosh Red *, NONSUCH *, Roseberry.	EMPEROR ALEXANDER †, Cox's Pomona.		Wealthy *, White Paradise *
	Rival.*	Cellini.*			
NOV.	Gambusnethan *, Malster.	Tamplin.	Gravenstein.		WASHINGTON.
		Cutler Grieve.*			
DEC.		CHAS ROSS.*, Heritage Pippin, Prince Edward, JEAFFE HARDY, Mrs. Phillimore, KING OF TOMKINS.		Scarlet Pearmain.	TWENTY OUNCE. Col. Vaughan.
		Foster's Seedling.*			
JAN.		Melon Apple.			Cornish Pine.
FEB.	Newtown Spitzenberg *		Cockington Calville, Upton Pyne, BEAUTY OF KENT, Sanspareil *		
MAR.	Wagener. ONTARIO. Granges Pearmain, Rome Beauty.				

IV.—GOLDEN NOBLE GROUP.

GOLDEN APPLES, NOT STRIPED.

* Bound and even.
† Turn creamy white.

	FLAT.	ROUND.	CONICAL.	OBLONG.	OVAL.
AUG.	Odlin.*	River's Early Peach.	English Codlin.	Summer Golden Pippin.*	
SEPT.		Sack and Sugar, Wormsley Pippin, Waltham Abbey.	Keswick Codlin.	Yellow Ingestrie.*	
OCT.	King's Acre Bountiful, Surprise.*†	Jolly Beggar, REV. WILKS.*†	Manx Codlin. Carlisle Codlin. Golden Spire. Thos. Rivers.		
NOV.	Hawthornden. Queen Caroline.*	Yorkshire Beauty. Golden Noble.* ARTHUR TURNER.* HOLLANDBURY. Barchard's Seedling. Histon Favourite.* NORFOLK BEAUTY.	YORKSHIRE BEAUTY. Bull Knot. King Harry.*	Mrs. Barron.	Royal Jubilee.
DEC.			DEWDNEY'S SEEDLING.		
JAN.		Small's Admirable.	Grantonian.		
FEB.	Galloway Pippin.* Wellington. High Canons. Newtown Pippin. March Pippin.	MONARCH.* Winter Peach	WINTER BANANA. Calville Blanche. d'Hiver.	Hormead Pearman.*	
MAR.					

2

† These both have a curious pinkish red.

	FLAT.	ROUND.	CONICAL.	OBLONG.	OVAL.
AUG.	Devonshire Quarrenden.		*Early Margaret.*		
SEPT.	Ben's Red.	Buddy.	Red Astrachan.*	Akero.†	GASCOYNE'S SCARLET.†
OCT.		RED VICTORIA.* Duchess' Favourite.*	Worcester Pearmain.*		
NOV.	Medenham Pippin, *Hereford Beefing,* Bosbury Pippin.	Ontler Grieve.	Mother.		
DEC.	CRIM, BRAMLEY, Baumann's Reinette.	Sops in Wine * Reinette Rouge Etoilee.*	Beaown. Pope's Scarlet Costard. Paroquet.*		
JAN.	Winter Quarrenden.	Bietigheimer.*†			
FEB.		FRAISE D'HOFFICE.	Northern Spy‡		
MAR.	Api,* Norfolk Beefing.	Fameuse.*	Delicious, William Crump, Calville Malingre.	Calville Rouge d'Hiver.	

REINETTES-RED AND RUSSET.

Key:
* Round, even.
† Angular.
‡ Deep sunk eye.

 FLAT.   **ROUND.**   **CONICAL.**   **OBLONG.**   **OVAL.**

	FLAT.	ROUND.	CONICAL.	OBLONG.	OVAL.
AUG.					
SEPT.		St. Everard.* Ellison's Orange.*		William's Favourite.	
OCT.	Coronation.* *Houblon.*	*Reinette Rouge* *Étoilée.* ENDSLEIGH BEAUTY.* Sir J. Thornycroft.* Ross Nonpareil.* Cox's Orange.* Bow Hill Pippin.*‡ Mannington Pearmain.*‡		*Red Ingestrie.*‡	
NOV.			Pine Apple Russet (of Devon).† AUTUMN PEARMAIN †	King of the Pippins.*‡	
DEC.	BLENHEIM ORANGE.*‡ Orange Pippin.* *Gipsy King.*		Allington Pippin.* *Margil.*†	*Scarlet-Golden Pippin*‡ Ribston Pippin.‡ *Loan's Pearmain.*† Barcelona Pearmain.*	Christmas Pearmain.* Mabbot's Pearmain.* St. Martin's.*
JAN.	Orleans Reinette.* Werder's Golden Reinette.†‡ Middle Green.* *Court of Wick.*‡	*Buxted Favourite.*‡ *September Beauty.* FORESTER.† Scarlet Nonpareil.* *New Rock Pippin.*† Golden Reinette.*	Lansberger Reinette.† Ribston Pippin.† Ard Cairn Russet. Ballinora.† Rosemary Russet.* Star of Devon.* Baxter's Pearmain.* Gabalva.† Bess Pool.† Wheeler's Russet.† BEDFORDSHIRE FOUNDLING.*‡	Ladies Finger of Lancaster.† *Pitmaston Golden* *Pippin.*‡ LADY HENNIKER.† BEAUTY OF HANTS.* Crawley Reinette. Adam's Pearmain.* Claygate Pearmain.* *Bereford.*‡ Baxter's Pearmain. Cobham.‡ Cornish Gilliflower.† *Kendll Swap.* Hubbard's Pearmain.* *Armeol.* *Lamb Abbey Pearmain.*	BELLE DE BOSKOOP.*‡
FEB.	May Queen.†‡ Golden Harvey.* Buxted Favourite.* Fearn's Pippin.*	Dutch Mignonne.* Chatley's Kernel. Roundway Magnum Bonum.†	Winter Queening.* Cornish Aromatic.* *Atalanta.* Nanny.†‡ Farmer's Seedling. Reinette Superfin *	*Pearson's Plate.* Wadhurst Pippin.‡ Shepherd's Pearmain.†	
MAR.	*Court Pendu Plat.*‡ *Hougen's Golden.* *Reinette.*† Allen's Everlasting.‡	WOODSTOCK PIPPIN.* Wanstall Pippin. Mr. Prothero. Brabant Bellefleur.* Granges Pearmain.	Easter Orange. Lord Hindlip. KING'S ACRE PIPPIN.† Sturmer Pippin.* Lord Burghley.‡ Hanwell Souring.† Hambledon deux Ans.†		*Beachamwell.* Barnack Beauty.*

VII.—RUSSET GROUP.
RUSSET WITHOUT RED.

* Round.
† Golden russet.
‡ Grey russet.
‖ Brown russet.

	FLAT.	ROUND.	CONICAL.	OBLONG.	OVAL.
AUG.					
SEPT.					
OCT.	Evagil.†* *Early Nonpareil.*‡	Egremont Russet.†	St. Edmund's Pippin.† King Harry.†		
NOV.	Franklin's Golden Pippin.†		*Lucombe Pine.**	*Pitmaston Pine Apple.*† *Pine Apple Russet.*†	
DEC.	Caraway Russet.† Braddick's Nonpareil.‡ Pitmaston Nonpareil.‖		*Forfar Pippin.*‡ *Nutmeg Pippin.*‖ *Cockle's Pippin.*‖ Aromatic Russet.† Diamond Jubilee.‡ Beauty of Stoke.‡ *Golden Pippin.*†		
JAN.	Wyken Pippin.† Duke of Devon.‡ *Syke House Russet.*†	*White Nonpareil.*‡ Belnette Grise.‡ Nonpareil.‡ Norman's Pippin.‡	Ashmead's Kernel.‡ *Boyal Russet.*† Brownlees Russet.‡ Boyal Late.‡		
FEB	*Golden Russet.*†	Boston Russet.‡	ROUNDWAY MAGNUM BEINETTE DE CANADA.‡ BONUM.‡ D'Arcy Spice.‡		
MAR.	Pomme Grise.† Ashmead's Kernel. Improved Ashmead's Kernel. Norfolk Stone Pippin.† Golden Knob.‖	Lodgmore Nonpareil.‡	Sturmer Pippin. Wheeler's Russet.		

APPLES.

ADAM'S PEARMAIN. *Her. Pom.*, I., 14. F., Rousse de Norfolk; G., Adam's Parmane. (Hanging Pearmain, Norfolk Pippin.) Dessert, December to March, medium, 2¼ by 2¼, conical. colour, deep yellow, red stripes and flush, with russet patches. Flesh, firm, yellow, very aromatic. Eye open, tips reflexed in a shallow plaited basin. Stem very short in a shallow even russet cavity. Growth slender, fertile. Leaf, medium, narrow oval, slightly up-cupped, boldly serrate, grey green, nearly smooth below. Origin probably English, brought to notice about 1826, and it was named after the donor of the grafts to the Royal Horticultural Society. This is one of the best late dessert sorts; it thrives in nearly all soils.

Akero : *see Akero.*

AKERO. *Svensk Pom.*, 15. (Akera, Okera.) Dessert, September to October, medium, 2¼ by 2¼, conical. Colour, pale creamy yellow with crimson peach-like flush and bloom. Flesh, white, firm, and juicy. Growth, moderate, fertility moderate. Leaf, rather large, upward folded, much twisted, coarsely crenate. Origin, probably Swedish. This is now rarely grown, but is of interest only from its remarkable coloration.

Albermarle : *see Newtown Pippin.*

ALBURY PARK NONSUCH. Cooking, December to March, medium, 3 by 2¾, round conical, ribbed, irregular. Colour, creamy yellow with faint stripes and flush. Flesh, crisp juicy, slightly yellow, sub-acid, no flavour. Growth, spreading. Leaf, medium, oval, sharply pointed, held-up, much up-folded, much twisted, coarsely serrate. Origin undiscovered. An award of Merit was given to this variety in 1892 to Mr. Leach. Not worthy of retention.

ALFRISTON. Ronalds p. 35. (Shepherds Pippin, Shepherds Seedling), culinary, keeps till April, large, 3¼ by 2¾, round, conical, flattened, irregular. Colour, green to yellow russet veined. Flesh, crisp, pale yellow, sub-acid. Growth, vigorous, fertile. Leaf, pea green, flat undulating, broadly serrate. Origin, raised by a Mr. Shepherd at Alfriston, Sussex, about the end of the eighteenth century. This apple cooks a tender, golden brown with a delicious pear-like flavour.

ALLENS EVERLASTING. *Gard. Chron.* 1899, p. 222. F., Eternelle d' Allen; G., Allens Dauerapfel. Dessert, April to May, 2¼ by 1¾, flat, regular. Colour. pale greenish-yellow, with brown red flush and russet netting. Flesh, crisp and juicy, greenish, excellently flavoured. Eye, large, open, in a wide angular basin. Stem rather slender in a very wide and deep cavity. Growth, dwarfish; fertile. Leaf, small, oval, flat, finely serrate. Origin, undiscovered; said to be a seedling from Sturmer Pippin. Known before 1870. One of the best late dessert sorts.

American Mother: *see Mother*.

ALLINGTON PIPPIN. The *Garden*, 1906, 131. (South Lincoln Pippin.) Dessert, October to December, Medium, 2½ by 2½, round, conical, regular. Colour, lemon yellow slight red flush and faint stripes. Flesh, crisp, juicy, pale yellow, sub-acid, pleasantly aromatic. Eye, slightly open, very long, tips reflexed in a slightly plaited, shallow basin. Stem medium in a moderately deep, even cavity. Growth, vigorous; very fertile. Leaf, narrow oval, grey green, upfolded undulating, coarsely rounded serrate, nearly crenate. Origin, raised in South Lincolnshire and introduced by Messrs. G. Bunyard & Co., Ltd., in 1896. A most valuable variety, which is now in the front rank. Thrives in nearly all soils. Its fault is in making rather too much lateral growth as a pyramid.

American Plate : *see Golden Pippin.*

American Red : *see Astrachan Red.*

Anglesea Pippin : *see Astrachan Red.*

Anis : *see Caraway Russet.*

ANNIE ELIZABETH. *Her. Pom.* 52. Culinary, December to June, medium to large, 3 by 2¼, oblong conical, irregular. Colour, pale yellow, flushed and striped brilliant red. Flesh, crisp, white, acid. Eye, closed in a rather broad and deep basin. Stem short in a fairly deep cavity. Growth, vigorous, upright. Fertility good when tree is developed. Leaf, large, long oval, dark, upfolded and twisted, regularly serrate. Origin, raised by Mr. Greatorex at Leicester about 1857, and introduced by Messrs. Harrison of Leicester about 1868. A valuable fruit deserving of extended cultivation. It can be recognised by the " hammered " appearance of the skin, especially marked on the sunny side.

ANTONOWKA. Culinary, October, December, 3 by 2¼, round conical, ribbed, five-sided, uneven. Colour, pale, whitish yellow, with dots under the skin, greasy. Flesh, white, loose grained, rather dry, aromatic. Eye, closed, on a level basin surrounded by knobs and beads. Stem, moderately long in a rather narrow, russet lined cavity, the russet spreading out. Growth, very vigorous, moderately fertile. Leaf, very large, little upfolded, sharply serrate. Origin, a very popular central Russian variety. This is hardly worthy of retention and is best described as a late edition of *White Transparent.*

17

API. *Ronalds*, 32. F., Api; G., Kleine Api. (Api rouge, Api petit, Lady.) Dessert, November to April, very small, 2 by 1¼, flat, regular. Colour, bright yellow, rich crimson flush. Flesh, tender, aromatic. Eye, half open in a shallow wide basin. Stem short in a rather wide cavity. Growth, upright, very slender making a small close tree, fertile. Leaf, small, oval, upfolded, shallow crenate. Origin, of great antiquity; possibly dating from Roman days. Known in this country in the seventeenth century. It is hardly worthy of cultivation except as a curiosity.

Api Petit : *see Api.*

Api Rouge : *see Api.*

Aporta : *see Emperor Alexander.*

Arbroath Pippin : *see Oslin.*

Aromatic Pippin : *see Kerry Pippin.*

ARD CAIRN RUSSET. *Garden*, 1911, 570. Dessert, January to February, medium, 2½ by 2¾, round conical. Colour, dark red, nearly covered with pale russet. Flesh, yellow, firm, good russet flavour. Eye, closed in a moderate even basin. Stem, very long and slender in a deep narrow cavity. Leaf, long oval, upfolded, coarsely serrate. Growth, rather upright, compact. Origin, an old Irish variety, introduced to notice by Messrs. Hartland, of Ard Cairn, Co. Cork.

ARMOREL. *Gard. Chron.*, 1893, March 4th. Dessert, February to May, very small, 2¼ by 1¾, oblong, regular. Colour, yellow, covered with russet. Flesh, crisp, of good flavour. Eye, closed in a deep and wide basin. Stem, short, in a medium sized cavity. Growth, moderate, fertility moderate. Origin, raised by Mr. Charles Ross, and introduced by Messrs. Cheal, in 1893. Now almost out of cultivation, as it is too small for present day needs.

AROMATIC RUSSET. *Her. Pom.*, p. 54. F., Rouge aromatisée. Dessert, December to February, medium, 2¼ by 2, round, conical, irregular. Colour entirely cinnamon russet, faint red showing through. Flesh, firm, aromatic, greenish white. Eye, very small, closed in a shallow basin. Stem, slender in a rather deep even cavity. Growth, weak ; fertile. Leaf, long, slightly upfolded, little undulating, coarsely crenate. Origin unrecorded, came into notice about 1830. A nice winter fruit, of Nonpareil flavour. There is some confusion about this fruit, it is probably the Aromatic Russet of Hogg, but not of Ronalds or Lindley. It is possibly the Petit Barbarie of Normandy.

Aromatic Russet : *see Caraway Russet.*

ARTHUR TURNER. Culinary, October to November, large, 4 by 3½, very even. Colour, yellow with brown red flush. Flesh, white, slightly acid, baking very well. Eye, open in a rather wide even basin. Stem, medium in a wide cavity. Growth, moderate, slightly upright ; fertility good. Leaf, narrow oval, grey green, little up-cupped, shallow serrate or crenate. Origin, introduced by Mr. Chas. Turner, in 1914, when it gained an Award of Merit. A very handsome apple, which deserves cultivation for an early winter cooking variety.

ASHMEAD'S KERNEL. *Ronalds*, p. 32. F., Semis d'Ashmead. G., Saemling von Ashmead. Dessert, December to March, medium, 2¼ by 2¼, round-square. Colour, greenish-yellow, faint brown flush, covered with russet. Flesh, firm, pale yellow, very aromatic. Eye, closed in a fairly deep and wide basin, which is slightly ribbed. Stem, variable in a deep wide cavity. Growth, moderate, fertile. Leaf, rather large, oval, up-folded, twisted, bi-serrate. Origin, raised by Dr. Ashmead, of Gloucester, about 1720. A valuable fruit for late use but a, poor cropper. A larger form exists known as Improved Ashmead's Kernel, *q.v.*

ASTRACHAN RED. *Ronalds*, p. V. (American Red, Anglesea Pippin.) Dessert, early August, medium, 2½ by 2¼, flattened round, fairly regular. Colour, deep crimson, unstriped. Flesh, crisp, white, sweet. Eye, closed in a shallow basin. Stem, short in a scaly russet cavity. Growth, moderate, fertility poor. Leaf, long oval, pale green, held flat, crenate. Origin, probably from the country of its name. Introduced to England in 1816. A most attractive fruit but too poor a cropper for general use.

ATALANTA. *Gard. Chron.*, 1893. Culinary or dessert, November to January, small, 2¾ by 2¼, conical, irregular. Colour, lemon yellow with red streaks. Flesh, firm, flavour moderate. Growth, moderate, very fertile. Origin, raised by Mr. Chas. Ross, from Scarlet Nonpareil, and introduced by Messrs. Cheal and Sons, in 1893. It has now dropped out of cultivation, presenting no marked advantages over other varieties of the same season.

AUTUMN PEARMAIN. *Ronalds*, p. 22. (as Royal Pearmain). F., Pearmain d'Eté. G., Sommer Parmaene. [American Pearmain, Royal Pearmain (in error).] Dessert or culinary, September to October medium, 2¾ by 2, conical, fairly regular. Colour, golden-yellow, partly covered with russet which is netted, and slight flush. Flesh, firm, yellow, highly flavoured. Eye, open in a very shallow, faintly ribbed basin. Stem, slender in a moderate cavity, always with a fleshy bump on one side, forcing the stem sideways. Growth, vigorous, upright, fertile. Leaf, roundish, pale, upfolded, undulated, finely serrate. Origin, an Old English variety mentioned by Parkinson, in 1629. It is the Summer Pearmain, of Hogg, but not of Continental Authors. It makes a fine standard tree.

AUTUMN ROUGE. Culinary. September, medium, 2½ by 2¼, round, conical, slightly flattened at eye. Colour, bright yellow, flushed with dull red faint stripes.

Flesh, close, pale yellow, acid. Growth, moderate, fertility moderate, makes a flat headed tree. Leaf, rather small, pale, upfolded, very undulated, boldly curved serrate. Origin, undiscovered. A worthless fruit.

Backhouse's Lord Nelson : *see Nelson Codlin.*

Baddow Pippin : *see D'Arcy Spice.*

Balgone Pippin : *see Golden Pippin.*

BALLINORA. Culinary or dessert, December to January, medium, 3 by 2¼, nearly even. Colour, golden-yellow, with bright red flush and very faint stripings. Flesh, firm, pale yellow, fair flavour, of Blenheim character. Eye, open in a shallow much ribbed basin. Stem, very short in a wide shallow cavity. Growth, vigorous, spreading. Leaf, large, flat, down hanging, roundish, boldly serrate. Origin, unrecorded. This apple may be called a Red Blenheim Orange, but it is not quite so good in flavour or so fertile.

Baltimore : *see Gloria Mundi.*

BARCELONA PEARMAIN. *Ronalds*, p. 21. G., Kleiner Casseler Reinette. (Speckled Golden Reinette, Speckled Pearmain.) Dessert, November to January, smallish, 2¼ by 2¼, roundish-oblong, regular, Colour, pale yellow, flushed with red. Flesh, crisp, pale yellow, aromatic. Growth, moderate ; fertile. Leaf, medium, flat, oval, with a long point, broadly serrate. Origin, continental ; country uncertain. It is now almost out of cultivation.

BARCHARDS SEEDLING. *Her Pom.*, p. 67. Culinary or dessert, October to November, 2¼ by 2¼, medium, irregular. Colour, pale yellow, with dull brown-red flush. Flesh, firm, yellowish, sub-acid. Eye, open in a shallow broad basin. Stem, rather long in a medium sized cavity. Growth, moderate ;

fertile. Leaf, rather small, much twisted, oval, shallow serrate. Origin, raised in the garden of J. H. Barchard, Putney, and introduced to notice in 1852. It is now little cultivated.

Bardfield Defiance : *see Waltham Abbey.*

BARNACK BEAUTY. *Gard. Chron.*, 1900, p. 251. Culinary or dessert, December to March, medium, 2¼ by 2¾, oval, regular. Colour, golden-yellow, dark red flush and faint stripes. Flesh, crisp, fair flavour, briskly acid, yellowish. Eye, large open in a shallow even basin. Stem, moderate in a very narrow russety cavity. Growth, vigorous ; fertile. Leaf, rather small, pale, slightly upfolded, very finely curved serrate. Origin, raised by a cottager at Barnack, Northants. Introduced by Messrs. Brown, of Stamford, about 1870. A useful and handy sort which does well on chalky sub-soils. Quite one of the most interesting fruits in February, as it keeps its acid flavour later than many.

Baroveski : *see Duchess of Oldenburg.*

Baron Wolseley : *see Dewdney's Seedling.*

BAUMANN'S REINETTE. *Fl. and Pom.*, 1879, p. 121. F., Reinette Baumann. G., Baumann's Reinette (Couronne des Dames, Reinette de Bolwyller). Culinary or dessert, December to January, medium, 2¼ by 2¼, round flattened, curving most to eye. Colour, almost covered with brilliant crimson flush with broad stripes. Flesh, white, crisp, juicy, slightly aromatic. Eye, small, closed, in a rather deep slightly plaited basin. Stem, rather thin, short, in a very wide russeted cavity. Growth, compact ; fertility remarkable. Leaf, rather large, very dark, held out, down cupped, finely curved serrate. Origin, raised probably by Van Mons, and generally cultivated in Germany in 1820. A remarkable cropper but of poor quality.

22

BAXTER'S PEARMAIN. Dessert or culinary, December to February, medium, 2¼ by 2¼, roundish conical, slightly flattened. Colour, pale yellow with red-brown flush and stripes. Flesh, yellowish, tender, pleasantly acid. Eye, open in a moderately deep and wide basin, which is slightly plaited. Stem, short, rather slender in an even basin. Growth, moderate; very fertile. Leaf, long, dark green, much upfolded, sharply serrate. Origin, a Norfolk variety, introduced to notice by Mr. G. Lindley, in 1821. It is rather too acid for some palates.

Bayfordbury Pippin : *see Golden Pippin.*

BEACHAMWELL. *Ronalds,* p. 27. G., Sämling von Beachamwell. (Motteux's Seedling.) Dessert, December to March, small, 2¼ by 2, flattened oval, regular. Colour, green-yellow, faint stripes with russet. Flesh, crisp, pale yellow, sugary. Eye, open in a shallow basin. Stem, medium in a narrow cavity. Growth, medium; fertile. Leaf, medium, ovate, faintly crenate. Origin, raised at Beachamwell in Norfolk, probably about the middle of the eighteenth century. It is now almost out of cultivation.

BEAUTY OF BATH. *Gard. Chron.,* 1900, p. 145. Dessert, early August, small to medium, 2¼ by 1¾, round, much flattened, even. Colour, pale yellow, red flush and stripes, a little rough to touch. Flesh, tender, yellowish, often stained with red, sweet and pleasant. Eye, closed, tips of the segments reflexed, in a round even, rather deep basin. Stem, stout, half inch in a rather shallow and even cavity. Growth, moderate; very fertile. Leaf, round oval, dark green, nearly flat, undulating, curved serrate. Origin, raised at Bailbrook, Batheaston, near Bath, and brought to notice by Messrs. Cooling, about 1864. This is a very attractive fruit, which is now largely grown for market purposes. Its chief fault is premature dropping which leads many growers to place straw beneath the trees to prevent injury.

BEAUTY OF BEDFORD. Dessert, September, fairly large, 2¼ by 2¼, round conical, flattened at eye. Colour, pale yellow with brown-red flush and stripes. Flesh, yellow, firm, juicy and sweet. Eye, closed, very broad segments, in a shallow, ribbed basin. Stem, unusually short, one-eighth inch set in a level or even on a raised bump, a very unusual feature. Growth, rather upright. Leaf, round, rather large, dark, up-folded, undulated, deeply curved serrate. Origin, raised by Messrs. Laxton, Lady Sudeley + Beauty of Bath.

BEAUTY OF HANTS. *Fl. and Pom.*, 1882, p. 89. F., Seedling Offine. Dessert, December to March, very large, 3 by 2¼, roundish square, rather irregular. Colour, dull yellow-green, brick red flush, russet patches. Flesh, very crisp, yellowish, highly aromatic. Eye, open in a broad even basin, which is rather deep. Stem, short and stout in a rather shallow cavity which is slightly russet. Growth, very strong, Leaf, up-cupped, round oval, dark green, boldly curved serrate. Origin, raised at Basset, Southampton, in Mrs. Eyre Crabbes garden, and introduced to notice about 1880. A fine form of Blenheim Orange. Barron places this as a synonym of Blenheim, which is quite wrong as is it perfectly distinct since the core of a Blenheim is axile and the seeds are long and pointed, while the core of Beauty of Hants is abaxile and the seeds are short and plump.

BEAUTY OF KENT. *Ronalds*, p. 15. F., Beauté de Kent ; G., Schöner aus Kent. (Worling's Favourite, Countess of Warwick.) Culinary, 3½ by 3, fairly large, till March, round conical, flattened at base, irregular. Colour, yellow green, bright red flush, broad dark stripes. Flesh, tender, yellowish, slightly acid. Eye, closed in a very wrinkled and knobbed basin. Stem, stout and long in a wide, shallow, russeted cavity. Growth, strong ; fertile. Leaf, rather large, dark, down held, flat, very deeply curved serrate. Origin, unknown, recorded first about 1800. A very valuable cooking apple for late use.

BEAUTY OF STOKE. Culinary or dessert. January to March, medium to fairly large, 2½ by 2½, round conical. Colour, pale greenish yellow, occasional faint brown flush and slight russet. Flesh, firm, rather dry, yellowish, pleasant flavour. Growth, vigorous, a little spreading; fertile. Leaf, narrow, oval, pea green, little upfolded, boldly curved serrate, little downy below, held out. Origin, raised by Mr. Doe, gardener to Lord Saville, Rufford Abbey; introduced by Messrs. Veitch. A valuable late variety, resembling Diamond Jubilee but distinct.

BEDFORDSHIRE FOUNDLING. *Ronalds*, p. 28. F., Trouvé dans le comté de Bedfordshire; G., Fundling aus Bedfordshire. (Cambridge Pippin.) Culinary, January to March, 3¼ by 2¾, large, square oval, slightly irregular. Colour, pale yellow-green, faint red flush. Flesh, tender, yellow, sub-acid. Eye, half open in a shallow wrinkled basin. Stem, rather long and thin in a wide and deep cavity, lined with faint russet. Growth, spreading, vigorous; moderately fertile. Leaf very large, dark, long oval, upward folded and twisted, sharply bi-serrate. Origin, uncertain. Probably arose about 1800, in Bedfordshire. An excellent cooker of the Blenheim style, but apt to canker.

BELLE DE BOSKOOP. *Ned. Boom.*, 43. G., Schoener aus Boskoop. (Reinette Monstreuse, Reinette von Montfort.) Culinary or dessert, December to April, medium to rather large, 2¾ by 2½, roundish oval, fairly regular. Colour, golden-yellow, brick red flush, with much thin russet. Flesh, firm, yellowish, flavour acid and aromatic. Eye, closed or slightly open in a rather deep basin. Stem, medium in a deep cavity lined with russet. Growth, moderate; fertile. Leaf, round, light, slightly upfolded, deeply curved serrate. Originated at Boskoop in Holland in 1856. It must not be confused with the Calville von Boskoop. Reinette von Montfort is considered by some authorities to be the correct name. A valuable fruit much grown for market in Holland and Germany, and worthy of trial for this purpose in England.

BELLE DE PONTOISE. G., Schoener von Pontoise. Culinary, December to February, large, 3¼ by 2¼, flat, irregular. Colour, pale yellow-green, red flush, and broad broken stripes. Flesh, tender, white, sweetish and juicy. Eye, open in a rather deep and wide basin. Stem, very long in an unusually wide and deep russet cavity. Growth, vigorous; very fertile. Leaf, very large, undulating, very coarsely serrate. Origin, raised at Pointoise, from a seed of Emperor Alexander, by M. Remy, and introduced in 1879. A very useful variety, keeping firm and acid, but rather tender and best for garden use.

Belle de Rome : *see Rome Beauty.*

Belle des Vennes : *see Wellington.*

Belle du Bois : *see Gloria Mundi.*

Belle Fille : *see Reinette Grise.*

Bell's Scarlet : *see Scarlet Pearmain.*

Belmont : *see Manks Codlin.*

Bennet's Defiance : *see Fearn's Pippin.*

BENONI. *Her. Pom.*, 47. Dessert, mid-September, small, 2¼ by 2¼, oval, regular. Colour, pale yellow, with crimson flush, and stripes. Flesh, tender, yellow, aromatic. Eye, small, a little open in a fairly deep even basin. Stem, short and rather slender in a deep even cavity. Growth, moderate, makes a roundish tree; moderately fertile. Origin, raised at Dedham, Mass., U.S.A., about the middle of the eighteenth century. Introduced to England about 1870. A very good early fruit.

BEN'S RED. *Gard. Chron.*, 1899. p. 261. Dessert, September, medium, 2¼ by 2, flat, a little irregular. Colour, pale yellow, almost entirely covered with darkest crimson flush and stripes. Flesh, firm, pale yellow, sweet, aromatic. Eye, closed in a wide shallow slightly wrinkled basin. Stem, very short in a wide and deep slightly russeted cavity. Growth, dwarf; fertility remarkable. Leaf, long oval, dark green, flat, a little down curved, neatly serrate. Origin, raised by Mr. Benjamin Roberts, of Trannack, Penzance, about 1830. A very useful fruit, valuable for its great cropping qualities.

BESS POOL. *Ronalds*, p. 23. (Black Blenheim, Stadway Pippin, Walsgrove Blenheim.) Dessert or culinary, November to March, medium, 2¼ by 2½, round, conical, irregular. Colour, greenish-yellow, nearly covered with crimson flush, darker stripes and russet. Flesh, tender, white sweet. Eye, nearly closed in a shallow much ribbed basin, generally showing five beads of flesh at the base. Stem, short in a shallow cavity, always with a knob at the side. Growth, vigorous, upward spreading, making a round headed standard; fertile when aged. Leaf, large, long, rather pale, upfolded, shallow serrate. Origin, a seedling found in a wood near Nottingham, and named after the young girl who discovered it. A good old sort, keeping firm and crisp to the last.

BETTY GEESON. Culinary, till March, medium, 2¾ by 2, flat, fairly regular. Colour, pea green to deep yellow, greasy. Flesh, firm, greenish-white, sub-acid, juicy. Eye, large, open in an unusually wide and deep basin. Stem, rather slender and short in a very wide and deep cavity. Growth, vigorous, slightly spreading, compact; fertile. Leaf, very broad, very coarsely serrate, dark, held flat but slightly undulating. Origin, said by Hogg to be a Worcestershire variety. Introduced to notice about 1854. A useful late variety now superseded by Bramley's Seedling and Newton Wonder.

Bide's Walking Stick: *see Burr Knot.*

BIELA BORODOWKA. Dessert or culinary, August to September, large 3¼ by 3, round, oblong, flattened both ends. Colour, pale milky yellow, pink flush with broken red stripes. Flesh, soft, yellow, pleasantly acid. Eye, closed, tips reflexed, in a boldly ribbed and deep basin. Stem, short and stout. Growth, compact, very upright; extremely fertile. Leaf, very large, oval, upward folded, down curved, coarsely curved serrate. Origin, Russian. Of the style of Duchess of Oldenburg, but not so attractive in appearance.

BIETIGHEIMER. F., Rouge de Stettin; G., Rother Stettiner. Synonyms number more than twenty-five. Culinary, November to February, large, 3 by 2¾, round flattened, regular. Colour, a rich crimson, with a curious milky tinge in the lighter portions. Flesh, firm, greenish-white, sweet but with no aroma. Growth, spreading; vigorous. Leaf, rather pale, flat, finely and sharply serrate. Remarkable for its distinct colouring. Not worthy of cultivation. The correct name is Rother Stettiner.

BISMARK. *Gard. Chron.*, 1898, p. 257. Culinary, November to February, large to very large, tapering to eye and sides, flat, angular. Colour, pale yellow, almost covered with dark crimson flush. Flesh, crisp, juicy and sub-acid. Eye, closed, in a much ribbed and angular basin. Stem, short, in a wide russet lined cavity. Growth, moderate, rather spreading. Leaf, very long, soft grey-green, lax, edges very undulated, shallow serrate or nearly crenate. Origin, raised at the German settlement of Bismark, in Hobart, in Tasmania. Another account claims it to have been raised by a Mr. Fricke, of Carisbrooke, Victoria, but the first is I presume correct. It must not be confused with the Bismark of Germany, which dates from 1877. A valuable fruit, cooking excellently.

Black Blenheim: *see Bess Pool.*

Black Blenheim: *see Hambledon Deux Ans.*

BLENHEIM ORANGE. *Ronalds* p. 31. F., Reinette de Blenheim; G., Goldreinette von Blenheim. (Kempster's Pippin, Northwick Pippin.) Culinary or dessert, November to January, 3¼ by 2¾, medium to fairly large, flattened, round, regular, Colour, yellow, flushed and striped dull red and fine russet. Flesh, crisp, yellow, sub-acid, with a characteristic flavour. Eye, large, open, in a broad even basin. Stem, medium in a rather deep even cavity. Growth, vigorous, spreading; fertile when aged. Makes a large flat headed tree. Leaf, large, broad, very dark, flat, sharply serrate. Origin, raised at Woodstock, near Blenheim, by Mr. Kempster. It came into notice about 1818, in the neighbourhood of London. There are doubtless many seedlings now in cultivation which closely resemble this fine variety, but are not quite identical. One of the best all round apples grown, cooking excellently, and of fine quality and texture for dessert.

BLUE PEARMAIN. *New York*, 80. Culinary or dessert, January to March, medium, 2¾ by 2½, round, conical, regular. Colour, yellow entirely covered with dull crimson flush and broad broken stripes, heavily covered with bloom on the tree. Flesh, tender, yellow, rather dry, highly aromatic and sweet. Eye, slightly open in a moderately wide and deep basin. Stem, rather short in a rather wide and deep cavity. Growth, moderate, rather spreading; fertile. Leaf, rather large, greyish-green, upfolded, finely serrate. Origin, American, date uncertain, known before 1800. A hardy variety worthy of further trial. It does well in Western Counties.

Blue Stone Pippin: *see Hambledon Deux Ans*.

Blumen Calville: *see Gravenstein*.

Bonne Rouge: *see Hollandbury*.

Borowinka: *see Duchess of Oldenburg*.

BORSDORFER. *Her. Pom.*, 3. F., Borsdorfer; G., Edelborsdorfer. (King George III., Queen Charlotte's Apple, etc., etc.) Dessert, December to February, small, 2 by 1¾, round-square, regular. Colour, milky yellow with dull red flush, slight russet veins. Flesh, firm, juicy, pale yellow, poor flavour. Eye, usually open in a shallow wide basin. Stem, slender, in a moderately deep cavity, slightly russeted. Growth, compact; fertile. Leaf, rather small, oval, held out flat, curved serrate. Origin, German, where it has been cultivated since the sixteenth century. Imported into England for Queen Charlotte, wife of George III. Recorded by Cordus in 1561. A worthless fruit in this country, except in very warm seasons.

BOSBURY PIPPIN. Dessert, December to March, small, 2¼ by 1¾, flat, fairly regular. Colour, golden yellow, with crimson flush, nearly covering fruit. Flesh, firm, pale yellow, sweet. Growth, moderate; fertile. Origin, unrecorded. Probably a West of England variety. Of the Baumann's Reinette type; it is not worthy of cultivation.

BOSTON RUSSET. *Her. Pom.*, 54. F., Reinette Rousse de Boston. (Roxbury Russet, Putnam Russet.) Dessert, January to March, medium, 2¼ by 2, flattened roundish, slightly conical, slightly irregular. Colour, entirely covered with dull brownish-green russet. Flesh, firm, juicy, greenish, of excellent flavour Eye, firmly closed in a wide plaited basin. Stem, moderately long in a wide shallow cavity. Growth, compact; very fertile. Leaf, rather large, roundish, dark, upfolded, curved serrate. Origin, supposed to have originated at Roxbury, Mass., early in the seventeeth century. The correct name is Roxbury Russet. A good late fruit. Reinette de Canada Grise is often wrongly called Boston Russet.

BOW HILL PIPPIN. Dessert, November to February, medium, 2¾ by 2¾, flattened round, even. Colour, golden-yellow, slight flush and broad broken stripes.

Flesh, firm, juicy, very yellow, good Blenheim flavour. Eye, open in a deep, wide, and slightly plaited basin. Stem, very long and thin, nearly one inch. Growth, rather slender, little spreading; moderately fertile. Leaf, narrow, rather pale, nearly flat, finely serrate. Origin, raised by Mr. A. S. White, of Bow Hill, near Maidstone, and introduced by Messrs. Bunyard & Co., about 1893. A very good winter fruit of Blenheim character.

BRABANT BELLEFLEUR. *Ronalds*, p. 31. F., Bellefleur de Brabant, ; G., Grosser Brabanter Belle Fleur. (Glory of Flanders, Iron Apple, Winter Bellefleur.) Culinary, till April, 3¼ by 3, fairly large, irregular. Colour, golden-yellow, orange red flush and stripes. Flesh, crisp, yellow, acid, Eye, open in a large wide basin. Stem, short in a deep russet cavity. Growth, moderate; fertile. Leaf, rather large, oval, curved serrate or crenate, held flat. Origin, probably Flemish. Brought to notice at the end of the eighteenth century, and imported into England about 1830. It is not the Brabant Bellefleur of Holland and Belgium, but is here known as the Westland Bellefleur. A useful late fruit.

BRADDICK'S NONPAREIL. *Ronalds*, p. 34. F., Nonpareille de Braddick; G., Braddicks Sondergleichen. (Ditton Pippin, Lincolnshire Reinette.) Dessert, November to April, 2¼ by 1¾, rather small, round, flattened, regular. Colour, greenish-yellow, flushed with brown red, with russet round eye especially. Flesh, firm, yellow, aromatic. Eye small, nearly closed in a wide shallow basin. Stem, short in a wide even russet cavity. Growth, slender; moderately fertile. Leaf, long oval, flat, edges twisted, very deeply and coarsely curved serrate. Origin, raised by Mr. Braddick, of Thames Ditton, about 1800. An apple of first class quality.

BRAMLEYS SEEDLING. *Her. Pom.*, 73. Culinary, November to March, large, 3½ by 2¾, flat, round, irregular. Colour greenish-yellow, red flush with broad broken stripes. Flesh firm, juicy, pale yellow, acid. Eye, closed in a broad, deep, slightly wrinkled basin. Stem, short, in a wide deep, slightly russet cavity. Growth, extremely vigorous; very regularly fertile when the tree is developed. Leaf, very large, dark, round, slightly upfolded, coarsely curved serrate. Origin, raised by Mr. Bramley, a shoemaker, of Southwell, Notts. Introduced by Messrs. Merryweather, in 1876. This is the most popular and profitable of cooking apples; ironclad in constitution, growing wherever apples will grow. It makes a very large spreading tree and should be planted at least thirty feet apart in orchards.

Brandy Apple : *see Golden Harvey.*

BROWNLEES RUSSET. *Her. Pom.*, 54. F., Reinette grise Brownlees; G., Brownlees Graue Reinette. Dessert, January to April, medium, 2¼ by 2, flat, conical, irregular. Colour, entirely covered with brownish-green russet, with faint brownish-red flush. Flesh, tender, greenish, sub-acid, of Nonpareil flavour. Eye, closed in a shallow uneven basin. Stem, short cavity. Growth, compact, rather upright; fertile. Leaf, very narrow, dark, upfolded, down hanging, coarsely crenate. Origin, introduced by Mr. Brownlees, a nurseryman, in 1848. A valuable fruit for winter use.

Brown's Queen Caroline : *see Queen Caroline.*

BUFF COAT. Culinary, December to March, large, 3¼ by 2¼, flat, conical, irregular. Colour, dull yellow-green, with large patches of thick russet. Flesh, firm, juicy, yellowish, sweet. Growth, sturdy; moderately fertile. Origin, unrecorded. An old variety. Resembles Alfriston, but is flatter.

Burlington : *see Newtown Spitzenburg.*

BURR KNOT. *Ronalds*, p. 39. (Bide's Walking Stick.) Culinary, October to November, large, 3¼ by 3, round, conical, irregular. Colour, golden-yellow, faint red flush. Flesh tender, yellow, acid. Growth moderate, compact; fertile. Leaf, small, oval, broadly serrate. Origin, uncertain. This name has been applied to many different fruits on account of the knots on branches, from which roots are easily emitted. Now rarely met with, save in old orchards. This is quite distinct from the Oslin, also called Burr Knot.

Burr Knot : *see Oslin.*

BUXTED FAVOURITE. Culinary, December to February, medium, 2¼ by 2¼, flattened round a little conical, even. Colour, pale golden yellow, slight brown red flush and stripes like a King of the Pippins; smooth. Flesh, yellow, crisp, rather acid, very little flavour. Eye open in a deep and wide plaited basin. Stem, short in a deep narrow russet cavity. A rather poor fruit with me, certainly not more than a cooking variety.

BYFORD WONDER. Culinary, November to December, very large, 3¼ by 2¼, flattened round, nearly regular. Colour, dull yellow with conspicuous russet dots. Flesh, loose, yellowish, sub-acid. Eye, closed in a rather deep basin which is a little puckered. Stem, short and stout in a deep and very wide russeted cavity. Growth, very vigorous; fertile. Leaf, very large, roundish, dark, little upfolded, sharply curved serrate. Origin, unrecorded. Introduced by Messrs. Cranstons, in 1894. A useful fruit often reaching enormous size on young trees.

Caldwell's Keeper ; *see Rymer.*

CALVILLE BLANCHE D'HIVER. *Ronalds*, p. 37. G., Weisser Winter Calville. (Glacé, Reinette à cotés, White Calville, etc.) Culinary or dessert, January to April, 3¼ by 3, medium, round—conical, irregular. Colour, pale yellow. Flesh, melting, pale

33

yellow, aromatic. Eye, closed in a deep and much ribbed basin. Stem, rather long in a deep cavity. Growth, weak; infertile. Leaf, rather large, roundish, finely and regularly serrate. Origin, uncertain; recorded in 1600. Probably French. Of delicate flavour and remarkably melting texture, but rarely well-finished in this country. Should be grown under glass or on a wall. Mr. Leake, of Wisbech, finds this to do excellently in his soil, which is almost free from lime.

CALVILLE MALINGRE. *Her. Pom.*, 56. G., Braunroter Winter Calville. Culinary, December to March, medium, 3 by 2¼, round, a little flattened. Colour, golden yellow, nearly covered with dark red flush and stripes. Flesh, firm, white. Eye, closed in a deep and ribbed basin. Stem, short and stout in a deep cavity. Growth, compact; remarkable fertile. Leaf, long, narrow, upfolded and undulating, crenate. Origin, doubtful. This apple has been always much confused. The variety described above is that known under this name in Britain. Of excellent flavour when cooked, the flesh then being soft and pinkish-yellow.

CALVILLE ROUGE D'HIVER. *Verger*, IV., 76. F., Calville Rouge; G., Roter Winter Calville. (Passe Pomme d'Hiver.) Culinary, December to March, medium, 2¾ by 2¼, round, conical, irregular. Colour, greenish-yellow, almost covered with dark crimson flush. Flesh, crisp, white with occasional red touches, juicy, sub-acid. Leaf, large, pale, upfolded, undulating, variable, finely to coarsely serrate. Eye, usually closed in a deep and wide basin. Stem, long and thin in a very deep cavity. Growth, compact; very fertile. Origin, one of the oldest varieties. Known in France, since 1600. Hardly worthy of cultivation nowadays.

CALVILLE DES FEMMES. G., Frauen Calville. Culinary, till June, very large, 3¾ by 3¼, round, conical, uneven. Colour, green to pale yellow, often with a brownish-red flush. Flesh, white in which greenish veins are noticeable, acid, firm. Eye, large, closed or open in a very large ribbed basin. Stem, usually very short, in a wide, deep cavity. Growth, very vigorous, making a roundish tree. Leaf, rather large, very dark, upfolded, down hanging, sharply serrate. Origin, uncertain, but very probably raised about 1850 in the garden of the Horticultural Society of Angers, France.

Calville Rouge Precoce : *see Reinette Rouge Etoilée.*

Cambridge Pippin : *see Bedfordshire Foundling.*

CAMBUSNETHAN PIPPIN. Culinary or dessert, October to December, medium, 3 by 2, flat, round, regular. Colour, pale yellow with broad, broken red stripes and flush. Flesh, soft, yellowish, fair flavour. Eye, open in a very wide even basin. Stem, of medium length in a fairly deep cavity. Growth, compact ; fertile. Leaf, roundish, upfolded, undulating, regularly crenate. Origin, raised by Mr. Paton, gardener at Cambusnethan House, about 1750. It is much appreciated in the North of England, but of no remarkable merit in the South.

CARDINAL. F., Pierre le Grand. (Peter the Great, Kiarolowski.) Dessert, mid-August-September, medium to large, 3 by 2¾, conical, regular. Colour, pale, creamy white, pinkish flush with broad stripes. Flesh, soft, white, juicy, remarkably sweet and aromatic. Eye, closed in an even and shallow basin. Stem, short and thick, in a narrow and deep cavity. Growth, sturdy, upright ; fertile. Leaf, pale, upfolded, down curved, very minutely serrate. Origin, a Russian variety from Riga, called Kiarolkowski introduced to England about 1880. It was also imported under the name of Peter the Great. A most attractive early fruit, worth growing if only for its beauty.

CARAWAY RUSSET. *Her. Pom.*, p. 21. F., Fenouillet Gris ; G., Grauer Feucher Apfel. [Anis, Fenouillet Anise, Aromatic Russet (of some) Spice Apple, etc., etc.] Dessert, November to March, small, 2 by 1½, flat, regular. Colour, yellow to orange, with russet; generally warted. Flesh, firm, yellow, aromatic. Eye, small, generally closed, in an even and shallow basin. Stem, short and thin in a rather small cavity. Growth, moderate; fertility moderate. Leaf, small, longish oval, upfolded, sharply and irregularly serrate. Origin, French, dating from the seventeenth century. The correct name is Fenouillet Gris. Leroy considers this the Epice d'Hiver of Olivier de Serres. A reliable sort still grown in old orchards.

CARLISLE CASTLE. Culinary, October to November, small, 1¾ by 2½, very flat, quite even. Colour, pale yellow, nearly covered with bright scarlet flush and stripes, smooth, greasy. Flesh, white, juicy, firm, sub-acid. Eye, closed in a deepish, wide and even basin. Stem, very short in a wide russet cavity. Of no value. Resembles Thorle, but the closed eye and deep basin serve at once to distinguish it.

CARLISLE CODLIN. *Ronalds*, p. 3. (Irish Codlin, Musk.) Culinary, August to December, fairly large, 3 by 3, conical, regular. Colour, yellow with slight red flush. Flesh, crisp, white and sweet. Eye, closed in a narrow ribbed basin. Stem, medium in a rather deep cavity. Growth, vigorous; fertility great. Leaf, large, sharply pointed, finely serrate. Origin, probably originated near Carlisle, before 1830. Now superseded by more modern sorts.

Carse O'Gowrie : *see Tower of Glamis*.

CATSHEAD. *Her. Pom.*, L. F., Tête du Chat; G., Schafsnase. (Katzenkopf, Catshead Greening.) Culinary, October to January, large, 3¼ by 3½, long oblong, conical, irregular. Colour, pale yellowish-green, faint brown flush. Flesh, tender, white, sub-acid. Growth, strong; fertile when aged. Leaf, large, round, pale, flat, curved serrate. Origin, Old English sort, known from seventeenth century. Not worthy of cultivation. Superseded by others such as Lord Derby.

Catshead Beaufin : *see Norfolk Beefing.*

Catshead Greening : *see Catshead.*

Cayuga Red Streak : *see Twenty Ounce.*

CELLINI. (Phillips' Seedling.) *Her. Pom.*, 12. Culinary, October to November, medium, 3 by 2½, round, slightly flattened, regular. Colour, pale yellowish-green, strongly striped, and flushed brown red. Flesh, tender white, sub-acid, with curious balsamic flavour. Growth, stocky and a little spreading; extremely fertile. Leaf, rather pale green, upfolded and twisted, boldly curved serrate. Origin, raised by Mr. Leonard Phillips, nurseryman, Vauxhall, and introduced about 1828. Regular cropping is its chief recommendation, but the curious flavour appeals to some.

Chalmer's Large : *see Dutch Codlin.*

CHARLES EYRE. Exhibition or culinary, October to November, enormous, 4 by 3½, roundish oval, even. Colour, pale greenish-yellow. Flesh, soft, greenish-yellow, Growth, vigorous, short jointed, a little spreading. Leaf, rather large, long pointed, oval, very minutely crenate, stipules large and leafy. Origin, raised by Mr. Charles Ross, and introduced to notice about 1911. Will probably be one of the largest apples grown. A larger Pott's Seedling.

CHARLES ROSS. Culinary or dessert, October to December, large, 4 by 3, round even. Colour, very pale yellow green, covered with a light red flush, and bold broken stripes over the whole of the fruit when fully exposed. Flesh, tender, short texture, fairly juicy, quite sweet, pleasant flavour. Eye, open in a shallow even basin. Stem, very short in a rather wide shallow cavity, which usually retains a greenish tinge when the fruit is ripe. Growth, upright, a little spreading; fertile. Leaf, narrow, pea green, nearly flat, finely shallow serrate. Origin, raised by Mr. Charles Ross, and introduced in 1899. This apple is of the

37

Peasgoods style, but is quite distinct, not showing so much bloom on the tree, the fruit being more upright and the carpels flatter and less curved. It is becoming a popular market apple and does extremely well on thin soils on chalk.

CHATLEYS KERNEL. Culinary, January to May, medium, 2¾ by 2, round, flattened, regular. Colour, yellowish-green, with brown red flush. Flesh, very crisp, greenish, acid. Growth, moderate; fertility, moderate. Leaf, grey-green, rather large, flat undulating, finely serrate. Origin, undiscovered. Hardly worthy of cultivation.

CHELMSFORD WONDER. *G. Mag.*, April 11th, 1891. Culinary, November to March, large, 3¼ by 3, round, very regular. Colour, deep yellow with crimson flush and stripes. Flesh, crisp and breaking, flavour, acid. Eye, closed in a shallow plaited basin. Stem, short in a moderate very evenly rounded cavity. Growth, sturdy, upright, spreading; fertility, fair. Leaf, much down folded. Origin, raised near Chelmsford, and introduced by Mr. Saltmarsh in 1891. A very useful fruit of the Wellington style in flesh; it keeps crisp to a very late season. The foliage is remarkably distinct.

Chiver's Seedling: *see Histon Favourite.*

CHRISTMAS PEARMAIN. Dessert, November to December, medium, 2¼ by 2, oval, conical, regular. Colour, dull yellow with brownish-red flush, slight russet and faint stripes. Flesh, firm, yellowish, pleasantly flavoured. Eye, wide open in a shallow even basin. Stem, short in a small round cavity. Growth, compact; extraordinarily fertile. Leaf, rather pale, slightly upfolded, undulated, rather small, finely serrate. Origin, a seedling raised by Mr. Manser, and introduced by Messrs. G. Bunyard & Co., in 1895. This fruit is valuable for small gardens on account of its free cropping powers.

Citron D'Hiver: *see London Pippin.*

CLARK'S SEEDLING. (Royal George.) Culinary, till March, fairly large, 3 by 2¼, round, slightly flattened at each end, fairly regular. Colour, yellow, with brownish red flush and faint stripes. Flesh, firm, juicy, pale, yellow. Growth, vigorous; fertility moderate. Leaf, rather small, very dark, upfolded, undulating, finely crenate or nearly serrate. Origin, raised by a Mr. Clark, at East Bridgeford, Notts., about 1800. This is considered an uncertain cropper in some districts but it is likely to be useful in the South. It is not the Clark's Pippin of Hogg. There is another apple called Royal George of the Warner's type.

CLAYGATE PEARMAIN. *Launche II.,* 72. F., Pomme de Claygate, G. Claygate Parmane. (Ribston Pearmain.) Dessert, December to February, medium, 2¼ by 2, roundish, flattened, regular. Colour, dull green, faint red flush with thin russet. Flesh, crisp, greenish-white, juicy and of excellent flavour. Eye, half open in a wide, rather shallow basin. Stem, rather long, thick in a wide cavity only slightly russeted. Growth, moderate; fertile. Leaf, rather large, horizontal, upfolded, sharply curved serrate. Origin, found in a hedge, near Claygate, by Mr. John Braddick, of Thames Ditton. This is one of the best late dessert apples and is of the highest quality.

Clifton Nonsuch: *see Fearn's Pippin.*

Clissold's Seedling: *see Lodgemore Nonpareil.*

Coates: *see Yorkshire Greening.*

COBHAM. (Pope's Golden Ducat.) Dessert, December to February, medium, 3¼ by 2¼, roundish-square, uneven. Colour, golden-yellow with brown-red flush and faint red stripes. Flesh, firm, yellow, juicy and of good flavour. Eye closed in a shallow, uneven basin. Stem, rather short in a wide russet cavity. Growth, stout, moderate, very fertile. Leaf, rather large, roundish, dark, flat, sharply curved serrate. Origin, said to have been raised in Sittingbourne, by a Mr. Pope, about 1790. Introduced to notice about 1828. It is now little grown, and hardly equal to Blenheim Orange, as stated by Dr. Hogg.

COCKLE'S PIPPIN. *Ronalds*, 23. G., Hahnen Peppin. (Nutmeg Pippin (error), Pilot Russet.) Dessert, December to March, smallish, 2¼ by 2¾, round, conical, regular. Colour, greenish-yellow, with thin cinnamon russet, which increases towards the base. Flesh, crisp, yellow, moderate flavour. Eye, closed in a shallow ribbed basin. Stem, stout and fleshy in a shallow cavity. Growth, moderate, upright, the long willowy shoots being very distinct ; fertile. Leaf, long, rather pale, flat undulating, very markedly doubly curved serrate. Origin, raised by a person named Cockle, in Sussex, probably about 1800. Of excellent flavour in warm seasons. Keeps well. Distinct from Nutmeg Pippin, with which it is often confused.

COCKINGTON CALVILLE. Dessert, January to April, medium, 2¼ by 2¼, round, conical. Colour, pale yellow, almost covered with deep crimson flush. Flesh, very firm, yellowish, sub-acid. Growth, moderate ; fertility moderate. Leaf, large, long, very sharply curved serrate, pea green, upfolded. Origin, uncertain. Grown at Cockington, near Torquay. Of the Calville Rouge type. Of no particular merit.

COLLOGET PIPPIN. (Lawry's Cornish Giant.) Culinary, October to November, very large, 3¼ by 3 (often much larger), flat, conical, very irregular, Colour, yellowish-green with red flush, and bold broken stripes. Flesh, yellow, firm, acid, flavourless. Eye, a little open in a rather deep and much ribbed basin. Stem, short in a rather wide cavity. Growth, extra vigorous, prolific. Leaf, undulating, flat, down hanging. Origin, an old Cornish variety named after the place of its origin. Of no particular merit.

40

COLONEL VAUGHAN. *Her. Pom.*, 74. G., Rother Kentische Peppin. (Kentish Pippin, Scarlet Incomparaable.) Culinary or dessert, November to January, medium, 2¼ by 2⅜, round oblong, Colour, golden-yellow, almost entirely with broad broken stripes of bright red and slight flush. Flesh, nearly white, firm, very juicy and sweet, often stained with a little red. Eye, closed or a little open in a shallow much ribbed basin. Stem, short in a fairly deep even cavity into which the coloured stripes run. Growth, moderate, makes a nice compact tree ; extremely fertile. Leaf, roundish, pea green, nearly flat, twisted, sharply curved serrate. Origin, this has been grown in Kent from the seventeenth century. It crops so well and is so useful for small gardens that it seems a pity that it is almost forgotten in these days.

Common Codlin : *see English Codlin.*

Copmansthorp Crab : *see Dutch Mignonne.*

Corby Seedling : *see Hormead Pearmain.*

CORNISH AROMATIC. *Ronalds,* p. 15. (as Aromatic Russet). Dessert, December to February, medium, 3 by 3, round, conical, uneven. Colour, golden-yellow with red flush and russet. Flesh, yellow, crisp, aromatic. Eye, very small, closed in a shallow ribbed basin. Stem, rather short in a wide russet cavity. Growth, compact, twiggy ; moderately fertile. Leaf, medium, rather long oval, crenate. Origin, originated in Cornwall, perhaps in the seventeenth century. This apple is of the highest quality, and appearance.

CORNISH GILLYFLOWER. *Her. Pom.*, p. 41. F., Calville d'Angelterre ; G., Cornwalliser Nelken (Regelans). Dessert, December to May, 2¾ by 3, medium, round, conical, irregular. Colour, greenish-yellow, streaked dull red with russet. Flesh, firm, pale yellow, very richly flavoured. Eye, closed in a deep ribbed basin. Stem, fairly long in a small cavity.

Growth, slender ; moderately fertile. Leaf, upward held, upfolded. Origin, probably Cornish, introduced to notice about 1813. Probably not the July flower of Evelyn. Of delicious flavour ; requires good treatment and a warm climate. Best as a standard or free bush.

CORNISH PINE. (Red Ribbed Greening.) Culinary, December to February, medium to large, 2¼ by 2¾, oblong, conical, very irregular. Colour, golden-yellow, with thick broken stripes. Flesh, firm, yellow, sweet, aromatic. Moderately fertile. Leaf, large, long, dark, upfolded, down held, finely serrate. Origin, raised at Exminster, Devon, from a pip of Cornish Gillyflower.

CORONATION. *Gard. Chron.*, 1905, p. 28. Culinary or dessert, October to December, 3¼ by 2¾, medium, round, flattened at top and bottom, slightly conical, very regular. Colour, yellow, dusted with dark red and thick blotchy stripes. Flesh, fairly firm, yellowish, fair flavour. Eye, closed or a little open in a shallow plaited basin. Stem, very long in an even russet rather wide cavity. Growth, upright, vigorous and fertile. Leaf, long oval, pale green, very regularly curved serrate, upfolded, falls early. Origin, raised by Mr. Prinsep, gardener at Buxted Park, Sussex. Introduced by Mr. Pyne, of Topsham. Not of great merit, but pleasantly flavoured in its earlier season but this soon goes off leaving it mealy and tasteless.

Councillor : *see Yorkshire Beauty.*

Countess of Warwick ; *see Beauty of Kent.*

Couronne des Dames : *see Baumann's Reinette.*

COURT OF WICK. *Ronalds*, p. 12. (Fry's Pippin, Golden Drop, Woods Huntingdon.) Dessert, December to March, small, 2¼ by 1¾, rounded, square, regular. Colour, pale yellow, flushed with rich orange. Flesh, crisp, yellow, richly flavoured, slightly acid. Eye, open in a wide basin. Stem, short, in a shallow russet cavity. Growth, medium, spreading; fertility good. Leaf, medium, long oval, sharply serrate. Origin, raised near Yatton, Somerset, and introduced to commence in 1790, by Messrs. Wood, of Huntingdon. A good old sort, now little grown.

Court Pendu Blanc : *see Orleans Reinette.*

COURT PENDU PLAT. *Ronalds*, p. 12. G., Koeniglicher Kurzstiel. (de Bertin, Garnons, Wise Apple, Court Queue, Wollaton Pippin, etc., etc.) Dessert, till April, smallish, 2¼ by 1¾, flat, regular. Colour, yellow covered with dull red flush and slight russet. Flesh, yellow, firm, rich flavour. Eye, open in a very deep even basin. Stem, very short in a deep cavity. Growth, small; fertility, good. The latest of all to flower, hence its name, Wise Apple. Leaf, rather small, much upward cupped, sharply serrate. Origin, of great antiquity; known in the sixteenth century, and possibly dating from Roman days. A valuable sort, its late flowering habit often enabling it to escape early frosts. One of the best for a heavy clay soil.

Court Queue : *see Court Pendu Plat.*

COX'S ORANGE. *Her. Pom.*, 16. F., Orange de Cox ; G., Cox's Orangen Reinette. Dessert, November to March, medium, 2¼ by 2½, round, conical, regular. Colour, golden yellow with brownish-red flush, and russet and faint stripes. Flesh, tender, yellow, juicy and of the highest flavour. Eye, half closed, segments reflexed, in a very shallow slightly ribbed basin, often russeted. Stem, moderately stout, in a wide shallow cavity, always a little russeted. Growth, slender ; fertility, moderate. Leaf, narrow, rather pale, undulated, upfolded, crenate. Origin, raised in 1825, by Mr. Cox, a retired brewer of Colnbrook Lawn, near Slough, and introduced by Mr. Charles Turner, about 1850. Generally considered to be the richest flavoured of English Apples.

COX'S POMONA. *Her. Pom.*, 12. F., Pomona de Cox. (Royal Portugee, Hill's Seedling.) Dessert or culinary, October to December, medium, 3 by 2, round, flattened, conical, irregular. Colour, yellow flushed and striped with crimson. Flesh, tender, white, sub-acid. Eye, open in a deep basin which has five prominent knobs. Stem, rather short in a very deep cavity. Growth, moderate; fertile. Leaf, medium, roundish, light green, nearly flat, broad shallow serrate. Origin, raised by Mr. Cox, in 1825, near Slough, Bucks., and sent out by Mr. Smale, Colnbrook nursery. A very attractive fruit.

CRAWLEY BEAUTY. Culinary, December to February, medium to large, 3¼ by 2¾, flattened round, even. Colour, pale creamy yellow, red flush and broken stripes. Flesh, firm, greenish-white, acid, good flavour when cooked. Eye, open in a deep and wide basin. Stem, medium in a broad and rather deep cavity. Growth, vigorous; very fertile. Leaf, round-oval, crenate or doubly serrate. Origin, raised in a cottage garden, near Crawley, Sussex, and introduced by Messrs. Cheal & Co. This promises to be a very useful variety, flowering very late.

CRAWLEY REINETTE. Dessert or culinary, December to March, medium, 3¼ by 3¼, round oblong, nearly regular. Colour, pale yellow, covered with rich red flush and faint inconspicuous stripes; general colouring being like King of the Pippins. Flesh, white, crisp, juicy, of fair flavour. Eye, open in a moderately deep, slightly ribbed basin. Stem, rather short in moderately deep, angular, russeted cavity. Growth, vigorous, little spreading; fertility said to be very good. Leaf, long, held flat, coarsely crenate. Origin, recent; introduced by Messrs. Cheal. This apple might be described as a later King of the Pippins, but I have not grown it sufficiently long to speak very definitely of its merits.

44

CRIMSON BRAMLEY. A form of Bramley's Seedling, differing only in the possession of a rich red colour all over the fruit. Originated as a bud sport in an orchard in Southwell, Notts.

Croft-en-Reich : *see Galloway Pippin.*

Croft-St. Andrews : *see Galloway Pippin.*

Culver Russet : *see Syke House Russet.*

Cumberland Favourite : *see Yorkshire Beauty.*

CUTLER GRIEVE. Dessert, November to January, medium, 2⅜ by 2¼, rounded, flattened, conical. Colour golden-yellow, almost covered with brilliant scarlet flush, under which are seen very broad stripes. Skin, greasy. Flesh, white, firm, close grained, juicy, sweet, but no particular flavour. Eye, closed in a medium, much ribbed basin. Stem, slender in a fairly deep, wide, cavity, which is often a little russeted. Growth, vigorous, rather upright ; fertility, good. Leaf, round-ish, finely curved serrate. Origin, raised by Mr. James Grieve, and introduced by Mr. Storrie. The brilliant appearance of this apple together with its season suggest that it is the successor of Worcester Pearmain, for which market growers have long been searching.

Dainty : *see Hoary Morning.*

D'ARCY SPICE. (*Her. Pom.*, 25. (Baddow Pippin, Essex Spice, Spice, Spring Ribston). Dessert, November to April, medium, 2¼ by 2¼, square-rounded irregular. Colour, green to yellow, with dull red flush, covered with russet. Flesh, firm, greenish, highly aromatic. Eye, slightly open in a deep wrinkled basin. Stem, short rather, deeply inserted in a russet cavity. Growth, weak ; fertility, moderate. Leaf, medium, dark, upfolded, sharply serrate or curved serrate. Origin, probably originated in Essex. Introduced to general notice about 1850. Of the finest quality, but not often found thriving out of East Anglia.

45

Dean's Codlin: *see Pott's Seedling*.

De Bertin: *see Court Pendu Plat*.

DELICIOUS. *Gard. Mag.*, 1914, p. 97. Dessert, November to January, medium, 2¼ by 2½, round, conical, angular. Colour, golden-yellow with dark crimson flush and stripes. Flesh, firm, yellow, juicy and highly flavoured. Eye, slightly open in a rather deep ribbed basin. Stem, medium in a fairly deep cavity. Growth, compact; fertile. Leaf, medium, long, oval, upfolded, deeply curved serrate. Originated in the garden of Mr. Jesse Hiatt, of Peru, Iowa, U.S.A., about 1880, and introduced into England about 1912. Extremely hardy in its native country, and likely to prove a valuable fruit for Great Britain.

Deux Ans: *see Hambledon Deux Ans*.

DEVONSHIRE QUARRENDEN. *Her. Pom.*, p. 3. F., Quarrendon du Comté de Devon; G., Englisher Scharlach Peppin. (Sack, Quarrington (error).) Dessert, end August-September, small to medium, 2¼ by 1¾, flat, irregular. Colour, covered with dark crimson flush. Flesh, crisp, greenish, aromatic. Eye, closed in a wide shallow basin. Stem, fairly long in a deep cavity. Growth, moderate, rather spreading; fertility irregular. Leaf, upfolded, undulating. Origin, this is mentioned by Worlidge, in his *Vinetum Britannicum* in 1678, and probably takes its name from Carentan, an apple district in Normandy. Of most distinct and refreshing flavour; rather subject to canker.

DEVONSHIRE QUEEN. *Ronalds*, p. 25. Culinary, October, medium, 3¾ by 2¼, flattened, round, irregular. Colour, bright yellow, flushed and striped with scarlet. Flesh, soft, yellowish-white, tinged with red. Eye, closed in a shallow much ribbed basin. Stem, medium, in a very deep cavity. Growth, moderate; fertile. Origin, probably from the county of its name. Known in 1820. Not worthy of cultivation.

DEWDNEY'S SEEDLING. (Baron Wolseley.) Culinary, December to January, large, 3 by 2¼, flat, conical, rather irregular. Colour, golden-yellow, with brownish-red flush. Flesh, firm, pale yellow, juicy and brisk. Eye, closed in a round, moderately deep slightly ribbed basin. Stem, rather short, stout in a wide cavity, nearly free from russet. Growth, straggling, vigorous; fertile. Leaf, moderate, dark, nearly flat, undulating, curved serrate .Origin, raised at Barrowby, near Grantham, by Mr. Dewdney, about 1850. A useful late cooking variety.

DIAMOND JUBILEE. Dessert or culinary, January to March, rather large, 2¾ by 2¾, round, conical, even. Colour, even grass green, changing to yellow. Flesh, firm, white, flavour rather good. Eye, nearly closed in a flat and shallow plaited basin, Stem, short, and moderately stout, in a very small cavity. Growth, rather upright, spreading, twiggy, making a round tree. Leaf, rather large, narrow, flat, a little twisted, undulating, curved serrate, held up. Origin, raised at Rainham, Kent, and introduced in 1901. A good late apple, which may be described as an earlier Beauty of Stoke. Royal Late which is sometimes said to be the same is quite distinct.

Diels Sommer König : *see Gravenstein.*

Ditton Pippin : *see Braddick's Nonpareil.*

Dr. Harvey : *see Waltham Abbey.*

DOCTOR HOGG. Culinary, September to February, fairly large, 3 by 3, oval, conical, regular. Colour, yellow with pale flush. Eye, open in a deep irregular basin. Stem, rather long in a wide cavity. Flesh, tender, white, sweet. Growth, moderate; fertile. Leaf, horizontal, upfolded. Origin, a supposed seedling from Calville Blanche. Raised by Mr. Ford, gardener at Leonardslee, Horsham, and introduced by Messrs. W. Paul & Son, about 1880. Now little grown, having been superseded.

Dolgoi Squoznoi : *see Sugar Loaf Pippin*.

DOMINO. Culinary, September to October, medium, 2¼ by 2¾, oblong, rounded, irregular. Colour, pale yellowish green with occasional faint flush. Flesh, yellowish-white, crisp, acid. Eye, closed in a moderately deep broad ribbed basin. Stem, short in a narrow fairly deep cavity. Growth, upright, compact and twiggy ; very fertile. Leaf, pale, long oval, shallow serrate, flat, twisted, falls early. Origin, unrecorded ; much grown around London ; probably from the Midland Counties. A useful fruit of the Codlin type.

D. T. Fish : *see Warner's King*.

DUCHESS' FAVOURITE. *Her. Pom.*, 69. Dessert, September to October, medium, 2¼ by 2, round, flattened, regular. Colour, pale yellow, almost entirely covered with crimson red. Flesh, crisp, yellow, brisk and pleasant, often tinged with red. Eye, open in a shallow wrinkled basin. Stem, moderately long in a rather deep evenly russeted cavity. Growth, upright ; very fertile. Leaf, rather small, light green, upfolded, finely crenate. Origin, raised by Mr. Cree, a nurseryman of Addlestone, before 1823. This apple is attractive in appearance and largely grown for market use.

DUCHESS OF OLDENBURG. *Ronalds*, p. 6. F., Borovitsky ; G., Charlamovski. (Baroveski, Borowinka.) Culinary or dessert, August to September, medium, 3¼ by 2¾, round, flattened, regular. Colour, palest yellow, with strong red stripes. Flesh, soft, white, sub-acid. Eye, closed in a deep even basin. Stem, slender in a deep narrow cavity. Growth, vigorous, upright ; fertility, good. Leaf, medium, upfolded, undulating, nearly serrate. Origin, Russian. Introduced into England in 1824. Of most attractive appearance, and a refreshing summer fruit.

DUKE OF DEVONSHIRE. Dessert, February to March, small to medium, 2¼ by 2, round, conical, fairly regular. Colour, dull golden-yellow, almost covered with russet. Flesh, firm, pale greenish-yellow, good flavour, rather dry. Eye, half open, almost on a level with the fruit. Stem, very short and stout in a small russet cavity. Growth, moderate, makes a fine standard; very fertile. Leaf, slightly upward folding, very boldly serrate, sometimes crenate. Origin, raised at Holker Hall, Lancs., by Mr. Wilson, gardener to the Duke of Devonshire, in 1835. It is quite indispensable for late use. Remarkable for the variegation of fruit, leaves and wood. This is best seen in young trees. Makes a fine standard tree.

Duke of Wellington : *see Wellington.*

DUMMELOUS SEEDLING. *Ronalds*, P. 19. (Belle des Vennes, Dumelow's Seedling, Duke of Wellington, Normanton Wonder.) Culinary, till March, medium, 3 by 2¼, flattened round, regular. Colour, creamy-yellow with scarlet flush. Flesh, crisp, white, acid. Eye, open in a flat wrinkled basin. Stem, very short in a very shallow cavity or almost on surface. Growth, vigorous; fertility fair. Leaf, fairly large, rather pale, nearly flat, very coarsely serrate or crenate. Origin, raised at Shakerstone, Leicester, by Mr. Dummelow, in the latter part of the nineteenth century. One of the best of cooking apples for those who like a brisk acidity. It is apt to canker.

Dummelow's Seedling : *see Wellington.*

Dunster Codlin : *see Tower of Glamis.*

DUTCH CODLIN. *Ronalds*, p. 36. G., Hollandische Kuchen Apfel. (Chalmers Large, White Codlin, Royal Codlin, Glory of the West (error).) Culinary, till November, large, 4 by 3¼, conical, oblong, very irregular. Colour, greenish-yellow, with faint orange flush. Flesh, firm, white, acid, Eye, closed in a very deep basin. Stem, long, in a narrow cavity. Growth, moderate; not very fertile. Leaf, very large, roundish oval, bi-serrate. Origin, probably Dutch. Brought to notice about 1783. Hardly worthy of cultivation nowadays.

DUTCH MIGNONNE. *Ronalds*, p. 26. F., Reinette de Caux ; G., Grosser Casseler Reinette. (Copmansthorp Crab, Pomme de Laak, Stettin Pippin, Paternoster, etc.) Culinary or dessert, till March, medium, 3¼ by 3, flattened, round, fairly regular. Colour, pale yellow, with bold red stripes and flush. Flesh, firm, yellow, moderate flavour. Eye, closed, in a moderate basin. Stem, rather long, in a narrow russet cavity. Growth, vigorous ; very fertile. Leaf, rather pale, slightly up-folded, boldly curved serrate. Origin, probably German. Brought into England about 1780. A most useful, fertile fruit. Considered by many to be worthy of dessert use late in the season. Grosser Casseler Reinette is the original name.

Dymond's Sugar Loaf : *see Sugar Loaf Pippin.*

Early Crofton : *see Irish Peach.*

Early Julien : *see Early Julyan.*

EARLY JULYAN. *Her. Pom.*, 41. F., Julien Précoce. (Early Julien, Fair Lady.) Culinary or dessert, August, 2¼ by 2, smallish, flattened, conical, angular. Colour, pale golden-yellow, occasionally with a slight flush. Flesh, crisp, yellow, acid. Eye, closed, in a much ribbed basin. Stem, thick, very hairy, in a deep cavity. Growth, rather dwarfish ; fertile. Leaf, roundish oval, narrow, undulating, sharply bi-serrate. Origin, uncertain. Known before 1800. Formerly much grown for market.

Early May : *see White Joaneting.*

EARLY NONPAREIL. *Her. Pom.*, 27. F., Nonpareille hative ; G., Frueher Nonpareil. (Hick's Fancy, Stagg's Nonpareil.) Dessert, October to December, small, 2¼ by 1¾, round, conical, regular. Colour, green to deep yellow, with russet. Flesh, tender, greenish, aromatic. Eye, slightly open in a shallow basin. Stem, rather long, in a small cavity. Growth, moderate, upright ; fertile. Leaf, medium, round oval, crenate. Origin, raised by a Mr. Stagg, of Caister Great Yarmouth, about 1870, from a seed of Old Nonpareil. A delicious fruit, seldom grown now.

Early Peach : *see River's Early Peach.*

Early Pippin : *see Yellow Ingrestrie.*

Early Red Calville : *see Reinette Rouge Etoilee.*

EARLY RED MARGARET. Dessert, early August, medium, 2¼ by 2¼, round, conical, tapering to eye. Colour, pale greenish-yellow with dull brown-red flush, not striped. Skin, smooth, greasy. Flesh, tender, greenish white, flavour flat, not so good as Red Juneating. Eye, open in a narrow ribbed basin. Stem, stout, quarter-inch, protruding. Growth, moderate, very fertile.

Early Victoria : *see Emneth Early.*

EASTER ORANGE. Dessert, February to April, medium, 2¼ by 2¼, round, a little flattened, regular. Colour, deep golden-yellow with flush and stripes of dark-red brown and marked scaly russet around stem. Flesh, firm, yellow, moderately juicy and of good flavour. Eye, closed in a shallow much puckered basin. Stem, medium, rather slender in a rather wide, round cavity which has a good deal of scaly russet. Growth, moderate ; fertile. Leaf, held flat, rather pale. Origin, introduced by Messrs. Hillier, of Winchester. A fruit of attractive appearance and good flavour for late winter and spring use.

Easter Pippin : *see French Crab.*

ECKLINVILLE. *Her. Pom.*, p. 17. G., Saemling aus Ecklinville. (Glory of the West.) Culinary, September to November, fairly large, 3¼ by 2¼, round, flattened, regular. Colour, pea green to yellow, with occasional red flush. Flesh, tender, white, acid. Eye, closed in a deep and wide basin. Stem, very short in a rather deep cavity, which is veined with russet. Growth, vigorous; fertile. Leaf, rather narrow, light green, flat, undulating, shallow serrate or crenate. Origin, raised at Ecklinville, Ireland, about 1820, by a gardener named Logan. A most excellent cooker. Rather apt to canker in some soils.

Edmonton: *see Kerry Pippin.*

EDWARD VII. *Garden*, 1911, 523. Culinary, December to April, large, 3¼ by 2¼, oblong, regular. Colour, pale yellow with faint brownish-red flush. Flesh, extremely firm, yellow, acid, juicy. Eye, open in a wide rather deep basin which is slightly ribbed. Stem, short in a fairly wide not deep cavity. Growth, vigorous; moderately fertile. Leaf, dark, held flat, undulating, roundish oval, crenate. Origin, said to be Blenheim Orange × Golden Noble. Introduced by Messrs. Rowe, of Worcester, about 1908. A valuable fruit, which should be more widely cultivated. Cooks dark red and transparent. It usually has a small raised line down one side as in Keswick Codlin.

Egg: *see Paradise White.*

EGREMONT RUSSET. Dessert, October to December, medium, 2¼ by 1¾, round, regular. Colour, yellow, golden-brown flush almost covered with russet. Flesh, firm, greenish yellow, of very distinct and good flavour. Eye, wide open, in a shallow even basin. Stem, very short in a very narrow cavity. Growth, neat, upright, well spurred; fertile. Leaf, rather small very narrow, upfolded, undulated, finely serrate, often curved serrate. Origin, unrecorded. Introduced to notice about 1880. A delicious fruit, especially suited for garden use.

ELLISONS ORANGE. Dessert, September to October, medium, 2¼ by 2¼, round, slightly conical. Colour, golden, yellow with crimson stripes and slight flush.

Flesh, tender, markedly yellow, of fair flavour. Eye, nearly closed in a shallow basin. Stem, long and slender in an even cavity. Growth, slender; fertility, fair. Leaf, long pointed, upfolded, undulated, very boldly crenate. Origin, raised by Rev. C. C. Ellison, Bracebridge, and Mr. Wipf, gardener at Hartshorne Hall (Cox × Calville Blanche). Introduced by Messrs. Pennell and Sons, 1911. Resembles Cox's Orange very closely in appearance and is of good flavour for a short period.

Embersons : *see Waltham Abbey.*

EMNETH EARLY. (Early Victoria.) Culinary, July to August, medium to large, 2½ by 2¾, conical, irregular. Colour, yellowish-green. Flesh, greenish-white, rather soft, cooking frothily. Eye, closed in a shallow knobbed basin. Stem, rather short in a rather wide and deep cavity, which has no russet. Growth, compact, upright, moderate. Leaf, rather large, pale. twisted, broadly serrate. Origin introduced by Messrs. Cross, Wisbech, in 1899. Said to be Lord Grosvenor × Keswick Codlin. The best of the early codlins for crop, vigour, and appearance.

EMPEROR ALEXANDER. *Ronalds* p. 25. F., Grand Alexandre ; G., Kaiser Alexander. (Aporta, English King.) Culinary or dessert, September to November, large, 4 by 3, round, conical, flattened on five sides. Colour, golden-yellow, with broad red stripes and flush. Flesh, pale yellow, tender, sweet. Eye, closed, in a rather deep and plaited basin, which is topped by five angular ribs. Stem, rather long in a deep and wide russet-lined cavity. Growth, vigorous, spreading ; fertility moderate. Leaf, large, roundish, pale grey-green, down hanging, nearly flat, very coarsely crenate. Origin, Russian. Imported into England in 1817. It has suffered often at the hands of re-christeners. Valued chiefly on the exhibition table. May be distinguished from Bismarck by the short round seeds.

Emperor Napoleon : *see Reynold's Peach.*

ENCORE. *Gard. Chron.*, 1907, p. 2. Culinary, till June, large, 3¼ by 2¼, much flattened, nearly regular, oblong round. Colour, grass-green, changing to pale yellow, with occasional brown flush and stripes. Flesh, fairly soft, greenish-white, slightly acid. Eye, closed or a little open, in a broad ribbed basin. Stem, very short in a deep narrow, russet cavity. Growth, vigorous; fertile. Leaf, oval, pale, slightly upfolded, undulating, finely serrate. Origin, raised by Mr. Charles Ross (Warner's King × Northern Greening). Introduced by Messrs. Cheal, in 1908. A very promising fruit, heavy and keeps with me later than either Bramley's Seedling or Lane's Prince Albert.

ENDSLEIGH BEAUTY. Dessert or culinary, October to December, large, 2½ by 3, round, much flattened each end. Colour, yellow with a faint brown-red flush and pale stripes, dusted with a little fine russet. Flesh, firm, pale yellow, of Blenheim style, without its flavour. Eye, closed in a wide shallow basin, slightly plaited. Stem, stout, knobbed at end, in a moderately wide and deep cavity, faintly russet. Growth, upright, spreading. Leaf, pea green, upfolded, sharply serrate. Origin, undiscovered. A handsome fruit of Blenheim style.

ENGLISH CODLIN. *Her. Pom.*, 31. (Common Codlin, Quodlin.) Culinary, August to September, medium, 3¼ by 2¼, conical, irregular. Colour, yellow with red flush and slight russet. Flesh, tender, white, acid, pleasant aroma. Eye, closed in a wide and deep ribbed basin. Stem, fairly long in a wide and deep cavity from which russet veining extends. Growth, moderate; fertility immense. Leaf, rather large, round oval, sharply serrate. Origin, English and of great antiquity; known before the seventeenth century. Very little grown nowadays. Much used in olden times for espaliers, and propagated by rooted branches.

Englische Granat Reinette : *see Ribston Pippin.*

English King : *see Emperor Alexander.*

English Nonpareil : *see Nonpareil*.

English Spitzenberg : *see Newtown Spitzenberg*.

Essex Spice : *see D'Arcy Spice*.

EVAGIL. Dessert or culinary, September to October, medium, 2¼ by 2, flat, even. Colour, an even golden-yellow. Flesh, pale yellow, rather hard and dry. Eye, open in a shallow wide basin. Stem, very short in a very narrow deep cavity. Growth, moderate ; fertility, poor. Leaf, small, roundish, sharply pointed, sharply curved serrate. Origin, found at Thielt by Dr. Vander Espt, and introduced in 1863, by Van Houtte & Sons. Not worthy of cultivation.

Eve : *see Mank's Codlin*.

Eve : *see Paradise White*.

Eve : *see Red Joaneting*.

Fair Lady : *see Early Julyan*.

FAMEUSE. *Ronalds*, p. I., F., De Neige. (Snow, Royal Snow, Sanguineous.) Dessert, November to January, small, 2¼ by 2¼, round, flattened, regular. Colour, brilliant red flush almost covering fruit. Flesh, crisp, white, flavour poor. Eye, a little open in a shallow ribbed basin. Stem, slender in a round even narrow cavity. Growth, vigorous ; fertility, good. Leaf, medium, narrow, held out, nearly flat, sharply serrate.
Origin, probably Canadian ; known before the seventeenth century. Known in England about 1800. Of no value in Britain. Notable for its white flesh.

FARMER'S SEEDLING. Culinary, till May, large, round, slightly conical, fairly regular. Colour, yellowish-green, with brick-red flush and faint stripes. Flesh, greenish-white, firm, acid. Eye, closed, the long segment tips reflexed in a wide boldly ribbed basin. Stem, fairly long, stout and woolly, in a deep russet cavity.

55

Leaf, large, long oval, boldly crenate, upward folded. Origin, unknown. Not worthy of retention. The appearance generally is that of a late Allington Pippin.

FEARN'S PIPPIN. *Ronalds*, p. 12. (Bennet's Defiance, Clifton Nonsuch.) Dessert, November to March, medium, 2¼ by 2, flat, regular. Colour, pale yellow, with dark crimson flush, crisp, yellowish, aromatic. Eye, open in a very wide shallow ribbed basin. Stem, short in a wide cavity. Growth, moderate; fertility good. Leaf, medium flat, edges down curved, rather coarsely bi-serrate. Origin, raised at Fulham, in the garden of Mr. Bagley, before 1780, according to Rogers. An excellent old sort which keeps well.

FELTHAM BEAUTY. *Gard. Chron.*, 1908, p. 178. Dessert, August to September, medium, 3 by 2¾, oblong conical, nearly regular. Colour, yellowish-green with red stripes and flush. Flesh, yellowish, crisp and very highly flavoured, sweet. Growth, slender, upright; fertile. Origin, raised and introduced by Messrs. Veitch, from Cox's Orange × Gladstone. A very promising fruit.

Fenn's Wonder : *see Lord Stradbrook.*

Fenouillet Anisé : *see Caraway Russet.*

Five Crown Pippin : *see London Pippin.*

FLANDERS PIPPIN. Culinary, November to January, moderately large, 3¼ by 2¾, flat conical, uneven. Colour, greenish-yellow with brick-red flush and broad crimson stripes. Flesh, firm, greenish-yellow, juicy and acid with balsamic flavour. Eye, closed in a much ribbed basin. Stem, medium, in a rather deep russet cavity. Growth, moderate; fertile. Leaf, rather large, roundish, pea green, nearly flat, sharply serrate. Origin, unrecorded. Probably continental. Often confused with Mère de Menage from which it is quite distinct.

FORFAR PIPPIN. Dessert, till March, small to medium, 2¼ by 2, roundish conical. regular. Colour, pale green to yellow, with russet dots and veins. Flesh, tender, greenish-yellow, sub-acid and pleasantly flavoured. Eye, closed in a shallow, wrinkled basin. Stem, fairly long, in a shallow cavity. Growth, compact; moderately fertile. Leaf, medium, oval, upfolded, finely serrate. Origin, uncertain; probably from the county after which it is named. A very excellent fruit, especially for those of riper years.

FORESTER. Culinary, December to January, large, 3¼ by 3, roundish, slightly flattened at each end, little angular, but ribs well rounded. Colour, green, fading to yellow with faint brown red flush, covered with little thin russet and large black dots. Eye, closed in a wide slightly deep basin. Stem, medium, in a wide shallow faintly russeted cavity. Flesh, greenish-white, soft in grain, somewhat acid. Origin unknown. A favourite in many parts of Shropshire and Worcestershire.

Formosa Pippin: *see Ribston Pippin*.

FOSTER'S SEEDLING. Culinary, November to March, medium, 2¼ by 2, flattened round, regular. Colour, golden-yellow, with deep brown flush and faint stripes. Flesh, tender, pale yellow, very juicy and slightly acid. Eye, very large, wide open in a broad deep basin. Stem, very short in a wide cavity. Growth, dwarf; fertility. extraordinary. Leaf, rather small, pea green, upcupped, undulating, irregularly crenate or serrate. Origin, a seedling raised at Maidstone, and introduced by Messrs. G. Bunyard & Co., about 1893. Resembles Cellini, but keeps longer.

FRAISE D' HOFINGER. G., Hofingers Himbeer Apfel. Dessert, November to March, rather large, 2¼ by 3, round, slightly rounded to eye. Colour, pale yellow, shaded nearly all over with rich carmine, approaching Gascoynes Seedling in colour. Flesh, greenish-white, slight musky flavour. Eye, closed, in a very deep and slightly irregular basin. Stem, short and stout, in a moderately deep cavity. rather irregular in shape. Growth, compact, upright spreading. Leaf, upheld and upfolded, regularly crenate. Origin, found by Liegel in the Rev. Hofinger's garden, at St. Peters, Brunau, before 1851. Of no merit except for its lovely colour.

FRANKLYN'S GOLDEN PIPPIN. *Ronalds*, p. 18. Dessert, October to December, small, 2¼ by 2, round, flattened. Colour, golden-yellow, Flesh, crisp, yellow, slightly acid. Eye open, in a wide shallow basin. Stem, short in a small round cavity. Growth, strong; fertile. Leaf, roundish oval, slightly upfolded, sharply serrate. Origin. I find the following note in my copy of Brookshaw's *Pomona Britannica*: "It was not Dr. Franklin, who introduced this apple but Mr. Franklyn, a florist, whose son and grandson, attended to Mr. Percival's tulips for many years. The grandson now lives at Highbury (1853)." Now almost out of cultivation.

FRENCH CRAB. *Ronalds*, p. 42. G., Gruener Oster. (Easter Pippin, Ironstone Pippin, Iron King, John Apple, Winter Greening (Hogg).) Culinary, keeps a year or more, medium, 3¼ by 2¼, round, fairly regular. Colour, pea green. Flesh, greenish, crisp, acid. Eye, closed in a shallow wrinkled basin with five prominent ribs at top. Stem, rather short in a russet cavity. Growth, vigorous; fertile. Leaf, large, round oval, upfolded, coarsely serrate. Origin unknown. Probably imported into England at the end of the eighteenth century. A valuable late season fruit, cooking excellently. The desire of Hogg to substitute the name Winter Greening has not been adopted. I therefore retain the name by which it is best known.

FROGMORE PROLIFIC. Culinary, September to December, medium, 3 by 2¼, round, conical, regular.

Colour, greenish-yellow, dusted with red and broad broken stripes. Flesh, soft, white, sub-acid. Eye, closed, in a shallow even basin. Stem, long, in a deepish cavity. Growth, moderate ; fertile. Leaf, oval, bluntly pointed, finely serrate. Origin, raised in the Royal Gardens at Frogmore, by Mr. Ingram. Now little grown.

Fry's Pippin : *see Court of Wick.*

GABALVA. *Gard. Chron.*, 1900, p. 165. Dessert or culinary, December to January, large, 3 by 2¾, roundish, conical, irregular. Colour, dull yellow, with shiny red flush, and often half covered with russet. Flesh, soft, yellow, aromatic, rather dry ; of Blenheim class. Eye, closed, in a shallow ribbed basin. Stem, very short, in a deep russet cavity. Growth, spreading ; not very fertile. Leaf, rather large, oval, pea green, upfolded, undulated, very finely and doubly serrate. Origin, introduced by Messrs. Treseder & Son, Cardiff, 1901. Not sufficiently good for retention.

GALLOWAY PIPPIN. *Fl. and Pom.*, 1872, p. 193. (Croft-en-Reich, Croft St. Andrews.) Culinary, till February, large, 3 by 2½, round, much flattened, regular. Colour, pale yellow, with slight brownish flush. Flesh, crisp, pale yellow, juicy. Eye, open, in a rather deep basin. Stem, medium, in a deep cavity. Growth, vigorous, and a regular cropper. Origin, supposed to have originated by a Crofter at St. Andrews, near Wigtown. Known in the South of England about 1872. Very valuable for the Northern counties.

Garnons : *see Court Pendu Plat.*

GASCOYNE'S SCARLET. Exhibition, September to January, large, 2¾ by 2¾, slightly flattened, oval, very slightly ribbed. Colour, entirely covered with brilliant scarlet, faintly striped, with a delicate bloom giving a blue tinge. Flesh, loose, pale with red stainings ; pleasant balsamic flavour. Eye, firmly closed in a deep much ribbed basin. Stem, long, stout, in a deep narrow cavity. Growth, vigorous, rather spreading and uneven, best as a standard or bush; fertility, poor, hence it is now rarely grown, except for decorative purposes. Leaf, large, pale, flat, lax, irregularly curved serrate. Origin, raised by Mr. Gascoyne, Bapchild Court, Sittingbourne, Kent, and introduced by Messrs. G. Bunyard & Co., Maidstone, in 1871.

German Nonpareil : *see Wyken Pippin*.

GIPSY KING. *Her. Pom.*, 69. Dessert, November to January, small, 2¼ by 2, round flattened, even. Colour, golden-yellow, with deep brown-red flush, and stripes and generally nearly covered with russet netting. Flesh, crisp, yellow, juicy, and pleasantly sub-acid, but poor in flavour. Eye, open, in a shallow wide basin. Stem, fairly long, in a deepish cavity. Growth, slender ; fertile. Leaf, small, oval, dark, nearly flat, flat crenate. Origin, unrecorded. A very nice little fruit with a brisk acidity. Of the Ross Nonpareil style.

Glace : *see Calville Blanche D'Hiver*.

GLADSTONE. F., Monsieur Gladstone. (Jackson's Seedling, Striped Quarrenden.) Dessert, July to August, medium, 2¼ by 2, round conical, irregular. Colour, greenish-yellow, almost covered with dark red, occasionally with broken stripes. Flesh, soft, greenish-white, pleasantly flavoured. Eye, closed, in a much ribbed basin. Stem, medium in a shallow cavity. Growth, moderate ; very regularly fertile. Leaf, rather small, roundish, pea green, upfolded, undulating, shallow serrate. Origin, found near Kidderminster, by Mr. Jackson, of Blakedown Nursery, and introduced by him in 1868. Much grown for market purposes, and a valuable early sort.

GLORIA MUNDI. *Ronalds*, p. 7. (as Mammoth). F., Josephine ; G., Gloria Mundi. (Baltimore, Belle du

Bois (error), Monstrous Pippin, Ox Apple, Grosse de St. Clement.) Culinary, till January, immense, 4 by 3¼, square conical, angular. Colour, grass-green, changing to straw-yellow. Flesh, tender, white, sub-acid. Eye open, in a deep wide, boldly ribbed basin. Stem, short, in a very wide and deep russet cavity. Growth, vigorous, upright; fertility very poor. Leaf, large, upcupped, undulating, boldly serrate. Origin, American. Introduced to England from America in 1817. There is some disagreement as to the origin of this apple. It was first recorded in America in 1804. Too uncertain a cropper in most parts. It cooks a brown colour, but is very sweet and rich.

Glory of Flanders : *see Brabant Bellefleur.*

Glory of the West : *see Dutch Codlin.*

Glory of the West : *see Ecklinvillle.*

Goff : *see Orange Goff.*

Golden Drop : *see Court of Wick.*

Golden Ducat : *see Cobham.*

GOLDEN HARVEY. *Ronalds*, p. 23. F., Harvey doré. (Brandy Apple, Round Russet Harvey,) Dessert, till May, small, 2 by 1¾, flattened, round, even. Colour, greenish-yellow with dull red flush, covered with thin russet. Flesh, firm, yellow, very sweet and rich. Eye, open in a shallow basin, Stem, moderately long, in a small cavity. Growth, moderate ; fertile. Leaf, rather small, nearly flat. Origin, English ; known early in the seventeenth century. The original tree was at the Royal Horticultural Show, at Chiswick, in 1821. One of the good old sorts which have been neglected.

GOLDEN KNOB. *Ronalds*, p. 32. (Old Maid, Old Lady.) Dessert, till May, very small, 2¼ by 1¾, round, flattened, regular. Colour, orange-brown, covered with russet. Flesh, firm, greenish-yellow, sub-acid, good flavour. Eye, open in a small shallow basin. Stem, very short in a very narrow cavity. Growth, moderate; fertile. Leaf, fairly large, very dark, slightly upfolded, coarsely serrate. Origin, probably English; popular in markets in the early nineteenth century. Still grown in Kentish orchards; of distinct flavour.

GOLDEN NOBLE. *Her. Pom.*, 23. G., Gelber Edel Apfel. (Lord Clyde, Lord Stanwick, John Peel, Rutlandshire Foundling.) Culinary, September to January, medium, 2¾ by 2¼, round, slightly flattened, regular. Colour, clear yellow, with slight russet. Flesh, tender, yellow, acid. Eye, small, closed, in a shallow plaited basin. Stem, very short in a rather wide slightly russet cavity. Growth, vigorous; fertile. Cooks frothily and of golden colour. Leaf, rather large, little upfolded, regularly crenate, pea green. Origin, uncertain: brought to notice in 1820. According to Boisbunel, this is the Drap d'Or of France (not of Hogg). See *Revue Horticole*, 1883. One of the very best cooking apples for colour and flavour. Can be distinguished from Queen Caroline by its closed eye.

GOLDEN PIPPIN. *Ronalds*, p. 18. F., Pépin d'Or; G., Englischer Gold Pepping. (American Plate, Balgone Pippin, Bayfordbury Pippin.) Dessert, November to March, small, 2 by 1¾, oblong-round, regular. Colour, golden-yellow, with slight russet. Flesh, crisp, yellow, aromatic. Eye, usually closed in a broad shallow slightly plaited basin. Stem, very short, in a small narrow cavity. Growth, weak; fertility, moderate. Leaf, rather small, narrow, pale, slightly upfolded, finely and sharply serrate. Origin, English, probably dating from the early seventeenth century. Imensely popular in the seventeenth and eighteenth centuries, but now seldom grown. There are many seedlings of this sort of doubtful distinctness. Only in warm years and on light soils does it reach first-class flavour.

GOLDEN RUSSET. *Ronalds,* p., 29. G., Vergoldeter Russet. Dessert, December to March, medium, 2¾ by 2¼, roundish, flattened. Colour, entirely covered with golden russet, with an occasional red flush. Flesh, yellow, firm, sugary, aromatic, a little dry. Eye, closed, or a little open, in a round even basin. Stem, short, in a rather deep round cavity. Growth, moderately vigorous, a little spreading; fertility, moderate. Origin, probably an old English variety of some 150 years or more. I have never been able to obtain this apple true and the above description is borrowed from Hogg and Ronalds. There has been much confusion with this apple, the English Russet and the Roxbury Russet.

GOLDEN SPIRE. *Fl. and Pom.,* 1884, 185. Culinary, September-December, medium, 2¼ by 3¼, oblong-rounded, irregular. Colour, of an even golden-yellow, very occasionally flushed. Flesh, pale yellow, juicy, soft, slightly flavoured. Eye, open in a fairly deep much ribbed basin. Stem, short, rather slender in a small russeted cavity. Growth, upright; remarkably fertile. Leaf, rather small, narrow, dark green, nearly flat, held up, broadly serrate. Origin, uncertain; probably from Lancashire, where it was much grown in 1850. Its regular cropping and neat habit make it a fruit highly recommendable for small gardens.

GOLDEN REINETTE. *Her. Pom.,* 49. F., Reinette Dorée. (Grosser Borsdorfer, Reinette Gielen, Wyker Pippin.) Dessert, November to March, medium, 2¼ by 2¾, flattened round, regular. Colour, golden-yellow, bright red cheek, russeted. Flesh, very firm, yellow, well flavoured. Eye, wide open, in a flat shallow basin. Stem, long, yellowish, in a very even cavity. Growth, vigorous; fertile. Leaf, medium, dark, nearly flat, curved serrate. Origin, an old variety, which has been known in England for several hundred years. It is widely grown on the Continent, and has over fifty synonyms. A nice fruit, but hardly of first-class quality now. It does well on clay soils.

GOLD MEDAL. (Ryland Surprise.) Culinary, end August to September, large, 4¼ by 3½, flat conical. Colour, yellowish-green. Flesh soft, white, slightly acid. Eye, closed, segments reflexed, in a shallow and ribbed basin. Stem, very short in a very wide and deep cavity. Growth, sturdy and compact, making twiggy shoots, which become tortuous when tree ages; fertile. Leaf, round, rather large, slightly upfolded, undulated, serrate. Origin, raised by Mr. Troughton, a nurseryman, at Preston, and introduced about 1882. Originally called Ryland Surprise. Now little grown, Grenadier having replaced it. It is often confused with this apple owing to their having been mixed when introduced; see under Grenadier.

Gold Reinette: *see Reinette du Canada.*

GOOSEBERRY. *Her. Pom.,* 43. Culinary, November to June, medium to large, 3 by 2¾, square round, irregular. Colour, pea green to pale yellow, with occasional slight brown flush. Flesh, tender, greenish, acid. Eye, half open, in a deep, wide much plaited basin. Stem, stout, fairly long, in a rather deep cavity from which russet veins spread out over the base of fruit. Growth, vigorous; fertile. Origin, undiscovered. Known for over 100 years. Not to be confused with the Gooseberry Apple of *Ronalds.* This apple is still to be found in old orchards.

GOSPATRICK. Culinary, till March, medium, 2¾ by 2¾, rounded-oblong, irregular. Colour, pale greenish-yellow. Flesh, sweetish, firm, pale yellow, of no particular merit. Growth, moderate; fertility, fair. Leaf, medium, long, narrow, pale, flat, doubly serrate. Origin, raised by Mr. Charles Ross, in 1875, from Golden Reinette, and introduced by Messrs. Bunyard & Co., Maidstone. Not worthy of retention.

Gowrie: *see Tower of Glamis.*

Grafen Apfel: *see Gravenstein.*

Grand Sultan: *see White Transparent.*

GRANGE'S PEARMAIN. Culinary or dessert, till May, rather large, 3½ by 2¾, round, a little flattened, tapering to eye. Colour, grass-green, fading to yellow with dull red flush and broken stripes. Flesh, pale yellow, crisp, very juicy, with good flavour. Skin, slightly rough. Eye, closed, in a round, moderately shallow, slightly ribbed basin, which is generally a little russeted. Stem, moderately long, in a rather wide russet cavity. Growth, rather upright; fertility, good. Leaf, dark, slightly upheld, upward cupped, undulated, medium, oval, serrate. Origin, according to Hogg, this was raised by a Mr. James Grange, of Kingsland, Middlesex, probably early in the nineteenth century. It was I think introduced by Messrs. Dickson, of Chester. This is a much neglected fruit. There are few apples which keep better and retain their crisp juicy flesh in the spring and it is probably the nearest approach we have to Newtown Pippin.

GRANTONIAN. Culinary, till March, medium, 3 by 2¼, flat, conical, irregular. Colour, pale yellowish-green with brownish flush. Flesh, firm, greenish-white, sub-acid. Eye, closed, in a shallow ribbed basin. Stem, short, stout, in a shallow cavity. Growth, vigorous, upright; fertile. Leaf, oval, long, upfolded, lax, shallow crenate. Origin, introduced by Messrs. Pearson & Son, Nottingham. Now little cultivated.

Grauer Rabau : *see Reinette Grise.*

GRAVENSTEIN. *Her. Pom.*, 39. (Blumen Calvill, Diel's Sommer König, Grafenapfel, Ohio Nonpareil, Paradies.) Dessert or culinary, October to December, medium, 3 by 2¾, rounded square, irregular. Flesh, crisp, yellowish-white, extremely juicy, of most distinct flavour. Eye, closed in a deep ribbed basin. Stem, short, thick in a large deep cavity. Growth, moderate; fertile. Leaf, medium, rather dark, upfolded, finely serrate. Origin, said to have been found at the Castle of Grafenstein, in Schleswig-Holstein. Introduced about 1760. A good dessert apple. Its fragrant aroma and digestible flesh make it deserving of wider cultivation. A form also exists which is much redder than the above and which arose as a bud sport. It has the unusual quality of ripening on the tree and yet keeping for several months. It very rarely sets any seed.

Gray Apple : *see Pomme Grise*.

GRENADIER. Culinary, August to September, large, round, conical, a little uneven. Colour, pale green fading to light yellow, smooth. Eye, closed, in a moderately deep basin which is rather puckered. Stem, stout, knobbed at end, in a deep narrow cavity. Growth, moderate ; fertility, excellent. Leaf, long, strap shaped, little undulated, boldly crenate, pale green. Origin, undiscovered, recorded about 1860. This variety has often been confused with Gold Medal and they are still mixed by some cultivators. They can be easily recognised in winter by the large red buds of Gold Medal. A very valuable cooking apple for August, its free bearing qualities and large size making it the most popular of market varieties. Cooks to a froth.

Green Blenheim : *see Hambledon Deux Ans*.

Green Cossings : *see Rymer*.

Greenups Pippin : *see Yorkshire Beauty*.

Grosser Borsdorfer : *see Golden Reinette*.

Grosse de St. Clement : *see Gloria Mundi*.

Gruener Reinette : *see Nonpareil*.

Hallingsbury : *see Hollandbury*.

HAMBLEDON DEUX ANS. *Ronalds*, p. 42. G., Dauer Apfel von Hambledon. (Black Blenheim, Green Blenheim, Stone Blenheim, Blue Stone Pippin, Grahams, Deux Ans (and phonetic renderings), Yorkshire Queen, etc., etc.) Culinary, January to August, fairly large, 3 by 2¼ oval conical, slightly irregular.

66

Colour, yellow, nearly covered with brown-red flush and faint stripes. Flesh, dry, hard, yellow, a little sweet. Eye, firmly closed in a shallow ribbed and knobbed basin. Stem, very short in a shallow russet cavity, always showing a lump on one side. Growth, moderate; fertility, moderate. Leaf, dark, slightly upfolded, very finely and regularly serrate. Origin, at Hambledon, in Hampshire, about 1750. A good late keeper.

HAMBLING'S SEEDLING. *Gard. Chron.*, 1893, p. 535. Culinary, January to March, very large, 3¼ by 2¾, round conical, fairly regular. Colour, even pale yellow. Flesh, tender, pale yellow, sub-acid, cooks frothily. Eye, open in a wide shallow basin, often almost level with surface. Stem, very short, in a wide russet cavity. Growth, sturdy, spreading, well spurred; fertile when mature. Leaf, rather large, pea green, upcupped, evenly serrate. Origin, raised by Colonel Hambling, Dunstable, and introduced by Messrs. G. Bunyard & Co., Maidstone, in 1894. A valuable late cooker, of remarkably good flavour; making a good standard tree.

Hampshire Greening : *see Newtown Pippin*.

Hanging Pearmain : *see Adam's Pearmain*.

HANWELL SOURING. *Ronalds*, p. 30. (Landmere Russet, Lawrence's Seedling.) Culinary, till April, medium, 3 by 2½, round, conical, irregular. Colour, greenish-yellow with a red flush, large conspicuous grey dots. Flesh, firm, white, acid. Eye. closed in a broad ribbed basin. Stem, short, in a deep russeted cavity. Growth, moderate; fertility, good, Origin, probably at Hanwell, near Banbury. Came into notice in 1820. A good late variety.

Haute Bonté : *see Reinette Grise*.

Hawley : *see Hawthornden*.

HAWTHORNDEN. *Her. Pom.*, 6. (Hawley, Lincolnshire Pippin, Old Hawthornden.) Culinary, October to December, medium, 3 by 2½, round, slightly flattened, irregular. Colour, creamy-yellow with faint red flush. Flesh, tender, white, sub-acid. Eye, closed, in a moderately deep and ribbed basin. Stem, short and very stout in a rather deep cavity. Growth, moderate; fertility medium. Leaf, very pale, nearly flat, rather large. shallow serrate. Origin, raised at Hawthornden, Scotland before 1790. One of the best cooking sorts, making a dwarfish flat tree.

HECTOR MACDONALD. Culinary, October to February, medium, to large, 3 by 2½, round slightly conical, fairly regular. Colour, pale yellowish-green with faint broken stripes. Flesh, very crisp, juicy, greenish, acid, good cooker. Eye, closed in a rather deep, wide and plaited basin. Stem, nearly always very short in a wide rather deep cavity without russet. Growth, very dwarf; very fertile. Leaf, large, long, dark, slightly upfolded and undulated, deeply curved serrate. Origin, raised by Mr. Charles Ross and introduced by Messrs. Pearson in 1906. Resembles Lane's Prince Albert, but it proves to be rather too poor a grower for market use.

HERRING'S PIPPIN. Culinary or dessert, November, medium to large, 3 by 2¾, round, conical, uneven. Colour, pale greenish-yellow with a brown-red flush. Flesh, pale yellow, tender, with a spicy aromatic flavour. Eye, open in a deep and regular basin. Stem, short, not protruding, stout, in a deep, round, slightly russet cavity. Origin, undiscovered. I have not grown this apple personally but the above description is taken from fruits kindly sent me by Mr. Pearson who thinks very highly of this variety.

HEUSGEN'S GOLDEN REINETTE. F., Reinette dorée de Heusgen; G., Peter Heusgen's Gold Reinette. Dessert, March to April, medium, 2½ by 2, round, conical, often rather flat. Colour, golden-yellow with bright crimson flush and faint stripes. Flesh, firm, yellow, very juicy, nice flavour. Eye, closed, or slightly open, in a shallow ribbed basin. Stem, very stout in a wide, deep russet cavity. Growth, compact, upright; remarkably fertile. Leaf, rather narrow, little upfolded, grey-green, broadly serrate. Origin, raised by the Pastor Henzen, and named after the pomologist Heusgen. Introduced about 1877. A valuable addition to late dessert sorts.

Hick's Fancy : *see Early Nonpareil.*

HIGH CANONS. *Gard. Chron.*, 1907, p. 113. Culinary, till April, medium, 3 by 2¼, flat, conical, irregular. Colour, pale yellow with faint red flush and spots. Flesh, extremely crisp, pale yellow, acid. Eye, closed, in a shallow wrinkled basin. Stem, short and stout in a shallow, strongly russet cavity. Growth, moderate; moderately fertile. Origin, raised by Mr. Thrower, of High Canons, Barnet, and introduced by Messrs. G. Bunyard & Co., about 1887. A good apple of the Wellington style, cooking well.

Hill's Seedling : *see Cox's Pomona.*

HISTON FAVOURITE. (Chiver's Seedling.) Dessert or cooking, November to December, medium, 2¼ by 2¼, round, slightly flattened, regular. Colour, pale yellow with red flush and faint stripes. Flesh, soft, pale yellow, juicy, slight aromatic flavour. Eye, closed in a shallow wide basin. Stem, fairly long, stout, in a wide and rather deep cavity, which always has a lining of yellow feathery russet. Growth, vigorous; fertility moderate. Leaf, long oval, pale, slightly upfolded, very bodily serrate. Origin, raised at Histon, Cambs., by Mr. John Chivers early in the nineteenth century. A nice fruit, but rather too small with me.

HITCHIN PIPPIN. Dessert, end-August-September, medium, 2¼ by 2¼, round, oblong, flattened, regular. Colour, greenish-yellow with crimson flush and irregular broken stripes. Flesh, moderately soft, pale yellow, pleasantly flavoured, very juicy. Growth, moderate compact, making a flat spreading tree; very fertile. Leaf, pea green, long, upfolded, very finely serrate. Origin, undiscovered. A very nice fruit which may be described as an early King of the Pippins.

HOARY MORNING. *Ronalds*, p. 28. F., Brouillard; G., Morgendust. (Dainty, Downy Apple, Sam Rawlings.) Culinary, October to December, small, to medium, 3¼ by 2¼, flattened conical. Colour, pale yellow with broad red stripes, entirely covering fruit. and with a remarkable bloom. Flesh, crisp, pale yellow, acid. Eye, closed, in a very shallow ribbed basin. Stem, short and thick in a wide deep cavity. Growth, moderate; fertility, moderate. Leaf, roundish, rather dark, down hanging, upfolded, undulating, serrate. Origin, probably from Somersetshire. First recorded about 1819. A favourite in the West of England; attractive in appearance, but of poor quality.

HOLLANDBURY. *Ronalds*, p. 40. F., Beau Rouge, G., Kirke's Schoener Rambour. (Bonne Rouge, Hallingsbury, Kirke's Scarlet Admirable, Red Flanders.) Culinary, November to December, large, 3¼ by 3¼, round, conical, flattened, irregular. Colour, clear yellow with scarlet flush. Flesh, tender, white, acid. Eye, closed, in a large basin. Stem, medium, in a wide and deep cavity. Growth, vigorous; moderately fertile, Leaf, held-up, upfolded, twisted, large, roundish, sharply serrate. Origin, uncertain; known at the end of the eighteenth century. A striking fruit but now superseded.

Holland Pippin: *see Pott's Seedling.*

HORMEAD PEARMAIN. (Corby Seedling.) November to March, a little above medium, size 3 by 3¼, round, conical, flattened at top. Colour, pale yellow-green, occasional slight brown-red flush, many conspicuous large dots. Flesh, firm, short, yellowish-white, especially under the skin. Eye, open, in a shallow

70

even basin. Stem, short in a shallow cavity. Growth, vigorous; extremely fertile. Leaf, rather large, narrow, pale, nearly flat, widely and bluntly serrate. Origin, this was received at the Royal Horticultural Society's garden in 1826, and is supposed to have been raised at Hormead, Herts. A very useful fruit; a smaller Hambling's Seedling.

HOUBLON. *Gard. Chron.*, 1902, p. 11. Dessert, December to January, small to medium, 2¼ by 1¾, flattened, round, very regular. Colour, orange-yellow with dark crimson stripes and russet veinings. Flesh, firm, yellow, of good flavour. Eye, closed, in a very shallow basin. Stem, long and thin in a moderately russet cavity. Growth, moderate; fertility moderate. Leaf, roundish, rather dark, flat, a little undulating, crenate or shallow serrate, variable. Origin, raised by Mr. Charles Ross, and introduced in 1901. An attractive fruit very nearly first-class in flavour.

HOUNSLOW WONDER. Culinary, December to March, medium, 3 by 2¼, flattened round, tapering to eye. Colour, pale yellow with dark spots, brown-red flush and broad broken stripes. Flesh, firm, crisp, after Wellington style. Eye, small, closed, in a shallow plaited basin. Stem, short in a narrow deep and russet cavity. Growth, moderate; fertility, good. Leaf, moderate, oval, deeply curved serrate. Origin, this new apple was introduced by Messrs. Spooner, of Hounslow, who find it a valuable market variety.

HUBBARD'S PEARMAIN. *Lind. Pom. Brit.*, 27. Dessert, November to March, small, 2¼ by 2, conical, regular. Colour, pale yellowish-green, occasionally flushed with dull brownish-red, slightly russet. Flesh, crisp, juicy, greenish, very richly flavoured. Eye, open, in a shallow basin. Stem, rather short in an even cavity. Growth, slender; very fertile. Leaf, small, oval, nearly flat, irregularly and finely serrate. Origin, a Norfolk variety, known before 1800. An old English variety deserving more recognition for late use.

HUNT'S EARLY. Dessert, mid-August, medium, 2¼ by 1¾, flattened, round, slightly ribbed. Colour, greenish-yellow, nearly covered with brown-red flush and faint stripes. Flesh, soft, pale yellow, pleasant flavour. Eye, closed in a wide, boldly ribbed basin. Stem, rather long and slender in a narrow and deep cavity, which has slight russet occasionally in marked rings. Growth, moderate; fertility good. Leaf moderate, round, oval, blunt pointed, greyish-green, slightly upfolded, shallow curved serrate, stipules, large, leafy. Origin, undiscovered. A Mr. Hunt was a raiser of many apples about 1800, and it is probably one of his seedlings. Esteemed for market use in some districts.

Hunt's Nonpareil : *see Nonpareil.*

Hutching's Seedling : *see Sugar Loaf Pippin.*

IMPROVED ASHMEAD'S KERNEL. Dessert, February to March, medium to rather large, round flattened, fairly regular, generally higher on one side. Colour, golden yellow almost entirely covered with reddish-brown russet with golden-brown flush. Flesh, firm, pale yellow, of pleasant sub-acid flavour. Eye, closed in a rather deep wide basin. Stem, short in a very wide cavity. Growth, moderate; fertility, moderate. Leaf, roundish, pale, nearly flat, deeply curved serrate. very large. Origin, undiscovered. Hogg considered this identical with the original Ashmead's Kernel, but it is certainly distinct and much larger.

Irish Codlin : *see Carlisle Codlin.*

Irish Codlin : *see Mank's Codlin.*

IRISH PEACH. *Ronalds*, p. 8. (as Early Crofton). F., Pêche de Irlande ; G., Irländischer Pfirsich. (Early Crofton.) Dessert, August, 2¼ by 1¾, small, flat, conical, irregular. Colour, pale yellow, washed and mottled with milky red, darker stripes. Flesh, yellow, tender, aromatic. Eye, closed in a deep ribbed basin. Stem, short and stout in a fairly deep cavity. Growth, slender ; moderately fertile. Leaf, medium, narrow, shallow serrate or almost crenate, undulating, slightly upcupped. Origin, an Irish variety, introduced to England early in the nineteenth century. A delicious early variety.

Iron Apple : *see Brabant Bellefleur.*

Iron King : *see French Crab.*

Ironstone Pippin : *see French Crab.*

Jackson's Seedling : *see Gladstone.*

JAMES GRIEVE. *Deutsh. Obstb.*, 1910., 133. Dessert, September to October, medium to large, 3 by 3, round, conical, slightly irregular. Colour, pale creamy yellow, with crimson flush and stripes. Flesh, tender, very juicy, yellow, of excellent flavour. Eye, closed in a rather deep even basin, of which the sides are a little plaited. Stem, moderately long, knobbed at end, in a deep rather narrow cavity. Growth, vigorous, rather upright ; very fertile. Leaf, rather long, dark green, very finely crenate. Origin, a seedling from Pott's Seedling, raised by Mr. James Grieve, and introduced by Messrs. Dickson, of Edinburgh, about 1890. A most excellent fruit quite the best of its season ; its faults in the South are liability to rot and to fall prematurely.

JAMES WELSH. Culinary, end-September, fairly large, 3¼ by 3, round, conical, irregular. Colour, pale greenish yellow. Flesh, firm, crisp, white, acid. Cooks white and frothy. Eye, small, closed in a moderately deep narrow, much ribbed basin. Stem, rather short, in a small not russet cavity. Growth, strong ; fertility, very good. Leaf, rather large, oval, twisted, curved serrate. Origin, raised by Mr. James Grieve from Ecklinville. Very subject to rot on tree in the South of England. The style of Lord Suffield.

JEANNE HARDY. *Rev. Hort.*, 1890, 324. Culinary or exhibition, November to February, very large, 4 by 3½, round, conical, much ribbed. Colour, pale creamy-yellow with brilliant carmine flush and stripes. Flesh, pale yellow, soft, juicy, sweet, no particular flavour. Eye, open set in a deep wide basin which is boldly ribbed. Stem, short in a very deep and unusually wide cavity. Growth, strong and compact. Leaf, very large, pale, crenate, upfolded, upheld, round-oval. Origin, raised at the School of Horticulture, at Versailles, in 1878, first fruited in 1882, and dedicated to Mlle. Jeanne Hardy. A very beautiful fruit, that may be best described as a large Cox's Pomona with the appearance of Emperor Alexander.

Jenetting : *see White Joaneting*.

John Apple : *see French Crab*.

John Apple : *see Northern Greening*.

John Peel : *see Golden Noble*.

JOLLY BEGGAR. *Her. Pom.*, 31. Culinary, August to November, medium, 2¾ by 3, round, conical, irregular. Colour, pale yellow with very slight orange flush. Skin, very smooth. Flesh, tender, white, sub-acid. Eye, closed, in a shallow basin, which has ten knobs at the top. Stem, moderately long in a narrow deep cavity, faintly streaked with russet. Growth, moderate ; rather spreading ; very fertile. Leaf, rather large, roundish, little up-cupped, boldly crenate. Origin, raised by Dr. John Lyell, Newburgh, Fife, and introduced about 1858. A useful variety ; now little grown.

JUNEATING. Dessert, end July, small, flattened round, even. Colour, pale greenish-yellow. Skin, slightly greasy. Stem, small. Growth, rather upright, moderate ; fertility, moderate. Leaf, small, irregularly serrate, sometimes crenate, little upfolded. Origin, a very old variety known from the seventeenth century. Not to be confused with the Red Juneating.

KANDIL SINAP. *Rev. Hort.*, 1892, 36. (Sari Sinope.) F., Candile Sinope. Dessert or culinary, till February, medium, 2¼ by 3¼, oblong, even. Colour, pale yellow, almost entirely covered with deep red flush and stripes. Flesh, white, crisp, tender, juicy, and slight flavour. Eye, open in a broad ribbed basin. Stem, short and slender in a deep narrow cavity. Growth, moderate; extremely fertile. This Russian fruit is remarkable for its elongated barrel shape and is occasionally met with. It is one of the most popular market varieties in the Crimea.

Katzenkopf : *see Catshead.*

Kempster's Pippin : *see Blenheim Orange.*

KENTISH FILL BASKET. *Ronalds*, p. 9. G., Weisser Kentischer Pepping. (Lady de Grey's, Potter's Large.) Culinary, November to January, very large, 4 by 3¼, flattened, round, angular. Colour, greenish-yellow with distinct red stripes and flush. Flesh, tender, greenish-white, acid. Eye, closed, in a very deep and wide russeted basin. Stem, medium in a wide deep cavity. Growth, vigorous; fertility, good. Leaf, roundish, nearly flat, dark, finely and sharply serrate. Origin, unknown. An old and good apple, now seldom grown.

Kentish Pippin : *see Colonel Vaughan.*

KERRY PIPPIN. *Ronalds*, p. 6. (Edmonton, Aromatic Pippin.) Dessert, September, small to medium, 2 by 2¼, roundish oval, regular. Colour, greenish-yellow with slight flush and red stripes. Flesh, very crisp, yellow, aromatic, brisk and juicy. Eye, closed, in a shallow basin. Stem, short in a very shallow cavity, or often on level. Growth, medium; fertility moderate. Leaf, oval, slightly upfolded, coarsely curved serrate. Origin, raised in Ireland and received in England in 1819. A good fruit of the sub-acid type.

KESWICK CODLIN. *Ronalds*, p. 3. G., Keswicker Kuchenapfel. Culinary, August to September,

medium, 2¾ by 2⅓, conical, regular. Colour, yellow
with faint red flush. Flesh, soft, palest yellow, acid.
Eye, closed, in a shallow basin which has five marked
knobs around the eye. Stem, short, in a rather narrow
even cavity, sometimes faintly russet with pearly spots
showing below the skin. Growth, medium, compact;
fertility immense. Leaf, long oval, curved serrate,
greyish-green. Origin, at Gleastone Castle, Ulverstone,
about 1790. Introduced by Mr. John Sander, Keswick.
Much grown in North Britain. Still appreciated for
culinary use and its reliable cropping habits. Nearly
always shows a raised line on one side of the fruit.

Kiarolowski : *see Cardinal*.

Killick's Apple : *see Stones*.

Killick's Apple : *see Warner's King*.

King : *see King of Tomkins County*.

KING'S ACRE BOUNTIFUL. *Gard. Chron.*, 1905,
p. 341. Culinary, October to November, rather large,
2¾ by 2¼, round, much flattened, fairly regular. Colour
pale yellowish-green, turning creamy-white, occasionally
faintly flushed. Flesh, firm, greenish-white. Eye,
closed in a rather deep, knobbed and ribbed basin.
Stem, short in a very shallow, wide cavity, slightly
russet. Growth, stout and compact; very fertile.
Leaf, oval, tapering to point, little upfolded, sharply
serrate, undulating. Origin, introduced by the King's
Acre Nurseries. Not of any remarkable merit, save
free cropping.

KING'S ACRE PIPPIN. Dessert, till March,
medium, 2¼ by 2, round-conical, irregular. Colour,
yellow with brown-red flush netted with russet. Flesh,
crisp, juicy, pale yellow, highly aromatic. Eye, closed,
in a shallow cavity which is surrounded by five prominent ribs. Stem, rather long in a moderately deep,
russet cavity. Growth, moderate; fertility, moderate. Leaf, medium, rich green, nearly flat, markedly

curved serrate. Origin, reputed Sturmer Pippin ×
Ribston. Introduced by King's Acre Nursery, in
1899. Quite one of the best late dessert sorts. It
is said by some to be a variety some 100 years old.

King George III.: *see Borsdorfer.*

KING HARRY. Dessert, October to November,
medium, 2¼ by 2¾, oval, conical, flattened sides. Colour,
pale yellow, with russet dots and patches. Flesh,
firm, yellow, good flavour. Eye, open in a shallow
basin. Stem, medium, in a shallow russet cavity.
Growth, moderate, upright; fertile. Leaf, pale,
nearly flat, sharply serrate, long oval. Origin, received
by the Royal Horticultural Society from R. Manning,
Esq., of London, who had it from the neighbourhood
of Woodstock, Blenheim. A distinct fruit of good
quality.

KING OF THE PIPPINS. *Her. Pom.,* 14. F.,
Reinette d Orée ; G., Winter Gold Parmane. (Shropshire Pippin.) Dessert, October to December,
medium, round, oblong, Colour, golden yellow, shaded
reddish-brown. Flesh, creamy-yellow, firm, juicy with
a distinct slightly bitter flavour. Eye, open, in a
shallow even basin. Stem, moderately long in an
even russet cavity. Growth, moderate, upright. Leaf,
rather small, slightly upfolded, finely serrate. Origin,
this apple is generally attributed to England, but the
history of this variety and the Reine des Reinettes of
France, is a tangle which I have not yet been able to
unravel. The name of King of the Pippins was given
by Kirke early in the nineteenth century. This is
the Golden Winter Pearmain of Hogg, the original
King being an earlier fruit. It cannot be the King
apple of Rea, as Hogg suggests as this ripens at the end
of June.

KING OF TOMKINS COUNTY. *New York*, 346.
(King, Winter King.) Dessert, till April, large, 3½ by 3¼,
oval, conical, irregular. Colour, golden-yellow with

bright red flush and broad broken stripes. Flesh, crisp, rather dry, tender, markedly yellow, sweet and of excellent flavour, slightly fragrant. Eye, closed, in a moderately ribbed basin, generally higher on one side. Stem, slender, in a wide slightly russeted cavity. Growth, vigorous, rather drooping; moderately fertile. Leaf, large, long-oval, upfolded, undulating, sharply serrate, down-hanging. Originated in New Jersey before 1800. Very delicious when well grown. This I have seen equal to American samples from a Sandstone soil.

Kirke's Scarlet Admirable: *see Hollandbury*.

Knight's Codlin: *see Wormsley Pippin*.

Lady: *see Api*.

Lady de Grey's: *see Kentish Fillbasket*.

Lady Derby: *see Thorle*.

Lady's Finger: *see Paradise White*.

LADY'S FINGER OF LANCASTER. Culinary, November to January, medium, 3¼ by 3¾, conical, uneven, flat-sided. Colour, pale yellow with very faint red flush. Flesh, pale yellow, rather dry and almost astringent. Eye, closed, in a shallow much ribbed basin. Stem, short, in a narrow cavity. Growth, vigorous; very fertile. Origin, unknown. This apple seems to be grown in many parts. I have seen trees near Oxford, and have frequently received fruit from Worcester.

LADY HENNIKER. *Her. Pom.*, 67. Culinary, November to January, large to very large, 3¼ by 2¾, roundish-oblong, irregular, Colour, golden-yellow with bright red flush and a few broad broken stripes. Flesh, tender, yellow, Blenheim flavour. Eye, closed in a wide, deep and boldly ribbed basin. Stem, moderately long in a deep, rather narrow russet cavity. Growth, vigorous, upright; fertile. Leaf, rather large, long, flat, sharply serrate, very dark green. Origin, raised by Lord Henniker, at Thornham Hill, Suffolk, about 1845. A good old sort still worth growing.

LADY SUDELEY. Dessert, August to September, large, 2¾ by 2¼, oblong-conical. Colour, bright golden-yellow, heavily splashed with brilliant scarlet stripes and flush. Flesh, yellow, tender, very juicy, of delicious flavour. Eye, closed in a deep and boldly ribbed basin. Stem, rather short in a deep russet cavity. Growth, moderate, compact; fertile. Leaf, medium, narrow, down-curved, upfolded, undulating, bi-serrate. Origin, raised by Mr. Jacobs, of Petworth. Introduced by Messrs. George Bunyard & Co., in 1885. This variety has sported since its introduction into a paler and slightly russet form, which keeps quite distinct when propagated.

Lady Suffield : *see Lord Suffield.*

LAMB ABBEY PEARMAIN. *Ronalds*, p. 21. Dessert, January to April, very small, 2¼ by 2, oblong, regular. Colour, clear yellow with dull red flush and stripes. Flesh, firm, pale yellow, sugary and rich. Eye, large and open in a wide basin. Stem, slender, in a russet cavity. Growth, vigorous, rather upright; fertile. Leaf, round, oval, very boldly bi-serrate, held flat. Origin, raised near Dartford, at the end of the eighteenth century from a pip of a Newtown Pippin. Of good quality but little grown now.

Lammas : *see Red Joaneting.*

Lancashire Crab : *see Minchall Crab.*

Landmere Russet : *see Hanwell Souring.*

LANDSBERGER REINETTE. *Her. Pom.*, 49. F., Reinette de Lansberg. Dessert, October to January, medium, 2¾ by 2¼, round conical, irregular. Colour, yellow with crimson flush. Flesh, tender, white, sweet. Eye, open or closed, in a broad basin. Stem, thin and long deeply inserted in a deep cavity.

Growth, strong; fertility moderate. Leaf, large, variable in shape, boldly crenate. Origin, German Raised by Councillor Burchardt, at Lansberg. Now little cultivated. It is said to be very firmly attached to the tree, thus withstanding autumnal gales.

Lane's : *see Lane's Prince Albert*.

LANE'S PRINCE ALBERT. *Her. Pom.* 52. G., Prinz Albert. (Prince Albert, Lane's.) Culinary, January to March, large, 3¼ by 3, round conical. Colour, yellowish-green with distinct red stripes and slight pinkish flush. Skin, remarkably smooth. Flesh, tender, greenish-white, acid. Eye, generally closed in a deep wide slightly ribbed basin. Stem, short in a wide deep, russet free cavity. Growth, dwarf, spreading; very fertile. Leaf, rather large, pale, lax, nearly flat, very coarsely serrate. Origin, found in a garden at Berkhampstead, and introduced by Messrs. Lane, of that town in 1857. Perhaps the most reliable cropper of all cooking apples.

LANGLEY PIPPIN. *Gard. Mag.*, September 3rd, 1898. Dessert, August to September, medium, 2¼ by 2¼, oblong-conical, fairly regular. Colour, yellow with crimson flush and broad broken stripes. Flesh, yellowish, soft; flavour moderate. Eye, open in a rather ribbed basin. Stem, long in a moderately deep cavity. Leaf, rather small, light green, very twisted, finely serrate. Origin, Cox's Orange × Mr. Gladstone. Raised and introduced by Messrs. Veitch, Chelsea. There are many better fruits of the same season.

Large American : *see Mrs. Barron*.

Lawrence's Seedling : *see Hanwell Souring*.

Lawry's Cornish Giant : *see Colloget Pippin*.

Leather Coat : *see Royal Russet*.

Leather Coat of Turic : *see Pomme Grise*.

Leder Apfel : *see Reinette Grise*.

LEMON PIPPIN. *Ronalds*, p. 10. G., Konigin Sophiensapfel. (Winter Queen, Quince, Reinette von Madeira.) Culinary, till March, medium, 2¾ by 2¼, oval, regular. Colour, green changing to lemon-yellow. Flesh, firm, greenish-white, acid. Eye, closed or a little open, in an irregular basin. Stem, very short, often enclosed by a fleshy protuberance, the cavity then being almost nil. Growth, moderate; fertility, moderate. Leaf, long oval, upfolded, undulating, serrate. Origin, probably before 1700. Named from its resemblance to the lemon in shape and colour. (This name has also been applied to other apples.) An old sort, now little grown.

Lincolnshire Pippin: *see Hawthornden*.

Lincolnshire Reinette: *see Braddick's Nonpareil*.

Livesay's Imperial: *see Lord Suffield*.

LOAN'S PEARMAIN. *Ronalds*, p. 22. Dessert, November to January, medium, 2¾ by 2¼, round oblong, regular. Colour, greenish yellow with red flush and stripes and slight russet. Flesh, crisp, greenish, sugary. Eye, open in a wide shallow basin. Stem, medium in a shallow cavity. Growth, moderate; fertile. An old English sort, known in the seventeenth century. Now almost out of cultivation.

Loddington: *see Stones*.

LODGEMORE NONPAREIL. *Her. Pom.*, 21. (Clissold's Seedling.) Dessert, till June, small, 2 by 1¾, flattened round, slightly conical. Colour, pale yellowish-green, nearly covered with russet. Flesh, crisp, greenish, sweet, juicy, and well flavoured. Eye, nearly closed in a shallow basin. Stem, very short, in a narrow cavity. Leaf, rather small, roundish, boldly curved serrate. Origin; raised by a Mr. Cook, at Lodgemore, near Stroud, in 1808. An excellent old sort, now almost out of cultivation.

London Major: *see Lord Derby*.

LONDON PIPPIN. *Ronalds*, p. 14. F., Pepin de Londres ; G., London Peppin. [Citron d'Hiver, Five Crown Pippin, Royal Somerset (error).] Culinary, till March, medium, 3 by 2¼, round conical, irregular. Colour, yellowish-green with dull brown-red flush. Flesh, crisp, white, acid. Eye, closed, in a shallow basin which has five prominent ribs. Stem, slender, rather short in a deep narrow cavity. Growth, vigorous ; fertile. Keeps without shrivelling, Leaf, oval, upfolded, undulating, held out, finely serrate. Origin, dates probably from the sixteenth century. A valuable late fruit little cultivated but much grown in Australia and exported to this country.

Lord Burghleigh : *see Lord Burghley*.

LORD BURGHLEY. *Her. Pom.*, 65. (Lord Burghleigh.) Dessert, till May, small, 2¼ by 1¾, flattened, round-conical, irregular. Colour, pale greenish-yellow with clear brown red flush. Flesh, firm, yellow, juicy and sweet. Eye, nearly closed in a shallow irregular basin. Stem, medium in a shallow cavity. Growth, slender ; moderately fertile. Leaf, long oval, slightly upfolded, slightly undulated, shallow serrate or nearly crenate. Origin, raised in the garden of the Marquis of Exeter, at Burghley, near Stamford. Distributed in 1865, by Mr. Hase, of Peterborough. One of the best late dessert varieties.

Lord Clyde : *see Golden Noble*.

LORD DERBY. *Her. Pom.*, 73. (London Major.) Culinary, November to December, large, 3½ by 3¼, oblong-conical, irregular. Colour, pea green, changing to lemon-yellow. Flesh, firm, pale yellow, sub-acid. Cooks a deep golden red. Eye, closed, in a very deep, wide and irregular basin. Stem, short, in a very wide and shallow cavity quite without russet. Growth, sturdy, upright ; extremely fertile. Leaf, long, rather dark, little upfolded, undulating, oval, serrate. Origin, raised by Mr. Witham, a nurseryman in Stockport, about the middle of last century. One of the most appreciated sorts for market purposes, as it is an almost certain annual cropper.

LORD GROSVENOR. Culinary, August to September, medium, 3¼ by 3¼, conical, distinctly ribbed, irregular. Colour, pale yellow, changing to white. Flesh, white, juicy, acid, cooking excellently. Eye, closed, in an unusually puckered and wrinkled basin. Stem, medium much swollen at end, in a wide deep, cavity. Growth, not very strong ; fertility, excellent. Leaf, very pale green, large, upfolded, very lax. Origin, unknown. One of the most prolific of all apples ; it generally needs thinning to secure well shaped fruit ; it does well on dry soil.

LORD HINDLIP. *Gard. Chron.*, 1896, p. 115. Dessert, till April, small to medium, 2¼ by 2¼, conical, regular. Colour, nearly covered with dark crimson flush and stripes and netted russet patches. Flesh, crisp, white, sub-acid, juicy, and pleasantly flavoured. Eye, open in a shallow basin. Stem, long, in a very even russet cavity. Growth, slender, upright, spreading ; fertility, good. Leaf, very narrow, very dark, slightly upfolded, shallow serrate. Origin, a seedling raised in Worcestershire, and introduced by Messrs. Watkins, of Hereford. Of very good quality and a good cropper ; a likely candidate for the desired late market dessert apple.

LORD LENNOX. Dessert, end-September, small to medium, 2¼ by 1¼, flat. Colour, dark brownish-red over a pale yellow-green groundwork ; striping very faint. Flesh, firm, slight green tinge. Eye, closed in a rather broad shallow basin, which is slightly ribbed. Stem, half-inch in a rather wide, fairly deep and even cavity. Origin, this is the variety grown around Northampton under this name, but does not agree with Dr. Hogg's description.

Lord Stanwick : *see Golden Noble.*

LORD STRADBROOK. *Gard. Chron.*, 1905, p. 20. (Fenn's Wonder.) Culinary, till February, large. Colour, crimson on greenish ground. Growth, free; very fertile. Leaf, rather long, upfolded, shallow crenate. Origin, a chance seedling found in Henham Gardens, Wangford, about 1900. Certificated as Fenn's Wonder.

LORD SUFFIELD. *Her. Pom.*, p. 6. (Lady Suffield, Livesay's Imperial.) Culinary, August to September, medium to large, 3¼ by 3, oval, conical, irregular. Colour, pale lemon-yellow. Flesh, tender, white, acid. Eye, small, closed, in a shallow plaited basin. Stem, slender, in a rather narrow cavity. Growth, moderate, making a compact twiggy tree; very fertile. Leaf, medium, oval, held out, slightly upfolded, coarsely bi-serrate. Origin, raised by Thomas Thorpe, Middleton, near Manchester, about 1820. It cankers badly and is very apt to rot on the tree. Now superseded by Early Victoria.

LUCOMBE'S PINE. · *Her. Pom.*, 47. (Pine Apple.) Dessert, November to December, small, 2¼ by 2, round-conical, regular. Colour, yellow with faint orange flush. Flesh, tender, white, with pine apple flavour. Eye, open in a shallow plaited basin. Stem, fairly stout, in a shallow round cavity. Growth, moderate; fertility rather poor. Origin, raised by Messrs. Lucombe Pince & Co., of Exeter, about 1800. Now almost out of cultivation.

MABBOTT'S PEARMAIN. *Her. Pom.*, 61. F., Pearmain de Mabbott; G., Parmane von Mabbott. Dessert, November to January, medium, 2¼ by 2¼, oval, regular. Colour, golden-yellow almost covered with rich crimson flush. Flesh, tender, juicy, yellowish, of good flavour. Eye, closed in a shallow ribbed basin. Stem, slender in a narrow russet cavity. Growth, compact; fertile. Leaf, rather small, pea green, little upfolded, curved serrate, sharply pointed. Origin, uncertain; known around Maidstone for many years.

MACKINTOSH RED. *New York*, II., 132. Culinary or dessert, October to December, 2¾ by 2¼, medium, round tapering to eye, even. Colour, pale yellow, almost covered with rich crimson stripes and flush. Skin smooth. Flesh, greenish white, firm, slightly sweet, juicy. Eye, nearly closed in a medium ribbed basin. Stem, medium, rather short in a large russet cavity. Growth, vigorous, rather spreading; fertility, fair. Leaf, rather large, slightly upfolded shallow serrate or crenate. Origin, a chance seedling of Ontario, and named after Allan Mackintosh, the owner of the estate, on which it was found. Another account says it is at least 115 years old. This resembles Wealthy in appearance and has not yet been sufficiently tested at Allington to decide upon its value for this country.

MAIDSTONE FAVOURITE. *Journ. Pom.*, Vol. I., No. 1. Dessert, end-August-September, medium, 2¾ by 2, oblate, curving to eye. Colour, pale creamy yellow covered with carmine stripes and flush. Flesh, creamy white, fine grained, sweet and juicy, very firm. Eye, closed or open, in a deep and wide even basin. Stem, very short and stout, in a rather wide cavity. Growth, moderately vigorous, rather spreading; fertility very good. Leaf, oval, upfolded, little twisted, held-out, shallow crenate. Origin, raised by Messrs. George Bunyard & Co., from a seed of Emperor Alexander. One of the most beautiful apples of Autumn, a little lacking in flavour but very promising for market culture as it fills the gap between Beauty of Bath and Worcestershire Pearmain, and travels well.

MALTSTER. Culinary or dessert, October to January, large, 3 by 2¼, round flattened and angular, irregular. Colour, greenish yellow with slight flush and few scattered broken stripes. Flesh, crisp to soft, yellowish, of quite good flavour about November. Eye, closed in a deep ribbed basin. Stem, medium in a rather deep cavity. Growth, moderate, rather spreading; fertility good. Leaf, oval, upfolded, boldly curved serrate. Origin, unrecorded. Known in 1830.

In warm seasons the flavour and texture approach the Newtown Pippin, but usually it is only good enough for culinary purposes. I think this will probably be found to be of continental origin.

Mammoth : *see Gloria Mundi.*

MANK'S CODLIN. *Ronalds,* p. 3. F., Codlin de Mank ; G., Manck's Kuchenapfel. (Belmont, Eve, Irish Codlin, Pitcher.) Culinary, August to November, medium, 2¾ by 2¼, oval-conical, irregular, five sided. Colour, yellow-green with slight red flush. Flesh, firm, white, acid. Eye, very small, closed in a ribbed basin. Stem, rather stout, in a fairly deep, wide cavity. Growth, very compact and dwarfish ; fertility great. Leaf, narrow-oval, broadly serrate. Origin, this was raised by Mr. Kewley, of Ballanard, Isle of Man, and first fruited in 1815. It is still much grown in the North of England and is one of the best cooking apples there.

MANNINGTON'S PEARMAIN. *Her. Pom.,* p. 14. F., Pomme de Mannington. Dessert, November to March, medium, 2¼ by 2, flattened round, regular. Colour, dull green-red with russet. Flesh, crisp, yellow, fair flavour. Eye, nearly closed in a shallow basin. Stem, fairly long in a rather deep cavity. Growth, moderate, making a compact well-spurred tree. Leaf, rather small, roundish, pea green, slightly upfolded, undulating, very boldly curved serrate. Origin, raised at Uckfield, Sussex, about 1770, and distributed by Mr. Cameron of the same town, in 1849. The flavour of this variety is only fair and as there are so many better at this season I consider it not worth growing.

MARCH PIPPIN. Dessert, till April, medium to fairly large, 2¼ by 2¼, round flattened, fairly even. Colour, rich golden-yellow with slight flush and a few broad faint stripes. Flesh, very firm, yellow, of good flavour. Eye, wide open in a very broad ribbed basin.

Stem, short in a deep russet cavity. Growth, vigorous, upright; fertility, poor. Leaf, round, light, flat, down-hanging, bluntly serrate, almost crenate. Origin, raised by Mr. Lane, of Kynaston, Ross, Hereford, before 1900, and introduced by Messrs. George Bunyard & Co., of Maidstone. A fine fruit of Newtown Pippin style, but too poor a cropper to retain.

Margaret : *see Red Joaneting*.

MARGIL. *Ronalds*, p. 12. F., Reinette Musquée; G., Muskat Reinette. (Reinette d'Hiver Musquée, Small Ribston.) Dessert, October to January, small, 2¼ by 2¼, rounded conical, angular. Colour, pale yellow with dull brown-red flush and russet. Flesh, firm, yellow, highly flavoured. Eye, very small, closed in a ribbed basin. Stem, slender, in a narrow cavity. Growth, very weak; fertility, moderate. Leaf, very narrow, much upfolded, dark, boldly crenate. Origin, doubtless Continental (probably Norman). Of the highest possible quality; it makes a small tree and should be given a trial in every garden. The name is derived from Marg=marle=marrow, according to one author.

MAY QUEEN. Dessert, till May, medium, 2¼ by 2¼, flat, fairly regular. Colour, golden-yellow with brown-red flush and russet. Flesh, very crisp, yellow, juicy, and of good flavour. Eye, open, in a broad shallow basin. Stem, medium in a very deep russet cavity. Growth, very dwarf; fertility, extraordinary. Leaf, rather dark, nearly flat, small, oval, rather boldly serrate. Origin, raised by Mr. Haywood, of Worcester, and introduced by Messrs. Penwill. A neglected fruit of great excellence and as a fruit for small gardens as cordons or bushes it can hardly be surpassed. It is eatable in November and keeps excellently. Making but few laterals pruning is reduced to a minimum.

MEDENHAM PIPPIN. Dessert, September to October, medium, 2¼ by 2¼, round, slightly conical and flattened. Colour, golden-yellow, flushed with brownish-red and with broad, indistinct stripes. Flesh, firm, yellow, juicy, of excellent flavour. Eye closed in a wide, slightly ribbed basin. Stem, short, in a very narrow deep russet cavity. Growth, moderate ; fertile. Leaf, oval, sharply pointed, held stiffly up, upfolded, twisted, bi-serrate, dark green. Origin, this was distributed in error with grafts of Norfolk Beauty, and is therefore occasionally confused with that sort. Of no particular merit.

Mela Januria : *see Reinette du Canada.*

MELON. *New York*, I., 204. Dessert, December to January, medium to large, 3 by 2¼, round conical. Colour, pale yellow with carmine flush and stripes. Flesh, pale yellow, tender, juicy, somewhat aromatic. Eye, open or closed, in a small basin. Stem, long and slender, in a deep and narrow cavity. Growth, moderate ; fertile. Leaf, light green, flat, undulating, coarsely curved serrate. Origin, raised in East Bloomfield, Ontario, in the orchard of Heman Chapin, and introduced by Messrs. Ellwanger & Barry, in 1845 ; it was introduced into England about 1850. A good useful late fruit now seldom met with.

Melville Pippin : *see Scarlet Pearmain.*

MÈRE DE MÉNAGE. Culinary, till March, very large, 3¼ by 2¼, flat conical, very irregular. Colour, yellowish-green almost covered with dull brown crimson and darker broad stripes, and conspicuous white dots widely spaced. Flesh, firm, greenish, acid. Eye, closed in a broad much ribbed, and chanelled basin. Stem, very short and stout, in a wide, irregular, much russeted cavity. Growth vigorous, makes a large spreading tree ; fertility moderate. Leaf, very large, curved serrate, little undulating, flat, grey-green. Origin, most probably Continental, but not the Mère de Ménage of France. It is grown in Belgium as Queen Emma and under other names. Much grown in East Anglia. A useful kitchen fruit, keeping well.

MIDDLE GREEN. *Gard. Chron.*, 1903, p. 291. Dessert, December to February, medium, 2¼ by 2, flat, slightly conical, regular. Colour, yellow streaked with red. Flesh, soft, yellowish, pleasantly sweet. Eye, closed in a shallow, wide, ribbed basin. Stem, fairly long, in a wide, shallow cavity, not russeted. Growth, moderate ; fertility moderate. Origin, raised from Frogmore Prolific × Blenheim Orange, by Mr. Seden, and introduced by Messrs. Veitch, of Chelsea. Of no particular merit.

MILLER'S SEEDLING. *Gard. Chron.*, 1906, p. 239. (The Shah.) Dessert, end August, medium, 2¼ by 2¼, round conical, nearly regular. Colour, creamy-yellow striped and flushed with bright crimson on one side. Flesh, crisp, juicy, pleasantly sweet. Eye, closed in a shallow ribbed basin. Stem, moderately long, thin, in a wide deep uneven cavity. Growth, rather compact, spreading ; fertility remarkable. Leaf, grey-green, nearly flat, round, sharply serrate, very large, little twisted, held out. Origin, raised at Newbury, Berks., by Mr. James Miller, nurseryman, in 1848, and introduced by him. A very sweet fruit, appreciated as a market variety in some districts.

MINCHALL CRAB. *Ronalds*, p. 33. G., Englische Rambour. (Lancashire Crab, Mincham's Crab, Minchull Crab.) Culinary, till March, large, 3¾ by 2¼, flattened round, irregular. Colour, green to yellow with slight red flush and stripes. Flesh, firm, white, sharply acid. Eye, open in a very wide, ribbed basin. Stem, medium, in a shallow cavity. Growth, makes a low spreading tree ; fertile. Leaf, rather large, oval, little upfolded, boldly curved serrate. Origin, English ; named after Minchall, in Cheshire, dating from the eighteenth century. A good old variety of the Bramley type.

Mincham's Crab : *see Minchall Crab.*

Minshull Crab : *see Minchall Crab.*

MONARCH. Culinary, till April, large to very large, 3¼ by 2¾, flattened round. Colour, pale yellow with bright red flush and fainter striping beneath. Flesh, greenish-white, firm, moderately acid. Eye, open in a wide, shallow basin, similar to Wellington. Stem, fairly short in a moderately deep, slightly russet cavity. Growth, vigorous, little spreading; fertility, excellent. Leaf, very large, round, very boldly doubly crenate. Origin, said to be a cross. Peasgood's Nonsuch and Wellington. Introduced by Messrs. Seabrook. I have not yet grown this apple myself but am indebted to the introducers for specimens from which the above description is made.

Monstrous Pippin : *see Gloria Mundi.*

MOTHER. *Fl. and Pom.*, 1883, 121. G., Mutter Apfel. (So many apples have the name "Mother" that Hogg distinguished this one by prefixing the country of its origin :—American Mother.) Dessert. October to November, medium, 2¼ by 2½, oval conical, slightly ribbed. Colour, golden-yellow with dull brownish-red flush and faint stripes. Flesh, soft and, juicy, very sweet, yellow or slightly green of distinct flavour, resembling Peardrops. Eye, very small, closed, in a small fairly deep basin. Stem, rather short, slender in a moderate cavity which is compressed on one side. Growth, moderate; fertility rather irregular. Leaf, rather large, pale, nearly flat, down-hanging, sharply serrate. Origin, rather uncertain, but recorded in America before 1848. A very choice dessert fruit, which often keeps good till mid January.

Mother : *see Oslin.*

Motteux's Seedling : *see Beachamwell.*

MR. PROTHERO. Dessert, till June, medium to fairly large, 3 by 2¾, round, slightly flattened. Colour, golden-yellow with medium red flush and broad stripes. Flesh, pale yellow, good flavour, very firm. Eye, closed in a shallow, slightly ribbed basin. Stem, rather long, slender in a shallow russet cavity. Growth, good ; fertility good. Leaf, large, round oblong, little undulating, upfolded, boldly doubly crenate. Origin, introduced by Messrs. Seabrook & Sons, in 1918. I have not been able to test this apple sufficiently to pass an opinion on it and am indebted to the introducers for specimens from which this description is made.

MRS. BARRON. *Fl. and Pom.*, 1884, 89. (Large American.) Culinary, October to January, fairly large, $2\frac{1}{4}$ by $2\frac{3}{4}$, rounded, oblong, irregular. Colour, clear golden-yellow. Flesh, tender, yellow, sub-acid. Eye, large, open in a shallow ribbed basin. Stem, very stout in a rather wide ribbed cavity. Growth, vigorous, a little spreading ; fertility, moderate. Leaf, very large, light pea green, long oval, very sharply and doubly serrate, upfolded. Origin, brought to notice at the Apple Conference of 1885, and there named Mrs. Barron. Not remarkable for any special merit.

MRS. PHILLIMORE. *Gard. Chron.*, 1900, p. 249. Dessert, till March, smallish, $2\frac{1}{4}$ by 2, flattened conical, irregular. Colour, pale yellow, covered with red flush and broad broken faint stripes. Flesh, very tender, greenish, remarkably sweet. Eye, open, tips reflexed. in a rather deep, boldly ribbed basin. Stem, medium in a very wide and deep russet lined cavity. Growth, upright, spreading, spurs well, moderate ; fertile. Leaf, undulating, little upcupped, long oval, deeply serrate. Origin, raised by Mr. Charles Ross from Lord Burghley and Gladstone, and introduced in 1900, by Messrs. George Bunyard & Co. A nice apple worthy of further trial ; it may be described as a smaller and sweeter Cox's Pomona.

MURFITT'S SEEDLING. Culinary, till March, medium, $2\frac{3}{4}$ by $2\frac{3}{4}$, round conical, fairly regular. Colour, pale greenish-yellow, remarkably greasy, surface of fruit hammered. Flesh, firm, greenish-yellow, rather acid. Eye, closed in a very shallow basin with small beads at base. Stem, stout and short, in a moderately deep cavity. Growth, very spreading; fertile. Leaf, medium, round, coarsely serrate, pea green, flat, undulating. Origin, brought to notice about 1884, and said to be a Cambridgeshire variety.

Musk : *see Carlisle Codlin.*

NANCY JACKSON. Culinary, till March, medium, 2½ by 2½, round conical, regular. Colour, dull yellow with red flush and a few broad crimson stripes. Flesh, tender, juicy, acid. Growth, moderate; fertility, moderate. Leaf, large, oval, held out flat, very coarsely crenate, undulating, upward folded. Origin, unrecorded according to Hogg it was much cultivated in Yorkshire.

NANNY. Dessert, December to February, medium, flattened, round, slightly conical, fairly regular. Colour, lemon yellow with red flush and broad broken stripes of crimson. Flesh, tender, greenish yellow, a little sweet, but of no remarkable flavour. Eye, open in a rather deep and even basin. Stem, moderately long, thin, in a narrow, deep cavity, which is strongly marked with thick scaly russet spreading out in veins. Growth, moderate; fertile. Leaf, roundish, pea green, nearly flat, boldly curved bi-serrate. Origin, a Sussex apple, not often met with in other parts of the country.

NELSON CODLIN. *Her. Pom.,* 10. (Backhouse's Lord Nelson, Wilson's Codlin.) Culinary, till January, fairly large, 3½ by 3½, oval conical, irregular. Colour, green to yellow. Flesh, soft, white, sub-acid. Eye, open in a deep ribbed basin. Stem, rather short in an uneven cavity. Growth, vigorous; very fertile. Leaf, medium, oval, sharply bi-serrate. Origin, named after the Wesleyan preacher Nelson, Hardly required. Remarkable for its magnificent flower.

NELSON'S GLORY. Culinary, November to February, medium to rather large, 3 by 2½, irregular. Colour, greenish-yellow with many dark spots. Flesh, loose, yellowish-white, acid. Eye, half open in a wide shallow basin. Stem, thick and fleshy in a rather shallow russeted cavity. Growth, moderate; very regularly fertile. Leaf, oval, very finely serrate. Origin. I am informed that this was originally known as Stoke Lump Lemon and was introduced by Messrs. Maule, of Bristol, as Nelson's Glory. This apple is often confused with Warner's King, but it is quite distinct from this variety. Grown in the Northern Counties of England.

NEW BESS POOL. *Her. Pom.*, 71. Culinary, January to March, medium, 2¾ by 2¼, round, slightly flattened. Colour, greenish-yellow almost covered with dull brown crimson flush and brown blotches of the same colour. Flesh, crisp, juicy, greenish-white, sub-acid Eye, open in a much ribbed basin. Stem, extremely short and stout, in a shallow cavity. Growth, vigorous; fertile. Leaf, roundish, pale, nearly flat, very finely serrate. Origin, raised by Mr. J. Stevens, of Stanton-by-Dale, before 1850. A useful late keeper similar to Cellini in appearance.

NEW HAWTHORNDEN. Culinary, October, large, flat, evenly rounded to each extremity. Colour, pale green, fading to yellow, with an occasional red flush. Flesh, greenish-white, acid, moderately tender. Eye, closed in a wide and rather deep basin. Stem, remarkably short in a wide and deep cavity. Growth, vigorous, rather spreading. Leaf, rather large, pale, nearly flat, undulating, boldly serrate. Origin, according to Hogg this apple was introduced by Messrs. Rivers, in 1847. This fruit resembles a Warner's King, but can of course easily be distinguished when the tree is examined.

NEW NORTHERN GREENING. *Her. Pom.*, 5. Culinary, till March, medium, 3 by 2, round, flattened. Colour, pale green with dull red flush and faint stripes and russet spots. Flesh, greenish, firm, acid. Eye, open in a large basin. Stem, generally short in a narrow cavity. Growth, strong, upright ; fertile. Origin, raised by Mr. J. Stevens, Stanton Grange, Derbyshire, before 1850. Only second rate ; very subject to spot and rot on the tree.

NEW ROCK PIPPIN. G., Neuer Stein Pepping. Dessert, till April, small, 2¼ by 1¾, round flattened, regular. Colour, pale yellow with golden-brown flush and almost covered with russet. Flesh, firm, juicy, excellently flavoured. Eye, firmly closed almost on level, slightly beaded and wrinkled. Stem, short in a shallow cavity. Leaf, medium, oval, serrate. Origin, raised by Mr. W. Pleasance, near Cambridge, and introduced to notice about 1821. One of the best late sorts.

NEWTON WONDER. *Gard. Chron.*, 1900, 45. Culinary, till March, large, 3¼ by 2¼, round flattened, regular. Colour, bright yellow with slight scarlet flush with broad, broken stripes. Flesh, crisp, juicy, yellow, acid ; cooks excellently. Eye, open in a wide rather ribbed basin. Stem, very short and stout in a shallow almost level cavity. Growth, vigorous ; fertile. Leaf, round, held stiffly out, undulating, very thick, deeply and doubly curved serrate. Origin, raised by a Mr. Taylor, of King's Newton, in Melbourne, Derby, and introduced by Messrs. Pearson & Co., about 1887. One of the best half-dozen cooking apples. Quite a welcome dessert fruit in March. Makes a fine spreading standard.

NEWTOWN PIPPIN. *New York*, p. 146. G., Köstliche Reinette von Newtown. (Albermarle, Hampshire Greening.) Dessert, till March, fairly large, 3¼ by 2¼, flattened round, fairly regular. Colour, straw yellow. Flesh, very crisp, yellowish-green, of rich pineapple flavour. Eye, closed in a shallow basin. Stem, slender, in a rather deep russet lined cavity. Growth, moderate ; fertility, poor in England. Leaf, large, flat, down-curved, coarsely bi-serrate. Originated at Long Island, early in the eighteenth century, and introduced to this country about 1760. This apple does not attain to the same flavour in this country as in America, even under the most favourable conditions. There is a green variety considered distinct, in which the fruits do not have the rich yellow and faint orange flush of this variety.

NEWTOWN SPITZENBERG. *Ronalds*, p. 10. (Burlington, English Spitzenberg.) Dessert, till January, medium to large, 3¼ by 2¼, round, regular. Colour, clear yellowish-red with red flush and faint stripes. Flesh, yellow, crisp, aromatic. Eye, open, in a shallow basin. Stem, very short, in a deepish cavity. Growth, moderate; fertility moderate. Origin,, probably introduced into England by William Cobbett. Very little grown in England nowadays.

NONPAREIL. *Her. Pom.*, 21. F., Nonpareille ancienne; G., Alter Nonpareil. (English Nonpareil, Hunt's Nonpareil, Original Nonpareil.) Dessert, till March, small, 2¼ by 2, round conical, regular. Colour, yellowish-green with red-brown flush and covered with russet, with some large conspicuous dots at base. Flesh, tender, greenish, aromatic. Eye, open, in a very shallow basin. Stem, fairly long in a moderate, even cavity. Growth, moderate, upright spreading; fertility, moderate; Leaf, medium, narrow, pea green, held up, much upfolded, boldly curved serrate. Origin, unrecorded; known in England since about 1600. This fruit is worthy of all commendation. The obovate cells and conspicuous dots serve to distinguish it from the White Nonpareil.

Nonpareille d'Angleterre : *see Ribston Pippin*.

NONSUCH. *Ronalds*, p. 37. Culinary, September, round flattened, medium, regular. Colour, yellowish-green with red flush and broad stripes. Flesh, tender, white, sweet. Eye, closed in a rather deep and regular basin. Stem, short, in a deepish cavity. Growth, moderate; fertile. Leaf, medium, oblong, finely serrate. Origin, doubtful; possibly French. Not to be confused with the Nonsuch Paradise apple, which is a reputed seedling from this variety. It is now superseded.

NORFOLK BEAUTY. *Gard. Chron.*, 1902, p. 453. Culinary, October to December, large, 3¼ by 2¼, round flattened, regular. Colour, pale lemon yellow with faint red flush. Flesh, loose, yellowish, cooks frothily. Eye, closed, in a moderately deep plaited basin, which has prominent knobs at the top. Stem, long and thin, woody, in an even and narrow cavity, which is feathered with russet. Growth, moderate; fertility, medium. Leaf, rather large, grey-green, little upfolded, undulated, sharply curved serrate. Origin, raised by Mr. Allan, gardener at Gunton Park, from Warner's King and Waltham Abbey. Introduced to commerce in 1902. A very excellent fruit worthy of extended cultivation, cropping well when the tree is formed.

NORFOLK BEEFING. *Ronalds*, p. 33. G., Schoener von Norfolk. (Catshead Beaufin, Red Beefing, Taliesin, Winter Beefing.) Culinary, till April, medium, 3 by 2¼, round flattened. Colour, green nearly covered with dull brown crimson. Flesh, firm, greenish-yellow, acid. Eye, open in a wide ribbed basin. Stem, very short, in a deep slightly russet cavity. Growth, vigorous, making a spreading open tree; fertile. Leaf, round, dark green, large, flat, coarsely curved serrate. Origin, Norfolk; brought into notice about 1800. A useful late fruit, keeping plump till the end.

NORFOLK DUMPLING. Culinary, September to October, large, 3¼ by 3, round, tapering to eye. Colour, pale green yellow; smooth and slightly greasy. Flesh, white, coarse grained, acid. Eye, closed in a ribbed basin, which is rather small. Stem, extremely short, in a flat cavity. Growth, good; very fertile. Leaf rather small, narrow, crenate or curved serrate, nearly flat, dark green. Origin, undiscovered.

Norfolk Pippin : *see Adam's Pearmain.*

NORFOLK STONE PIPPIN. (White Pippin, White Stone Pippin.) Dessert, or culinary, till June; medium, 2¾ by 2, flat, angular, irregular. Colour, pale yellow, more or less covered with cinnamon russet. Flesh, very firm, pale yellow, sub-acid, aromatic and very distinct in flavour. Eye, open, in a shallow basin. Stem, slender in a medium, deep cavity. Growth, vigorous; very fertile. Origin, an old variety first described by Lindley in his "Guide to the Fruit Garden." A good old sort still grown in Norfolk.

NORMAN'S PIPPIN. Dessert, January to March, medium, 2¾ by 2, round, regular. Colour, pale greenish-yellow with russet markings and occasional faint flush. Flesh, firm but soft, yellowish, of rich flavour. Eye, open in a shallow even basin. Stem, very long and thin, in a rather narrow, deep cavity. Growth, compact; fertile. Leaf, upfolded. Origin, unrecorded; generally considered to be a monastic importation. An excellent variety deserving of wider cultivation. The very long stem and remarkable dots on fruit render it easily distinguishable.

Normanton Wonder: *see Wellington.*

NORTHERN GREENING. *Her. Pom.*, 43. F., Verte du Nord; G., Gruener Englischer Pepping. (John Apple, Walmer Court.) Culinary, till April, medium, 2¾ by 2¾, oval, conical, regular. Colour, pea green to pale yellow with red stripes and faint brown flush. Flesh, tender, greenish, acid. Eye, closed in a deep rather ribbed basin. Stem, fairly long, in a deepish cavity, often with a swelling at one side. Growth, vigorous, upright; very fertile. Leaf, long, dark green, boldly curved serrate, upheld and upfolded. Origin, probably English. Known in the seventeenth century. Still one of the best late cooking apples.

NORTHERN SPY. *Fl. and Pom.*, 1862, 8. G., Spaeher des Nordens. (Spy.) Dessert, till March, medium, 2½ by 2¾, round conical, almost regular.

Colour, greenish-yellow, almost covered with faint red stripes and flush. Flesh, loose, juicy, greenish-yellow, of good flavour. Eye, very small, closed in a shallow ribbed basin. Stem, very long, slender in a very wide and deep cavity, faintly russet veined. Growth, upright, compact ; only moderately fertile. Leaf, oval, nearly flat, undulating. Origin, at the orchard of Mr. R. Humphrey, East Bloomfield, New York, soon after 1840. This apple only does well in England in very favourable years.

Northwick Pippin : *see Blenheim Orange.*

NUTMEG PIPPIN. (Cockles Pippin (error).) Dessert, till March, small, 2 by 2, flattened conical, irregular. Colour, pale yellow almost covered with cinnamon russet, with faint brown red flush. Flesh, crisp, pale yellow, juicy and pleasantly flavoured. Eye, open in a shallow basin which has prominent knobs. Stem, very short in a very narrow, shallow russet cavity. Growth, slender ; fairly fertile. Origin, unrecorded. Lindley considered this to be the same as Cockles Pippin, but the fruit grown in Kent is quite distinct. A nice little fruit in March.

Ohio Nonpareil : *see Gravenstein.*

Okera : *see Akero.*

Old Hawthornden : *see Hawthornden.*

Old Lady : *see Golden Knob.*

Old Maid : *see Golden Knob.*

ONTARIO. *New York,* I., 240. Culinary or dessert, till April, medium, 2¾ by 2, flat, irregular. Colour, pale yellow with bright red flush and faint stripes. Flesh, crisp, juicy, pale yellow, sub-acid. Eye, very small in a broad rather deep basin. Stem, moderately long, rather slender in an extremely wide ribbed cavity. Growth, vigorous and sturdy; fertility remarkably regular. Leaf, rather large, rich green, very long oval, upcupped, much undulating, coarsely serrate. Origin, a cross between Wagener and Northern Spy, made by Mr. Charles Arnold, in Ontario before 1874. An excellent late variety, worthy of extended cultivation. It does not shrivel when kept long.

ORANGE GOFF. (Goff, Pork Apple.) Culinary, till March, medium, 3¼ by 2¼, roundish, slightly flattened. Colour, yellow with crimson flush and darker stripes. Flesh, crisp, yellow, rather acid. Eye, open in a shallow ribbed basin. Stem, short in a shallow or hardly perceptible cavity. Growth, sturdy; fertile. Origin, known for many years in Kentish orchards. A very old variety of excellent cooking qualities.

ORANGE PIPPIN. *Ronalds*, p. 16. Dessert, till January, medium, 3 by 2, flattened round, regular. Colour, orange-yellow, flushed with red. Flesh, tender, yellow, of fair flavour. Eye, closed in a shallow basin. Stem, slender in a fairly deep cavity. Growth, good; fertile. Origin, unknown. It has been grown in England at least 200 years. It is now little cultivated. There seem to be two varieties under this name, the above and a large fruit of the Blenheim style.

Original Nonpareil : *see Nonpareil.*

Original Pippin : *see Oslin.*

ORLEAN'S REINETTE. *Lauche* I. 40. (Reinette Triumphant, Court Pendu Blanc.) Dessert, till February, medium to fairly large, 2¾ by 2¼, flattened, very even. Colour, golden-yellow with slight red flush. Skin, covered with patches of fine russet. Flesh, yellow, very crisp, sweet, juicy and of the highest flavour intermediate between Blenheim Orange and Ribston Pippin. Eye, open in a wide, shallow, slightly ribbed basin. Stem, short and stout, in a moderately deep wide russeted cavity. Growth, strong, upright, spreading; fertility fair. Leaf, large, oval, dark green, boldly curved serrate, held nearly flat. Origin, uncertain but it was first described by Knoop in 1776. This apple has been much confused with others and I first received it mixed in with Blenheim Orange to which it is very similar in some respects, but is quite distinct the flavour being much better. It has received numberless synonyms and I regret that my firm added one by calling it Winter Ribston until the real name was discovered. This magnificent fruit cannot be too highly recommended.

OSLIN. *Ronalds*, p. 6. (Arbroath Pippin, Burr Knot, Mother, Original Pippin, Summer Oslin.) Dessert, August, medium, 2½ by 2, flattened round, regular. Colour, pale yellow, thickly spotted. Flesh, crisp, yellowish, sweet, aromatic. Eye, closed, in a shallow basin. Stem, short in a narrow cavity. Growth, good; fertility, good. Leaf, medium, round, irregularly serrate. Origin, Scotch? (possibly French) probably dating from the seventeenth century. Of no particular merit.

Ox Apple : *see Gloria Mundi.*

Oxford Peach : *see Scarlet Pearmain.*

Paradies : *see Gravenstein.*

PARADISE. The name Paradise has been applied to a large number of different varieties which are used for stocks. None of them, however, possess any special value from the culinary or dessert standpoint.
For description of the fruits see *Journal R.H.S.*, Vol. XLII., parts II. and III.

Paradise : *see Thorle.*

PARADISE WHITE. *Ronalds*, p. 2. (Egg, Eve, Lady's Finger.) Dessert, October to November, 2½ by 3½, medium, oval conical. Colour, red with faint stripes. Flesh, tender, flavour fair. Eye, open in a shallow basin, Stem, fairly long in a narrow round cavity. Growth, free ; fertility, moderate. Leaf, small, little upfolded, very finely serrate. Origin, undiscovered. An old variety which is yet found growing in old orchards particularly in Ireland. Not worth growing now. The synonyms of this apple are much confused. Eve and Lady's Finger being also used for distinct fruits.

PAROQUET. Culinary or dessert, till January, medium, 2¼ by 2¼, round conical. Colour, entirely covered with rich crimson red with russet markings. Flesh, tender, yellowish ; flavour, fair. Eye, wide, open in a wide very shallow basin. Stem, short and stout, in a small shallow cavity. Growth, compact ; fertile. Leaf, roundish, light green, upcupped, undulating, finely and deeply doubly curved serrate. Origin, a chance seedling raised by Mr. Charles Ross, and introduced by Messrs. Cheal, of Crawley. Attractive on account of its rich colour, but its flavour is not good enough as grown at Allington.

Passe Pomme d'Hiver : *see Calville Rouge d'Hiver.*

Paternoster : *see Dutch Mignonne.*

PAUL'S WINTER HAWTHORNDEN. *Her. Pom.,* 10. Culinary, till February, medium, 3 by 2¼, flattened round, tapering markedly to eye, even. Colour, pale green with faint red flush, smooth. Flesh, firm, pale green, acid ; flavour nil. Eye, closed almost on surface of fruit, basin a little ribbed and rounded. Stem, moderately long in a very deep, wide cavity. Growth, dense and compact ; fertility, good. Leaf, large, round oval, flat, pale green, shallow serrate. Origin, undiscovered. Makes a well spurred round headed tree.

PEARSON'S PLATE. *Her. Pom.,* 47. Dessert, till March, very small, 2 by 1¾, square-conical, regular.

Colour, greenish-yellow with brown-red flush and stripes and russet. Flesh, crisp, yellow, rich. Eye, open in a shallow ribbed basin. Stem, long in a moderately even cavity. Growth, moderate; fertile. Leaf, rather small, oval, bi-serrate. Origin, unknown. Robert Thompson considered de Hanovre to be identical with this. Now very little grown.

PEASGOOD'S NONSUCH. *Her. Pom.*, 61. F., Sanspareille de Peasgood. Culinary and exhibition, September to November, large, 3¾ by 2½, round flattened, remarkably regular. Colour, golden-yellow with faint flush and a few broad broken stripes. Flesh, tender, yellowish, of pleasant flavour and cooks frothily. Eye, nearly closed in a deep round, even basin. Stem, short in a very wide russet cavity. Growth, vigorous; fertile. Leaf, rather large, roundish, pea green, flat lax, finely crenate, falls early, turns greenish-yellow. Origin, raised by Mrs. Peasgood, of Stamford, in 1858, from a seed of the Catshead Codlin. First fruited in 1872. The original tree is still growing at Stamford. One of the most beautiful fruits grown; first rate for cooking. It makes a flat spreading tree. Rather liable to canker.

Peter the Great: *see Cardinal.*

Phillip's Seedling: *see Cellini.*

Pilot Russet: *see Cockle's Pippin.*

Pine Apple: *see Lucombe's Pine.*

PINE APPLE RUSSET OF DEVON. Dessert, September, fairly large, 2¾ by 2½, flat conical. Colour, creamy-yellow, golden-red flush and thin russet patches and veinings. Flesh, yellow, rather dry, rather hard, pleasant flavour of pine. Growth, compact; fertile. Leaf, rather small, roundish, slightly upfolded, very coarsely crenate, undulating. Origin, long grown in Devonshire and Cornwall. A very distinct fruit.

The Devonshire variety Sops in Wine much resembles this but is distinct and rather smaller. It must not be confused with the Pine Apple Russet of Hogg.

PINE APPLE RUSSET. Dessert, October to November, medium, 2 by 2½, oblong rounded, nearly even. Colour, greenish-brown covered with fine russet. Flesh, pale yellow, firm, a little dry. Eye, open in a shallow, even basin, tips laid back. Stem, moderately long, thin, in a small even cavity. Fertility, moderate. Leaf, rather small, upfolded, boldly crenate. Origin, found in a garden belonging to Mr. Hardingham, of Norwich, in 1780, and first described by Lindley. This is I presume Lindley's apple though he speaks of its abundant juice (and Hogg copies him almost verbatim), but as grown to-day, it is rather dry. The apple of the same name from Devon is quite distinct and I venture to add the name Devon to distinguish that variety. The flavour distinctly recalls the Pine Apple.

Pitcher : *see Mank's Codlin.*

PITMASTON GOLDEN PIPPIN. Dessert, till January, small, 2¼ by 2½, round, flattened at top. Colour, pale golden-yellow with russet and very faint brown-red flush. Flesh, yellow, very crisp and juicy, nicely flavoured. Eye, wide open in a very broad and shallow basin. Stem, very slender and short in a very even and narrow cavity. Growth, moderate ; fertile. Origin, raised by Mr. Williams, of Pitmaston, about 1838, " probably from a seed of the Golden Pippin." A very nice little fruit now seldom met.

Pitmaston : *see Pitmaston Nonpareil.*

PITMASTON NONPAREIL. *Her. Pom.,* 33 (as Pitmaston Russet). F., Nonpareille de Pitmaston. (Pitmaston, Pitmaston Russet, Pitmaston Russet Nonpareil.) Dessert, till January, medium, 2¾ by 2, roundish, flat, regular. Colour, heavily covered with bronze russet, occasionally with red flush. Flesh, tender, pale yellow, russet flavour. Eye, open in a shallow ribbed basin. Stem, rather short in a round, even cavity. Growth, compact, upright; fertile. Leaf, little upfolded, long oval, deeply serrate. Origin, raised by John Williams, of Pitmaston, near Worcester, and introduced to notice in 1818. A very good fruit of the flavour usually found in " russets ": now very little grown.

PITMASTON PINE APPLE. Dessert, till December, small, 2 by 2, oblong, conical, shape of Adam's Pearmain. Colour, golden-yellow, almost covered with very fine cinnamon russet. Flesh, yellow, firm, juicy with a most deliciously scented and honeyed flavour. Eye, closed, in a very shallow basin or level with surface surrounded by many minute ribs. Stem, rather stout, half-inch, in a narrow, shallow, very round cavity. Origin, this was first shown at the Royal Horticultural Show, in 1845, and the origin then given was that it was raised from the Old Golden Pippin, more than sixty years ago, by Mr. White, of Witley, steward to Lord Foley. Hogg says it was raised by Mr. Williams, of Pitmaston, but this is evidently wrong as it was only sent to London by him. This is one of the old fruits which have been neglected on account of their small size, but its distinct and delicious flavour should give it a place in the gardens of connoisseurs.

Pitmaston Russet : *see Pitmaston Nonpareil.*

Pitmaston Russet Nonpareil : *see Pitmaston Nonpareil.*

Plumderity : *see Venus Pippin.*

Pomme de Cuir : *see Pomme Grise.*

Pomme de Laak : *see Dutch Migonne.*

POMME GRISE. *Ronalds,* 16. (Gray Apple, Leather Coat of Turic, Pomme de Cuir.) Dessert, till March, small, 2¼ by 1⅓, flat, regular. Colour, brown-gold russet with dark red flush. Flesh, crisp, yellowish, aromatic. Eye, open in a shallow even basin. Stem, moderately long in a shallow cavity. Growth, weak; fertile. Origin, probably Canadian. Introduced to England in 1794. An excellent russet.

Pope's : *see Cobham.*

POPE'S SCARLET COSTARD. Culinary or dessert, till March, medium, 2¼ by 2½, conical, fairly regular. Colour, pale yellow, almost covered with dark brownish crimson. Flesh, crisp, juicy, greenish, pleasantly flavoured. Eye, closed, in a shallow ribbed basin, much knobbed at top. Stem, short in a small very russet cavity. Growth, vigorous; fertility, moderate. Leaf, roundish, flat, undulating, shallow serrate. Origin, unrecorded. Not worthy of cultivation.

Pork Apple : *see Orange Goff.*

Portugal : *see Reinette du Canada.*

Potter's Large : *see Kentish Fillbasket.*

POTTS' SEEDLING. *Her. Pom.*, 10. (Dean's Codlin, Holland Pippin.) Culinary, October to November, large, 3 by 3, round, regular. Colour, light green to chrome yellow; skin very smooth. Flesh, firm, white, acid. Eye, closed, in a wrinkled basin with prominent knobs at top. Stem, short, stout, in a wide and rather deep cavity. Growth, dwarf; fertility, remarkable. Leaf, pale, upfolded, undulating, rather large, shallow crenate. Origin, named after its raiser, who lived at Ashton-under-Lyme. Dates from 1849. A useful kitchen fruit. Most valuable for small gardens. Rather liable to canker.

Primiting : *see White Joaneting.*

Prince Albert : *see Lane's Prince Albert.*

PRINCE EDWARD. Culinary or dessert, till February, medium, 2¾ by 2¼, round conical, irregular. Colour, golden-yellow, with red flush and broad broken stripes. Flesh, tender, juicy, pale yellow, sub-acid. Growth, compact; fertile. Leaf, pale, medium, little upcupped, boldly crenate. Origin, raised and introduced by Messrs. Rivers. Of no particular merit.

Putnam Russet : *see Boston Russet.*

Quarrington : *see Devonshire Quarrenden.*

QUEEN. *Her. Pom.*, 39. (Saltmarsh's Queen, The Claimant.) Culinary, October to December, large, 3¼ by 2¼, flat, irregular. Colour, pale lemon-yellow with distinct red stripes and flush. Flesh, very tender, white, sub-acid, excellent cooker. Eye, closed in a deep, wide basin. Stem, short, in a very wide and deep cavity, which has scaly russet. Growth, strong and spreading; fertile. Leaf, large, flat, coarsely serrate or crenate. Origin, raised by Mr. W. Bull, a farmer of Billericay, in 1858, and introduced by Mr. Saltmarsh, of Chelmsford, in 1880. A useful fruit; does well as a standard, making a large flat headed tree.

QUEEN CAROLINE. (Spencer's Favourite, Brown's Queen Caroline.) Culinary, till December, fairly large, 3 by 2¾, flattened round, regular. Colour, pale greenish-yellow. Flesh, firm, juicy, yellow. Eye, large, open in a wide even basin. Stem, medium, in a rather deep cavity. Growth, moderate; fertile. Leaf, rather large, dark green, round oval, regularly serrate, upfolded, undulating. Origin, raised by Mr. T. Brown, a nurseryman of Measham, near Ashby-de-la-Zouch, about 1820, and named after the much discussed Queen. A good cooker, makes a good standard and bears well thus.

Queen Charlotte's Apple : *see Borsdorfer.*

Quince : *see Lemon Pippin.*

Quodlin : *see English Codlin.*

RAMBOUR PAPALEU. *Arbor. Belge,* 1882, p. 33.
Culinary or dessert, till March, very large, 3½ by 3,
oblong-conical. Colour, pale yellow, green with bold
red striping and flush. Flesh, pale yellow, crisp, juicy,
sweet. Eye, open, in a wide ribbed basin. Stem,
rather short, in a shallow cavity. Growth, very stout
and compact, upright; fertility, excellent. Leaf,
large, dark, flat, regularly serrate. Origin, raised
by Col. Hartwiss, of Nitika, in the Crimea, about 1853,
and named after M. Papaleu, of Ghent.

Red Astrachan : *see Astrachan Red.*

Red Beefing : *see Norfolk Beefing.*

Red Flanders : *see Hollandbury.*

Red Hawthornden : *see Yorkshire Beauty.*

RED INGESTRIE. *Ronalds, Pl.* 1. F., Ingestrie
Rouge ; G., Roter Pepping von Ingestrie. Dessert,
September to October, small, 2½ by 2, square, regular.
Colour, golden-yellow with red flush and faint stripes.
Flesh, crisp, juicy, yellow ; flavour, good. Eye, open,
in a moderately deep basin. Stem, slender in a narrow
cavity. Growth, vigorous, spreading. Leaf, medium,
oval, regularly serrate. Origin, raised by T. A. Knight,
about 1800 (Orange × Golden Pippin). Now rarely
met with.

RED JOANETING. *Ronalds,* P. 6. F., Marguerite ; G., Roter Morgareten. (Eve, Lammas,
Striped Quarrenden, Margaret.) Dessert, early August,
small, 2½ by 2½, oval, slightly irregular. Colour,
greenish-yellow, nearly covered with red stripes and
flush. Flesh, soft, greenish-white, sub-acid. Eye,
open, in a shallow, slightly ribbed basin. Stem, short
and stout, in a wide, not russet cavity. Growth,
moderate, making a shapely upright spreading tree ;
fertility great. Leaf, large, roundish, pea green,
upheld and upcupped, deeply bluntly serrate or nearly

crenate. Origin, probably English, dating from the seventeenth century. The second earliest of all apples. The Red Margaret is I think a red sport from this apple as it agrees in all respects save the colour is very much deeper and unstriped.

Red Margaret : *see Red Joaneting.*

Red Ribbed Greening : *see Cornish Pine.*

RED VICTORIA. *Gard. Chron.*, 1908, p. 297. Culinary, September, large, 3¼ by 2¾, flattened round, a little irregular. Colour, rich crimson, red all over. Flesh, pale, soft, sub-acid. Eye, open in a deep and uneven basin. Stem, short and thick, in a deep and wide cavity. Growth, moderate, Leaf, rather large, long oval, nearly flat, undulated, doubly curved serrate. Origin, a chance seedling which originated near Wisbech, about 1884. Introduced by Messrs. Miller, Wisbech, Remarkable for its high colour, which approaches that of Gascoynes Scarlet.

Regelans : *see Cornish Gillyflower.*

Reinnette a Cotés : *see Calville Blanche d'Hiver.*

Reinette De Bolwyller : *see Baumann's Reinette.*

Reinette De Canada Grise : *see Royal Russet.*

Reinette D'Hiver Musquée : *see Margil.*

REINETTE DU CANADA. *Ronalds*, P. 11. F., Reinette du Canada ; G., Pariser Rambour Reinette. (Some forty-eight synonyms exist ; Gold Reinette, Mela Januria, Portugal, Reinette Grandville.) Dessert, till April, large, 3¾ by 3, round conical, slightly angular. Colour, greenish-yellow with thin russet and slight brown flush. Flesh, firm, pale yellow, of rich flavour. Eye, open, very large, in a very wide ribbed basin. Stem, short and thick, not protruding from a very wide cavity. Growth, vigorous, rather spreading ; fertility, moderate. Leaf, rather large, dark, upfolded, undulated, oval, sharply pointed, very deeply curved serrate. Origin, uncertain ; known in France before 1771. Excellent in warm seasons. Very subject to canker.

Reinette Etoilée : *see Reinette Rouge Etoilée.*

Reinette Gielen : *see Golden Reinette.*

Reinette Grandville : *see Reinette du Canada.*

REINETTE GRISE. *Ronalds*, P., 32. G., Grau Franzosische Reinette. (Belle Fille, Grauer Rabau, Haute Bonté, Leder Apfel.) Dessert, till March, medium, 2 by 2, oblong round, regular. Colour, yellowish-green with dull red flush covered with russet. Flesh, crisp, yellow, aromatic. Eye, closed, in a rather deep basin. Stem, short in a very deep cavity. Growth, vigorous ; fertile. Origin, of great antiquity ; recorded in the sixteenth century in France, its country of origin. An apple of excellent quality.

Reinette Monstreuse : *see Belle de Boskoop.*

REINETTE ROUGE ETOILEE. *Fl. and Pom.,* 1884, 169. F., Reinette Rouge Etoilée ; G., Roter Stern Reinette. [Calville Rouge Précoce (error), Early Red Calville, Reinette Etoilée.] Dessert, October to December, small, 2½ by 2, flattened round, regular. Colour, rich yellow, almost covered with carmine red with broad broken stripes. Flesh, firm, juicy, pale yellow with suffused red below skin, sub-acid, of slight strawberry flavour. Eye, open, in a very even, regular basin. Stem, very short, in a narrow russet cavity. Growth, compact ; fertile. Leaf, rather dark, long oval, held flat, tip down curved, very finely curved serrate. Origin, it has been grown in Eastern Belgium for some 100 years or more. It was introduced to England probably about 1830. It is the Early Red Calville of Hogg. Of fair quality and most attractive in appearance.

REINETTE SUPERFINE. Culinary or dessert, till March, medium, 2½ by 2¼, round, markedly conical, regular. Colour, pale yellow almost covered with red flush and faint stripes. Flesh, pale yellow, firm, juicy, of pleasant flavour. Leaf, long, greyish-green, down hanging, boldly curved serrate. Origin, uncertain; introduced by Transon Frères, of Orleans, in 1866. An attractive fruit of some merit.

Reinette Triomphant : *see Orleans Reinette.*

Reinette Von Madeira : *see Lemon Pippin.*

Reinette Von Montfort : *see Belle de Boskoop.*

RENOWN. *Gard. Chron.*, 1908, p. 292. Dessert or culinary, October to November, fairly large, 3¾ by 2¾, broad conical, uneven. Colour, golden-yellow, almost covered with red flush, Flesh, pale yellow, firm, of pleasant flavour. Eye, closed, in a broad shallow basin. Stem, short, in a round even russet cavity. Growth, vigorous; very fertile. Leaf, round oval, medium, held up, flat, boldly curved serrate. Origin, raised by Mr. Charles Ross from the same cross as produced the apple Charles Ross.

REYNOLDS PEACH. (Emperor Napoleon.) Culinary or dessert, August, 2½ by 2¼, flat, conical, irregular. Colour, entirely covered with the brightest carmine with heavy bloom. Flesh, loose, pale yellow, sub-acid. Eye, closed, in a very ribbed irregular basin. Stem, short and thick not protruding. Growth, dwarf; fertile. Leaf, rather large, pea green, upfolded, boldly crenate. Origin, an old West Country apple much grown in Devonshire orchards. Remarkable for its earliness and unusual appearance on the tree, but of no value.

REV. W. WILKS. *The Garden*, 1910, 572. Culinary, September to November, very large, 3½ by 3, flat conical, slightly irregular. Colour, pale creamy-white with slight flush and stripes. Flesh, tender, white, sub-acid, cooks frothily, pale yellow. Eye, closed or slightly open, in a wide ribbed basin. Stem,, short, in a deep, narrow, slightly russet cavity. Growth, stout and dwarf ; fertility extraordinary. Leaf, large, dark, lax, undulated, doubly curved serrate. Origin, raised by Messrs. Veitch, from Peasgood Nonsuch and Ribston. A very large and promising fruit, of excellent cooking qualities.

RHODE ISLAND GREENING. *New York.*, I. 282. F., Verte de Rhode Island. Dessert or culinary, till April, medium to large, 3 by 2¼, round, slightly conical. Colour, pea green fading to pale yellow. Flesh; crisp, very juicy, pale yellow, spicy flavour. Eye, closed, in a medium basin. Stem, rather long, in a narrow cavity. Growth, sturdy and compact ; regularly fertile. Leaf, long oval, very dark green, upfolded, very sharply curved serrate. Origin, American, probably over 150 years old. A useful late fruit of the Newtown Pippin style. Quite good for dessert in March and April when well ripened.

Ribston Pearmain : *see Claygate Pearmain.*

RIBSTON PIPPIN. *Ronalds*, P. 27. F., Pepin Ribston ; G., Englische Granat Reinette. (Formosa Pippin, Nonpareille d'Angleterre, Travers Pippin.) Dessert, till January, medium to fairly large, 3 by 2¼, round conical, irregular. Colour, yellow with dull brownish-red flush and few stripes and russet. Flesh, firm, yellow, highly aromatic. Eye, a little open, in a deep uneven basin. Stem, rather long, in a narrow russet cavity. Growth, moderate ; fertility, medium. Leaf, very dark, and densely woolly below, upcupped, edges twisted, shallow serrate. Origin, English. Raised at Ribston Hall, Knaresborough, about 1709, from seeds brought from Rouen. One of the richest flavoured apples when well ripened.

RIVAL. Culinary or dessert, October to December, fairly large, 3 by 2¼, round flattened, regular. Colour, pale yellowish-green with carmine flush and a few broad stripes. Flesh, firm, juicy, white, flavour pleasant. Eye, half open, in a very deep and wide basin, which is a little plaited on the sides. Stem, short, in a very deep, round and even cavity. Growth vigorous; fertility, moderate. Leaf, medium, flat serrate, long oval, held flat, undulating, turns pale yellow. Origin, raised by Mr. Charles Ross, from Peasgood Nonsuch. Introduced by Messrs. Clibran, Altrincham. A most attractive fruit of great promise.

River's Codlin : *see Thomas Rivers.*

RIVERS' EARLY PEACH. Dessert, mid-August, medium, 3¼ by 2¾, flat conical, falling away to eye in flat sided angles. Colour, palest creamy-yellow with sometimes a faint flush. Flesh, white, granular, sweet, aromatic, apt to be a little dry. Eye, closed in a broad slightly ribbed basin. Stem, very short in a wide shallow cavity, a green tinge remains round stem when fruit is ripe. Growth, distinctly upright. Leaf, narrow, oval, down-hanging, flat, finely crenate, falling early. Origin, raised by Mr. Rivers.

Roman Beauty : *see Rome Beauty.*

Rome : *see Rome Beauty.*

ROME BEAUTY. *New York*, I. p. 290. (Belle de Rome, Roman Beauty, Rome.) Culinary or dessert, till May, large, 3 by 2¾, nearly round, even. Colour, pale yellow, almost covered with bright red flush and some broad broken stripes showing through. Flesh, palest yellow, crisp, juicy, a little sweet, not any marked flavour. Eye, closed, in a shallow, slightly ribbed basin. Stem, always long, in a shallow russet cavity. Growth, medium, at first upright, then slightly dropping. Leaf, long oval. Origin, raised by Mr. Gillett, in Lawrence, Ohio Co. Introduced in 1848. This American variety is under trial and so far seems promising, and if it crops sufficiently well and is resistent to canker it should be a valuable late market variety.

ROSEBERRY. Dessert, October and in the North till December, medium, 2½ by 2½, round-conical, uneven. Skin, smooth, a little greasy, Colour, almost entirely covered with bright scarlet flush and bright stripes. Flesh, pale yellow, very tender, sweet. Eye, medium, firmly closed, set in a shallow ribbed basin. Stem, variable, half to one inch, in a shallow, narrow, faintly russet cavity. Fertility good. Origin, raised by Mr. Storrie in his nursery, at Glencarse.

ROSEMARY RUSSET. *Ronalds*, P., 16. Dessert, till February, small to medium, 2½ by 2, round conical, flattened at base, regular. Colour, yellowish-green with slight red flush, covered with light russet. Flesh, crisp, yellow, very rich and brisk. Eye, a little open, in a small even basin. Stem, unusually long, in a wide cavity. Growth, moderate ; fertility, moderate. Leaf, rather large, light, held flat, boldly curved serrate. Origin, unknown ; first recorded by Ronalds, in 1831. Quite the best of late winter apples.

ROSS NONPAREIL. *Her. Pom.*, 21. F., Nonpareille de Ross. Dessert, till January, medium, 2½ by 2, round regular. Colour, greenish-yellow, with crimson flush and stripes, covered with russet. Flesh, tender, greenish, aromatic, strongly scented. Eye, wide open like a clove in a shallow regular basin. Stem, long and slender, in a narrow deep cavity. Growth, slender, making a compact tree ; fertile. Leaf, rather small, pea green, held up, flat, very irregularly serrate, often nearly entire. Origin, Irish ; introduced to England in 1820. A first rate garden fruit, as good in flavour as it is attractive in appearance. Makes a nice round headed standard.

Round Russet Harvey : *see Golden Harvey*.

ROUNDWAY MAGNUM BONUM. Dessert or culinary, till March, large, 3 by 2½, flat, conical. Colour, yellowish-green with dull brown flush and a few broad broken stripes. Flesh, firm, greenish-yellow, rather dry, flavour very sweet and pear like. Eye, a little open in a broad irregular basin. Stem, stout in a wide deep cavity. Growth, spreading ; fertility, moderate. Leaf, large, dark, held out, slightly upcupped and undulating, boldly curved serrate, very downy below. Origin, raised at Roundway Park, Devizes, and brought to notice about 1864. A fruit of remarkable flavour, deserving wider cultivation.

ROUND WINTER NONSUCH. *Her. Pom.*, 61. Culinary, till February, large, 3 by 2¼, round flattened, fairly regular. Colour, pale greenish-yellow with slight flush and broad broken stripes. Flesh, soft, greenish-white, sweet. Eye, closed, on a level with the surface, Basin a little wrinkled. Stem, short and stout, in a round, moderately deep, very slightly russet cavity. Growth, upright and free ; fertility, said to be good. Leaf, large, upfolded, reflexed, irregularly serrate. Origin, unrecorded ; known in 1842. A useful cooking variety, but hardly needed.

Rousette Royale : *see Royal Russet.*

Roxbury Russet : *see Boston Russet.*

Royal Codlin : *see Dutch Codlin.*

Royal George : *see Clark's Seedling.*

ROYAL JUBILEE. Culinary, October to December, medium, 2¼ by 2¾, oval, conical, very slightly ribbed. Colour, pale lemon yellow occasionally with the faintest orange flush. Flesh, firm, yellow, sub-acid : cooks well. Eye, closed, in a narrow much ribbed basin. Stem, short and stout, in a rather wide, slightly russet cavity. Growth, very dwarf ; extremely fertile. Leaf, medium, tapering to petiole, little down-folded, coarsely crenate. Origin, raised by Mr. John Graham, of Hounslow, was introduced by Messrs. G. Bunyard & Co., Maidstone, in 1893. Valuable for its late flowering and regular cropping habits.

ROYAL LATE. *Gard. Chron.*, 1896, p. 114. Culinary, till March, large, 3 by 2¼, round conical, slightly irregular. Colour, pale yellowish-green with russet nettings. Flesh, soft, yellow, juicy (almost Reinette like), sub-acid. Eye, open, in a very shallow basin. Stem, short and stout, in a shallow cavity. Growth, strong, wide spreading; fertility, fair. Origin, found in the Royal Gardens, at Frogmore, and said to have been raised by Mr. Powell. It has now been given up as it is very liable to canker.

Royal Pearmain : *see Autumn Pearmain.*

Royal Portugee : *see Cox's Pomona.*

ROYAL RUSSET. *Ronalds*, P. 29. F., Reinette Grise Royale; G., Koeniglicher Russet. (Leather Coat (of some), Reinette de Canada Grise (an error), Rousette Royale.) Culinary, till March, fairly large, 3¼ by 2¼, flattened round, irregular. Colour, entirely green, covered with brown russet. Flesh, tender, greenish-yellow, sweet. Eye, closed in a wide and shallow basin. Stem, slender in a very wide cavity. Growth, vigorous; fertile. Leaf, long oval very dark, upfolded and undulated, broadly curved serrate. Origin, probably English. First recorded in 1597. One of the best of its class.

Royal Snow : *see Fameuse.*

Royal Somerset : *see London Pippin.*

RUDDY. Early September, medium, 2¼ by 2¼, round flattened, fairly regular. Colour, palest yellow-green, almost covered with rich crimson flush, faintly mottled. Flesh, of loose texture, white, fairly sweet and slightly aromatic. Growth, compact; fertility, moderate. Leaf, long oval, undulating, curved serrate, grey-green. Origin, raised by Mr. Charles Ross from Ecklinville and Mère de Ménage. It resembles Red Astrachan but is of no particular merit.

Russian Ice Apple : *see Astrachan White.*

Rutlandshire Foundling : *see Golden Noble.*

Ryland Surprise : *see Gold Medal.*

RYMER. *Ronalds*, P. 41. (Caldwell's Keeper, Green Cossings.) Culinary, till March, fairly large, 3¼ by 2¾, flattened conical, slightly irregular. Colour, covered with deep crimson red flush and faint stripes. Flesh, tender, yellow, acid. Eye, closed, or a little open, in a deep wide ribbed basin. Stem, extra short, often only three-eights-of-an-inch, in a small, shallow cavity, or often level with the surface, or often raised. Growth, strong ; fertility moderate. Leaf, large, flat, down curved, round oval, doubly shallow serrate. Origin, named after its raiser, Mr. Rymer of Thirsk, Yorkshire, about 1750. Now almost out of cultivation, but a good fruit. This apple has probably the shortest stem of any.

Sack : *see Devonshire Quarrenden.*

SACK AND SUGAR. *Ronalds*, P. 1. Dessert or culinary, September, medium, 2¼ by 2¼, round, tapering to eye, irregular, showing one rib more prominent than the rest. Colour, pale yellowish-green, sprinkled with prominent dark green dots. Flesh, pale yellow, very tender, juicy, with pleasing aromatic flavour. Eye, closed, segments reflexed, in a fairly deep rather uneven basin, which is slightly ribbed. Stem, always very short and stout, not protruding from cavity which is moderately deep, rather narrow, free from russet. Origin, a very old West country apple.

ST. EDMUNDS PIPPIN. (St. Edmunds Russet.) Dessert, October to November, small, 2¼ and 2, flattened conical, even. Colour, entirely covered with golden russet. Flesh, pale yellow, very juicy and fine flavoured. Eye, closed, in a small even basis. Stem, slender, in a narrow cavity. Growth, medium, upright spreading, making a good garden tree. Leaf, medium, narrow, pale, upfolded, undulating, blunt serrate. Origin, raised at Bury St. Edmunds by a Mr. Harvey, about 1870. Quite the best early russet.

St. Edmunds Russet : *see St. Edmunds Pippin.*

ST. EVERARD. Dessert, September, medium, 2¼ by 2¼, round, regular. Colour, yellow, almost covered with deep crimson, with faint stripes. Flesh, crisp, yellow, juicy and of excellent flavour. Eye, closed in a shallow or almost level basin with a few radiating puckers. Stem, short and stout, protruding from a wide shallow cavity. Growth, sturdy and compact. Leaf, medium, dark, upcupped, coarsely curved serrate. Origin, raised by a gardener at Papworth Everard near Cambridge, supposedly from Cox's Orange by Margil and introduced in 1910, by Messrs. Veitch & Co. This apple is of great promise and should be included in all collections.

ST. MARTINS. Dessert, till February, medium, oval, tapering to eye, very even. Skin, smooth, faint russet in patches. Colour, golden yellow almost covered with brownish red and greyish general appearance. Flesh, moderately firm, pale yellow, juicy, remarkably sweet. Eye, closed in a rather shallow basin. Stem, medium, rather thin, in a narrow cavity. Leaf, long, narrow, regularly crenate, upfolded and twisted. Origin, raised and introduced by Messrs. Rivers. Perhaps the sweetest of all apples.

Salopian : *see Warner's King.*

Saltmarsh's Queen : *see Queen.*

Sam Rawlings : *see Hoary Morning.*

SANDRINGHAM. Culinary, till February, large 2¾ by 2¼, round conical, regular. Colour, yellow, with occasional faint flush. Flesh, firm, but soft, yellowish, sub-acid. Eye, closed in a rather deep slightly ribbed basin. Stem, slender in a moderately deep, very even slightly russet cavity. Growth, moderate, rather upright ; fertile when adult. Leaf, rather small, narrow, upfolded, undulated, minutely serrate. Origin, raised by Mr. Perry, of Sandringham Gardens, and introduced by Messrs. Veitch & Sons, in 1884. A useful fruit which does well in the Western Counties.

Sanguineous : *see Fameuse.*

SANSPAREIL. *The Garden*, 1911, 523. Culinary or dessert, till April, medium, 2¾ by 2¼, round-conical, irregular. Colour, orange-yellow with brilliant scarlet flush and stripes. Flesh, crisp, yellow, sweet, juicy and aromatic. Eye, half open, in a rather deep and ribbed basin. Stem, slender in a narrow russet-free cavity. Growth, compact ; very fertile. Leaf, oval, rather pale, upfolded, undulated, held out, irregularly and finely serrate. Origin, unknown. It has been cultivated in this country for thirty years at least. A most valuable late sort, keeping well without shrivelling It deserves to be more widely known.

Sapsovine : *see Sops in Wine.*

Sapson : *see Sops in Wine.*

Sari Sinope : *see Kandil Sinap.*

SCARLET GOLDEN PIPPIN. *Her. Pom.*, 37. Dessert, till March, very small, 1¾ by 1¼, square round. Colour, yellow, nearly covered with scarlet flush. Flesh, crisp, yellow, aromatic. Eye, open, in a shallow basin. Stem, rather long, and slender in a small cavity. Growth moderate ; fertile. Origin, as a bud sport of Golden Pippin in Scotland, about 1820. Now little grown and of no remarkable merit.

Scarlet Incomparable : *see Colonel Vaughan.*

118

SCARLET NONPAREIL. *Ronalds*, P. 34. F., Nonpareil Ecarlate; G., Scharlachroter Nonpareil. Dessert, till March, small to medium, 2¼ by 2, round conical, regular. Colour, yellow covered with dull red and russet. Flesh, firm, pale, yellow, sweet, rather good flavour. Eye, open in a shallow regular basin. Stem, rather long, in an even russet cavity. Growth, slender, a little upright, compact; fertile. Leaf, very narrow, sharp pointed, held out flat, light green, boldly crenate, nearly smooth below. Origin, probably raised at Esher, Surrey, about 1773, from a seed of the Old Nonpareil. A good old sort worthy of retention.

SCARLET PEARMAIN. *Ronalds*, P. 8. F., Pearmain Ecarlate; G., Scharlach rote Parmane. (Bell's Scarlet, Melville Pippin, Oxford Peach.) Dessert, September to November, medium, 2¼ by 2¼, square-conical, regular. Colour, crimson scarlet flush with faint stripes. Flesh, tender, yellow, red tinged, of crab apple flavour. Eye, open, in a deepish basin. Stem, medium, in a narrow cavity. Growth, slender, rather spreading making a close twiggy tree; fertility good. Leaf, long, narrow, upfolded, coarsely serrate. Origin, introduced to notice about 1800, by Mr. Bell, Agent to the Duke of Northumberland. A useful fruit of distinct flavour, but should be eaten soon after gathering.

SCHOOLMASTER. *Fl. and Pom.*, 1882, 169. Culinary, October to January, fairly large, 3 by 2¾, conical. Colour, bright green with slight flush. Flesh, crisp, white, slightly acid. Eye, closed, in a deep basin. Stem, very short, in a small irregular cavity. Growth, vigorous; fertile. Origin, raised in 1855 from the seed of a Canadian apple. The original tree grew in Old Stamford Grammar School Garden. Introduced by Messrs. Laxton, in 1882. Now little grown in the South.

SEATON HOUSE. Culinary, September to January, medium, 2¼ by 2, flat. Colour, pale milky-yellow with a faint flush and a few broken stripes. Flesh, crisp, juicy, pale yellow, flavourless. Eye, small, closed, in a very shallow basin, which is slightly plaited. Stem, stout, in a wide and deepish cavity, slightly russet lined. Growth, compact; fertility remarkable. Leaf, medium, long oval, pale, held flat, sharply serrate. Origin, raised at Seaton House, Arbroath, Scotland. Of the Hawthornden class, valuable only for its remarkable cropping powers, rather tender skin. It often keeps till March.

SEPTEMBER BEAUTY. Dessert, September to January, medium, 2¼ by 2, round flattened, slightly irregular. Colour, lemon-yellow with very bright crimson flush and broad broken stripes. Flesh, tender, yellow, of no particular flavour. Growth, moderate, makes a nice upright spreading tree. Leaf, long oval, nearly flat, undulating. Origin, introduced by Messrs. Laxton, about 1885. It is now superseded.

SHEPHERD'S PEARMAIN. Dessert or culinary, till March, large, 3¾ by 3¼, markedly conical, irregular. Colour, golden-yellow with brown red flush and patches of russet. Flesh, firm, rather dry, yellow, of good flavour. Growth, moderate; fertile. Leaf, rather dark, nearly flat, little undulated, oval, finely shallow serrate. Origin, an old sort still grown in the Eastern counties.

Shepherd's Pippin : *see Alfriston.*

Shepherd's Seedling : *see Alfriston.*

Shropshire Pippin : *see King of the Pippins.*

SIGNE TILLISCH. Culinary, October to December, fairly large, 2¾ by 3¼, round conical, ribbed and angular on sides. Colour, pale milky-yellow with faint brown-red flush, very greasy. Flesh, white, moderately firm, a little sweet. Eye, closed, in a deep and much ribbed basin. Stem, short in a narrow and deep cavity, free from russet. Growth, upright, spreading, moderately vigorous. Leaf, rather large, upfolded, twisted, sharply serrate. Origin unknown.

SIR JOHN THORNYCROFT. Dessert, October to December, medium, 2¾ by 2¼, round flattened. Colour, rich yellow with pinkish red flush. Flesh, crisp and juicy, yellowish; flavour, pleasantly aromatic Eye, closed, in a rather deep, slightly ribbed basin. Stem, moderately long in a wide shallow russet cavity. Growth, upright and free; fertile. Leaf, oval, dark, nearly flat, very finely crenate. Origin, raised by Mr. Collister, gardener to Sir John Thornycroft, at Bembridge, Isle of Wight, and introduced by Messrs. G. Bunyard & Co., in 1913. An attractive fruit.

Small Ribston: *see Margil.*

SMALL'S ADMIRABLE. *Her. Pom.,* 73. Culinary, till February, round, rather flattened, medium, 2¼ by 2¼, Colour, pale yellow, greasy, dotted with large russet dots. Flesh, firm, crisp, juicy, not very acid, nearly white. Eye, small, fast closed, in a very shallow basin which has a few beads at base. Stem, short, in a rather wide cavity. Growth, dwarf and compact; very fertile. Leaf, large, long, little upfolded, twisted, doubly crenate. Origin, raised about 1850, by Mr. Small, a nurseryman, of Colnbrook, near Slough. I think it doubtful if Hogg describes the right variety as it keeps much later than he states.

SMART'S PRINCE ARTHUR. *Gard. Chron.,* 1899. p. 123. Culinary, till March, large, 2¾ by 3¼, remarkably conical, and contracted at the top of the fruit, irregular. Colour, yellow, almost covered with red flush and wide stripes. Flesh, firm, dry, very yellow, rather flavourless. Eye, open in a deep much ribbed basin. Stem, stout, rather long, in a narrow, deep cavity. Growth, vigorous, weeping; fertile. Leaf, pea green, flat, undulating, long oval, curved serrate. Origin, raised by Mr. Smart, near Sittingbourne. A heavy good keeping sort; it stands rough usage well.

Snow: *see Fameuse.*

SOPS IN WINE. *Fl. and Pom.*, 1882, 105. (Sapson, Sapsovine.) Culinary, October to December, medium, 2¾ by 2, round, slightly flattened. Colour, greenish-yellow almost covered with dark crimson flush. Flesh, tender, white, much stained with red; flavourless. Eye, a little open in an even shallow basin. Stem, medium in a very deep cavity. Growth, vigorous; fertile. There are many red fleshed apples to which this name has been applied. This I believe to be the Old English apple so called. It is of no particular merit.

South Lincoln Pippin : *see Allington Pippin.*

Speckled Golden Reinette : *see Barcelona Pearmain.*

Speckled Pearmain : *see Barcelona Pearmain.*

Spencer's Favourite : *see Queen Caroline.*

Spice : *see D'Arcy Spice.*

Spice Apple : *see Caraway Russet.*

Spring Ribston : *see D'Arcy Spice.*

Spy : *see Northern Spy.*

Stadway Pippin : *see Bess Pool.*

Stagg's Nonpareil : *see Early Nonpareil.*

STAR OF DEVON. Dessert, till February, small to medium, 2¼ by 1¾, round conical, regular. Colour, golden-yellow, almost covered with red flush and bright carmine stripes. Flesh, soft, nearly white, of poor flavour. Eye, closed, in a shallow slightly ribbed basin. Stem, often very long, in a narrow, deep russet cavity. Growth, moderate; fertility, moderate. Leaf, upfolded. Origin, raised by J. Garland, Esq., Broad Clyst, Devon, and introduced to notice in 1905, by Mr. George Pyne, Topsham. Up to the present no particular merit has been discovered.

Stettin Pippin : *see Dutch Mignonne.*

STIRLING CASTLE. *Her. Pom.* 5. G., Schloss Stirling. Culinary, September to October, fairly large, 3½ by 2½, round flattened, regular. Colour, pale green. Flesh, soft, white, acid. Eye, open, in a remarkably wide and deep basin. Stem, slender in a deep cavity which has russet veins. Growth, compact but spreading; extremely fertile. Leaf, long, pale, nearly flat, shallow serrate. Origin, raised at Stirling, Scotland, about 1830, and introduced by Messrs. Drummond, of that town. A valuable fruit, remarkable for its fertility, a little liable to canker.

Stone Blenheim: *see Hambledon Deux Ans.*

STONE'S. *Her. Pom.*, 20. (Loddington, Killick's Apple.) Culinary, till January, large, 3 by 2¾, oblong conical, slightly irregular. Colour, pale yellowish-green with brown-red flush and broad broken stripes. Flesh, crisp, white, very juicy, acid. Eye, large, closed in a very deep ribbed basin. Stem, rather thin, in a very deep cavity. Growth, vigorous; very fertile. Leaf, very large, dark, nearly flat, very boldly serrate. Origin, raised at Loddington, near Maidstone, by Mr. Stone. A useful fruit, but rather apt to canker and now little planted.

STRIPED BEEFING. *Her. Pom.* 35. F., Beaufin Strié; G., Gestreifter Beaufin. Culinary, till May, fairly large, 3½ by 3, round, conical, irregular. Colour, pale green almost covered with wide red stripes. Flesh, firm, greenish-yellow, sub-acid. Eye, nearly closed, in a deep irregular basin. Stem, short, in a medium cavity. Growth, vigorous; fertile. Leaf, large, roundish, dark, slightly upcupped, very boldly curved serrate. Origin, probably English. Found in Norfolk and introduced to general cultivation about 1850. A useful old sort.

Striped Quarrenden: *see Gladstone.*

Striped Quarrenden: *see Red Joaneting.*

Stubb's Seedling: *see Winter Quarrenden.*

STURMER PIPPIN. *Her. Pom.*, 25. F., Pépin de Sturmer; G., Sturmer Pepping. Dessert, till May, medium, 2¼ by 2, round conical, regular. Colour, greenish-yellow with dull brown flush with slight russet. Flesh, crisp, juicy, greenish, brisk and pleasantly flavoured. Eye, closed, in a fairly deep ribbed basin. Stem, rather long, in an even russet cavity. Growth, slender; fertile. Leaf, rich green, little upfolded, very coarsely serrate. Origin, raised by Mr. Dillistone, a nurseryman, at Sturmer, near Haverill, Suffolk; and introduced about 1843. An indispensable fruit for late use. It should be left on the tree as late as possible. It does well on either light or heavy soils.

SUGAR LOAF PIPPIN. F., Pain de Sucre; G., Zuckerhut Apfel. (Dolgoi Squoznoi (original name) Dymond's Sugar Loaf, Hutching's Seedling.) Culinary, August, medium, 2¼ by 2⅜, tall, oblong, nearly regular. Colour, pale whitish-yellow. Flesh, soft, very juicy, greenish white, sweet. Eye, closed, in a deep, wide and slightly ribbed basin. Stem, rather short, in an even non russet cavity. Growth, spreading; fertile. Origin, probably Russian. Known in England since the early part of last century. Of no particular value, but very refreshing and sweet.

SUMMER GOLDEN PIPPIN. *Lind. Pom. Brit.*, 50. F., Pepin d'Or d'Eté; G., Sommergold Pepping. Dessert, mid to end August, small, 2 by 2, round, flattened each end, slightly conical. Colour, lemon-yellow with slight orange flush. Flesh, yellow, crisp juicy, pleasantly flavoured. Eye, open, in a very, shallow, slightly ribbed basin. Stem, medium in a shallow sloping russet cavity. Growth, moderate, upright spreading; fertility, moderate. Leaf, medium, oval, curved serrate, held flat, Origin, probably English, known before 1800. A delicious early fruit, worthy of extended cultivation; quite distinct from Yellow Ingestrie.

Summer Golden Pippin: *see Yellow Ingestrie.*

SURPRISE. Culinary, October to November, medium, 2¼ by 2¾, round conical, tapering much to eye. Colour, pale creamy-yellow with slight brown-red flush; skin smooth a little greasy. Flesh, soft, juicy, slightly yellow, a little sweet. Eye, open, almost on level with surface, basin a little wrinkled. Stem, moderately long and stout, in a rather deep and wide cavity which is faintly russet lined. Origin, undiscovered. This is not the Surprise of Downing.

Sussex Ducks Bill: *see Winter Queening.*

SYKE HOUSE RUSSET. *Ronalds*, P. 38. F., Reinette de Syke House; G., Englischer Spitals Reinette. (Culver Russet.) Dessert, till February, small, 2¾ by 2¼, round flattened, regular. Colour, yellow covered with russet. Flesh, firm, yellow, rich. Eye, open, in a very shallow basin. Stem, medium, in a rather shallow cavity. Growth, moderate; fertile. Leaf, rather small, oval, rather coarsely crenate or serrate, upcupped, held up. Origin, English. Named after a village in Yorkshire, and dating from 1780. Possibly introduced by Messrs. Perfect, of Pontefract, who sent it to Lee, of Hammersmith. A nice little fruit.

Taliesin: *see Norfolk Beefing.*

TAMPLIN. Dessert, November, large, round tapering to eye, slightly uneven. Skin, smooth, greasy. Colour, deep crimson red all over with dark broken stripes. Flesh, yellowish, very poor flavour. Eye, closed, in a very shallow basin, which has beads at base. Stem, short in a small round cavity. Origin, undiscovered.

The Claimant: *see Queen.*

The Shah: *see Miller's Seedling.*

THOMAS RIVERS. (River's Codlin.) Culinary, September to December, medium, 2¾ by 2¼, round conical, irregular. Colour, pale yellow with slight brownish flush. Flesh, crisp, yellowish, acid, cooks extremely well. Eye, open in a very small shallow basin. Stem, slender, fairly long, in a moderately deep cavity, which is free from russet. Growth, vigorous; very fertile. Origin, raised by Messrs. Rivers, and introduced in 1894. This apple is most valuable for its cooking qualities, having a distinct pear flavour with an almost quince like acidity.

THORLE. *Ronalds*, P. 2. F., Thorle d'Eté; G., Wirtel Apfel. [Paradise (error), Watson's New Nonsuch, Whorle, Lady Derby.] Dessert, August to September, small, 2¼ by 2¼, flat, regular. Colour, yellow with crimson stripes all over. Flesh, crisp, juicy, yellow; flavour brisk. Eye, open in a very shallow russet basin. Stem, short, in a wide cavity. Growth, moderate; fertility, moderate. Leaf, small, round oval, irregularly serrate. Origin, Scotch. A very old variety.

TIBBETT'S PEARMAIN. Culinary, till March, large, 3¼ by 2¾, round, conical, tapering markedly to eye. Colour, pale green to yellow with a very slight flush and a few very broad stripes round entire fruit. Flesh, greenish-white, tender, little sweet. Eye, very small closed in a very small ribbed basin, almost on surface. Stem, rather short, not protruding from a very deep narrow cavity which is faintly russet. Growth, vigorous, upright; fertility, regular. Leaf, large, bright green, upcupped, very undulated, crenate. Origin, this is found in many old orchards but I have not been able to find any account of its history. This is quite a useful apple and cooks very well, but the colour is rather brown. It requires little sugar.

Tom Potter : *see Tom Putt*.

TOM PUTT. *Her. Pom.* P. 6. (Tom Potter.) Culinary, September to November, medium, 3 by 2¼, round conical, much ribbed around eye. Colour, covered with red flush, broad blotches and stripes.

Flesh, crisp, acid, greenish white, cooking excellently. Eye, closed, in a medium much ribbed basin. Stem, short and stout, in a medium russet cavity. Growth, robust; fertility fair. Leaf, broad, round, upfolded, sharply crenate or serrate, very large. Origin, raised by the Rev. Tom Putt, Rector of Trent, Somerset, at the end of the eighteenth century. A great favourite in the Western counties. The fruit described by Hogg is not, I think, the true variety.

TOWAR OF GLAMIS. *Her. Pom.*, 10. F., Tour de Glammis; G., Schloss Glammis. (Carse o'Gowrie, Dunster Codlin, Gowrie.) Culinary, till April, large, 3¼ by 3, round conical (variable), irregular. Colour, dull green with brown-red flush. Flesh, crisp, white, acid. Eye, closed in a rather deep basin. Stem, fairly long, in a deep narrow cavity. Growth, vigorous, spreading; very fertile. Leaf, large, long oval, boldly serrate. Origin, probably Scotch. Known before 1800. A valuable apple, can be recognised by its unusual heaviness.

Transparent : *see Astrachan White.*

TRANSPARENT DE CRONCELS. Culinary or dessert, October to December, large, 3¼ by 3, round oblong, flattened considerably at each end. Colour, very pale milky-yellow with an occasional slight brown-red flush; no stripes. The dots show up as large and red when flushed. Flesh, pale yellow, crisp, tender, juicy, with a distinct flavour. Eye, open in a deep, wide, much ribbed basin. Stem, short in a moderately deep and very even cavity. Growth, strong, a little spreading; fertility, moderate. Leaf, large, round, dark, flat, edges undulated, very coarsely serrate. Origin, raised in 1869, by M. Ernest Baltet, and introduced by his firm. One of the few apples in France which was quite uninjured by the great frost of 1879.

Transparent de St. Leger : *see White Transparent.*

Travers Pippin : *see Ribston Pippin.*

TWENTY OUNCE. *New York*, V. 2., p. 228. F., Dix-huit onces. G., Zwanzig Unzen. (Cayuga Red Streak.) Exhibition, till January, large, 3 by 3, round, slightly conical, nearly regular, with a curious hammered appearance. Colour, pale yellow with slight flush and broad broken stripes. Flesh, loose, pale yellow, sub-acid, fairly juicy. Eye, a little open or closed, in a shallow ribbed basin. Stem, rather short and slender, in a deep narrow russeted cavity. Growth, moderately vigorous, makes a nice spreading tree; moderately fertile. Leaf, rather large, little upfolded, undulating, curved serrate. Origin, raised in America, early in the nineteenth century. Of value only for exhibition and pot culture.

TYLER'S KERNEL. Culinary, till March, large, 2¼ by 3, markedly conical, slightly angular, very variable in shape and size. Colour, soft, pale yellow, sweetish. Eye, a little open, in a very deep basin. Stem, generally extremely short, in a medium russet cavity. Growth, robust; fertility, moderate. Leaf, large, roundish, very dark, flat, boldly and sharply serrate. Origin, a Mr. Tyler, of Hereford, introduced this fruit to notice in 1884. A useful late fruit rather subject to canker.

UPTON PYNE. Exhibition, till March, large, conical. Colour, golden-yellow, striped with pale pink. Flesh, firm, white, juicy, of brisk pine flavour. Eye, closed, in a shallow, much wrinkled basin. Stem, short and stout, in a moderate, russet free cavity. Growth, strong, rather upright; fertile. Leaf, long, pale, upfolded, held up, nearly serrate. Origin, raised by Mr. Pyne, of Topsham, and introduced in 1910. Of very distinct flavour and likely to become popular.

VENUS PIPPIN. *Gard. Chron.*, 1899, p. 261. (Plumderity.) Dessert or culinary, September to October, medium, 2¾ by 2¾, roundish oblong, fairly regular. Colour, pale yellow-green. Flesh, tender, pale yellow, juicy and refreshing flavour. Eye, closed, in a medium basin. Stem, long and thin in a shallow cavity, which is faintly russet. Growth, vigorous, rather upright; fertile. Leaf, rather large, greyish-green, nearly flat, curved serrate. Origin, said to have been raised about 1800. Rather too soft for market use and hardly worth retention.

WADHURST PIPPIN. *Pom. Belge*, 1856, 49. F., Reinette de Wadhurst. Dessert or culinary, till March, medium to large, 2½ by 2¼, fairly regular, oblong-conical. Colour, creamy-yellow with carmine flush and faint irregular stripes. Eye, closed, in a deep basin. Stem, medium stout, in a fairly deep cavity. Growth, moderate; fairly fertile. Origin, presumably raised at Wadhurst in Sussex, before 1850. Of no particular merit.

WAGENER. *New York*, I., 354. G., Wageners Preis Apfel. (Waggoner (error).) Dessert or culinary, till April, medium, 2¾ by 2, flat roundish, irregular. Colour, golden-yellow, with bright pinkish carmine flush and faint stripes. Flesh, firm, juicy, yellow, pleasantly flavoured. Eye, closed, in a deep rather broad ribbed basin. Stem, rather long, slender, in a deep irregular, slightly russet cavity. Growth, compact; fertile. Leaf, long, pale, upfolded and twisted, regularly curved serrate. Origin, raised in a garden of Abraham Wagener, about 1796, at Dover, New York State. One of the best late varieties, keeps well without shrivelling.

Waggoner : *see Wagener.*

Walmer Court : *see Northern Greening.*

Walsgrove Blenheim : *see Bess Pool.*

Walsgrove Wonder : *see Yorkshire Beauty.*

WALTHAM ABBEY. *Her. Pom.* 17. F., Semis de l'Abbaye de Waltham; G., Saemling der Abtei Waltham. (Bardfield Defiance, Dr. Harvey,

Embersons.)   Culinary, September to December, fairly
large, 3¼ by 2¾, round conical, irregular. Colour, pale
yellow, with faint red flush. Flesh, tender, yellow,
sweet. Eye, closed or nearly so, in a rather deep,
irregular basin, which is much ribbed. Stem, long
and slender, in a narrow and deep cavity, always rayed
with scaly russet. Growth, moderate ; fertility good
when old. Leaf, small, oval, finely serrate. Origin,
raised at Waltham Abbey, by Mr. J. Barnard, about
1810, from seed of Holland Pippin. This is an excellent
cooking fruit and can always be distinguished by its
plump, roundish, very light brown seeds.

WANSTALL PIPPIN.   Dessert, till June, medium,
2 by 2¼, round, tapering a little to eye. Skin, rough.
Colour, yellow partly covered with dark brown-red
flush and darker stripes and few patches and veinings
of russet. Flesh, yellow, firm, very richly flavoured.
Eye, closed, in a rather wide ribbed basin.   Stem,
fairly long in a fairly deep and russet cavity. Leaf,
rather small, deep green, upfolded and undulated,
sharply curved serrate. Origin, said by Hogg to have
been raised by a tailor, named Wanstall, in Sittingbourne, in the early nineteenth century. A very useful
late dessert fruit which deserves to be better known.

WARNER'S   KING.   *Her. Pom.* 23.   (D. T.
Fish, King, Killick's Apple, Salopian, Weavering.)
Culinary, till February, very large, 4 by 3, flat conical,
irregular. Colour, pale green to pale yellow. Flesh,
tender, white, acid, Eye, closed in a very broad
and deep basin. Stem, fairly long, in a very deep,
slightly russet cavity. Growth, vigorous ; fertility,
moderate. Leaf, large, very long oval, very dark,
very undulating, nearly flat, sharply serrate. Origin,
generally considered Kentish, but very uncertain.
Dating from the early nineteenth century. This
apple is rather liable to canker.

Warwickshire Pippin : *see Wyken Pippin.*

130

WASHINGTON. Culinary, October to December, large, 3 by 2¼, oval oblong, flattened at top. Colour, pale yellow, only slightly greasy, dark red flush and bold broken stripes. Flesh, tender, fairly juicy, sub-acid, no flavour. Eye, closed, in a broad, deep basin. Stem, rather short in a narrow, deep cavity. Growth, makes a wide spreading tree. Leaf, large, long, very dark, much upfolded, undulated, shallow serrate. Origin, raised in Washington County, U.S.A., on the farm of Job Whipple, and first exhibited in 1849. Introduced from America, in 1812. This is known in America as Washington Strawberry, there being other varieties called Washington. It has hardly the dessert quality attributed to it by Dr. Hogg and now figures rarely except as an exhibition fruit.

Watson's New Nonsuch : *see Thorle.*

WEALTHY. Dessert, October to November, fairly large, 3 by 2¼, round, a little flattened each end. Colour, pale golden-yellow almost covered with brilliant crimson flush and broad stripes which extend right into the cavity. Flesh, white, often slightly stained with red, loose grained, juicy, very sweet, with a pleasant strawberry flavour. Eye, very small, closed, in a deep and rather narrow, slightly ribbed basin. Stem, very slender, rather long, in a remarkably narrow and deep cavity. Growth, rather slender, vigorous, little spreading ; fertility, excellent. Leaf, rather dark, flat undulating, shallow serrate or almost crenate. Origin, raised in Minnesota by a Mr. Peter Gideon, about 1860. This apple is almost worth growing for its appearance alone, and to those who like a tender fleshed variety it will be acceptable ; it is rather too soft for market use.

Weavering : *see Warner's King.*

Wellington : *see Dummelous Seedling.*

WERDER GOLDEN REINETTE. *Lauche,* 2, 95. G., Werdersche Wachs Reinette. Dessert, till March, medium, 2¼ by 2¼, round, very regular, flat. Colour, golden-yellow, striped with crimson. Flesh, firm, yellowish, sweet and well flavoured. Eye, open, sepals reflexed, in a flat, shallow basin. Stem, very short and stout, in a wide fairly deep cavity. Growth, vigorous; fertile. Leaf, moderately large, little upfolded, held up, crenate. Origin, raised at Werder, near Potsdam, Germany. It is probably not the fruit figured in the *Fl. and Pom.*, 1882, 73. A nice little fruit resembling a small Blenheim Orange.

WHEELER'S RUSSET. *Her. Pom.*, 33. F., Reinette Grise de Wheeler. Dessert, till April, medium, 2¼ by 2¼, round conical, irregular. Colour, yellow with reddish-brown flush, covered with russet. Flesh, firm, greenish, sweet. Eye, closed in a shallow plaited basin. Stem, medium, in a rather deep cavity. Growth, moderate; fertility, moderate. Origin, uncertain. Known in 1717. English. Of no particular merit.

White Calville : *see Calville Blanche d'Hiver.*

White Codlin : *see Dutch Codlin.*

WHITE JOANETING. *Ronalds*, P. 1. (Early May, Jenetting, Primiting.) Dessert, mid-July, small, 2 by 1¾, round slightly flattened, regular. Colour, straw-yellow with occasional faint red flush. Flesh, crisp, white, flavour fresh. Eye, a little open or closed, in a shallow, even basin. Stem, long and slender, in a shallow cavity. Growth, moderate, upright; fertility, fair. Leaf, small, irregularly serrate or crenate, little upfolded. Origin, English; before 1600. The earliest apple of all.

WHITE MELROSE. Culinary, October to December, fairly large, 3 by 3, roundish, conical, ribbed. Colour, palest yellow with an occasional reddish flush. Flesh, pale yellow, juicy, slightly acid. Eye, closed, in a deep ribbed basin. Stem, short in a deep russet cavity. Growth, vigorous, upright; very fertile.

Origin, according to Hogg, this is an old Scotch apple, probably introduced by the monks of Melrose Abbey. This is highly thought of in the North and Midlands, but with me is of no special excellence compared with the number of good fruits ripening at the same period.

WHITE NONPAREIL. *Her. Pom.* 21. F., Nonpareille Blanche; G., Weisser Nonpareil. Dessert, till February, small, 2¼ by 1½, flat, regular. Colour, pale greenish-yellow with slight brown flush, covered with russet. Flesh, tender, nearly white, aromatic. Eye, closed, in a fairly deep, plaited basin. Stem, slender, in a wide cavity. Growth, moderate; fertile. Leaf, oval, pointed, dark, upfolded, tip down-curved, very boldly serrate. Origin, probably English. A fruit of good flavour. The quite round cells distinguish it from the Old Nonpareil.

White Paradise: *see under Paradise White.*

White Pippin: *see Norfolk Stone Pippin.*

White Pippin: *see Yellow Ingestrie.*

White Stone Pippin: *see Norfolk Stone Pippin.*

WHITE TRANSPARENT. F., Transparente jaune. (Grand Sultan, Transparent de St. Leger, Yellow Transparent.) Culinary or dessert, early August, fairly large, 3 by 2½, round, conical, irregular. Colour, palest milky-yellow. Flesh, greenish-white, crisp, acid. Eye, closed, in a moderately deep, plaited basin with distinct knobs. Stem, medium, rather thin, in a narrow, deep cavity, occasionally with light russet. Growth, vigorous; fertile. Leaf, very large, greyish-green, lax, upfolded, undulated, finely serrate or crenate. Origin, Russian. Introduced early in the nineteenth century. A delicious summer fruit, brisk and digestible.

Whorle: *see Thorle.*

WILLIAM'S FAVOURITE. Dessert, August, medium, 2¼ by 2¼, round to oblong, conical, irregular. Colour, pale greenish-yellow, nearly covered with very dark crimson flush and broad stripes. Flesh, soft, greenish, aromatic. Eye, closed, segments reflexed at tips, in a moderate basin, at the base of which are a few round bead-like knobs. Stem, fairly long, much knobbed each end, in a shallow cavity. Growth, moderate, rather straggling, spurring well; fertile. Leaf, rather large, round, pale, down-hanging, undulating, serrate. Origin, at Roxbury, U.S.A., about 1750. Probably introduced to England, about 1828. One of the best early dessert apples and well worthy of culture.

WILLIAM CRUMP. *Gard. Chron.*, 1909, p. 21. Dessert, December to February, medium, 2¼ by 1¾, round conical, regular. Colour, greenish-yellow, almost covered with dark brown-red and light russet. Flesh, rather firm, greenish-yellow, of good flavour. Eye, closed in a round even basin. Stem, short in a deep and rather narrow cavity. Growth, moderate, upright. Leaf, rather large, dark, horizontal upfolded, little twisted, boldly serrate. Origin, raised by Mr. W. Crump from Cox's Orange and Worcester Pearmain, and introduced by Messrs. Rowe, of Worcester. A good addition to the late dessert sorts. So far it is not very fertile with me at Allington, but it crops well with its raiser.

Wilson's Codlin : *see Nelson Codlin.*

Winter Beefing : *see Norfolk Beefing.*

Winter Bellefleur : *see Brabant Bellefleur.*

WINTER BANANA. *Year Book Dept. Agr., U.S.A.,* 1913, 112. Dessert, till March, very large, 3 by 2¼, round, rather flattened, tapering to eye. Colour, pale golden-yellow with slight red flush. Skin, very smooth. Flesh, pale yellow, a little coarse grained, juicy, aromatic. Eye, slightly open, in a broad, slightly ribbed basin.

Stem, rather slender, fairly long, in a wide deep cavity, which is sometimes rather russet. Growth, vigorous. Leaf, narrow, flat, pale, crenate. Originated about 1876, with Mr. David Florey, near Adams Boro, Indiana. Introduced in 1890. The very fine specimens of this fruit sent from the States have led us to test this variety but at present the quality and fertility which it will attain in this country are somewhat doubtful.

Winter Greening : *see French Crab*.

Winter King : *see King of Tomkins County*.

WINTER MAJETIN. Culinary, till April, medium, 2¾ by 2⅜, round, tapering a little to eye, uneven. Colour, grass-green, fading to yellow with a strong brown flush. Flesh, greenish-white, crisp, sub-acid. Eye, closed, in a shallow much ribbed basin, around which five prominent ribs stand up. Stem, rather slender, fairly long, in a very deep, narrow, slightly russet cavity. Growth, upright spreading, well spurred ; fertility, excellent. Leaf, large, flat, down-curved at tip, bi-serrate. Origin, this variety is supposed to have originated in Norfolk, and has a reputation there of resisting American Blight, and is used as a stock in Australia with this object. For a free cropping late culinary variety, it deserves to be better known though it is a little small for modern standards.

WINTER PEACH. *Fl. and Pom.*, 1883, 153. F., Pêche d'Hiver. Culinary, till March, medium, 2¾ by 2, round flattened, fairly regular. Colour, palest creamy-yellow with faint scarlet blush. Flesh, crisp, yellowish, juicy, slight spicy flavour. Eye, open, in a rather deep basin. Stem, very short in a deep cavity. Growth, moderate ; fertility, moderate. Leaf, pale, little upfolded, large, very coarsely curved serrate. Origin, an American variety of uncertain origin ; known in England in 1853. This apple keeps well but it is not of particularly good flavour, and being apt to canker it is only second rate.

WINTER QUARRENDEN. (Stubb's Seedling.) Dessert, November to December, medium, 2¼ by 2¼, flat, nearly even. Colour, bright crimson. Flesh, pale greenish-yellow, crisp, poor flavour. Eye, a little open in a shallow round basin, slightly wrinkled. Stem, rather slender in a wide and deep cinnamon russeted cavity. Growth, moderate, upright spreading ; not very fertile. Leaf, long, narrow, upfolded, undulating, shallow crenate. Origin, introduced by Messrs. Pearson, of Nottingham. It has now been consigned to Limbo.

Winter Queen : *see Lemon Pippin.*

WINTER QUEENING. *Her. Pom.*, p. 14. Dessert or culinary, till March, medium, 2¼ by 3, conical. Colour, yellow, nearly covered with dull red stripes and flush. Flesh, firm, yellow, sub-acid. Eye, open, in a shallow, much wrinkled and lined basin. Stem, moderate length, in a rather narrow wrinkled cavity. Growth, vigorous ; fertile. Leaf, rather small, greyish, upfolded, twisted, shallow serrate or crenate. Origin, an old Sussex variety, probably of great antiquity. I fancy the Sussex Duck's Bill, usually quoted as synonymous with this variety is really distinct.

Winter Red Calville : *see Calville Rouge d'Hiver.*

Wise Apple : *see Court Pendu Plat.*

WITHINGTON FILLBASKET. Culinary, October to November, very large, 3¾ by 3, round, flattened on sides. Colour, pale yellow ; skin a little rough. Flesh, pale yellow, firm, rather dry. Eye, closed, in a deep angular ribbed basin. Stem, very short, in a very wide, deep russet cavity. Growth, vigorous, spreading ; fertile. Leaf, very large, upfolded, very sharply serrate. A large rather coarse fruit, hardly required in these days.

Wood's Huntingdon : *see Court of Wick.*

WOODSTOCK PIPPIN. Dessert or culinary, till April, large, fairly large, 3 by 2¼, round, flattened, fairly regular. Colour, pale yellowish-green with rarely a faint flush. Flesh, crisp, yellow, juicy, rather acid. Eye, open, in a shallow, wide basin, slightly plaited. Stem, short and thick in a moderately deep regular, russeted cavity. Growth, strong, rather spreading; fertility, poor. Leaf, large, round, sharply pointed, curved serrate, held down, flat. Origin, uncertain. Generally considered by pomologists as identical with Blenheim Orange, but is distinct from that in many respects.

Woodstock Pippin (error): *see Blenheim Orange.*

Woollaton Pippin: *see Court Pendu Plat.*

WORCESTER PEARMAIN. *Her. Pom.*, P. 2. Dessert, September to October, medium, 2¼ by 2¼, round conical, regular. Colour, bright crimson on golden-yellow ground. Flesh, crisp, greenish, very sweet, with a pleasant strawberry flavour. Eye, closed, in a shallow ribbed basin. Stem, short, in a rather narrow russeted cavity. Growth, moderate; very regularly fertile. Leaf, rather pale, oval, upfolded, undulating, coarsely serrate. Originated at Swan Pool, near Worcester, by a Mr. Hale, Introduced by Messrs. Smith, of Worcester, in 1874. An esteemed market variety, seldom failing to crop. The flavour of this fruit is greatly underrated by many, as it is usually gathered and eaten far before it is ripe. Makes a neat, round-headed standard.

Worling's Favourite: *see Beauty of Kent.*

WORMSLEY PIPPIN. *Ronalds*, P. 3. (Knight's Codlin.) Culinary, September to October, fairly large, 3¼ by 2¼, flat conical, regular. Colour, yellow with orange flush. Flesh, crisp, yellowish, sub-acid, Eye, open, in a rather deep ribbed basin. Stem, short, in a deep russet cavity. Growth, vigorous; fertility, fair. Leaf, large, oval, bi-serrate. Origin, raised by Mr. T. A. Knight, and introduced in 1811. Seldom grown now.

WYKEN PIPPIN. *Ronalds*, P. 41. F., Pepin de Warwickshire. (Warwickshire Pippin, German Nonpareil.) Dessert, till February, small, 3 by 2, flattened-round, regular. Colour, greenish-yellow, Flesh, tender, yellow, aromatic. Eye, open, in a wide, shallow basin. Stem, very stout in a very narrow cavity, which is often rather warted. Growth, moderate, very upright when young; fertility, good. Leaf, very small, grey-green, upcupped, undulating, curved serrate. Origin, introduced into England from Holland, about 1720. It is not now recognised as any Continental variety.

Wyker Pippin : *see Golden Reinette.*

YELLOW INGESTRIE. *Her. Pom.* P. 2. F., Ingestrie jaune; G., Gelber Peppin von Ingestrie. (Early Pippin, Summer Golden Pippin (error), White Pippin.) Dessert, end-August to September, small, 2 by 1¾, square-rounded, regular. Colour, golden-yellow. Flesh, firm, yellow, sweet. Eye, almost closed, in a shallow wide basin. Stem, slender, in a shallow, even cavity. Growth, slender; fertile. Leaf, rather small, roundish, oval, broadly serrate. Origin, raised by Mr. T. A. Knight (Orange Pippin × Golden Pippin), about 1800. Summer Golden Pippin is distinct *q.v.*

Yellow Transparent : *see White Transparent.*

YORKSHIRE BEAUTY. *Her. Pom.*, P. 20. (Councillor, Cumberland Favourite, Red Hawthornden, Walsgrove Wonder, Greenups Pippin.) Culinary, September to December, large, 3¼ by 3, round conical, irregular. Colour, pale yellow with scarlet flush and russet. Flesh, tender, yellow, sub-acid. Eye, closed in a deep ribbed basin. Stem, short, in a broad cavity. Growth, moderate; fertile. Origin, raised near Keswick, at the end of the eighteenth century, by a shoemaker, named Greenup. Introduced by Messrs. Clarke & Atkinson, of Keswick.

Yorkshire Cockpit : *see Cockpit.*

Yorkshire Goose Sauce : *see Yorkshire Greening.*

YORKSHIRE GREENING. *Ronalds*, P. 11. (Coates, Yorkshire Goose Sauce.) Culinary, till March, large, 4 by 3, flattened, round, sides angular. Colour, pea green to yellow with strong dark red stripes, and slight flush. Flesh, greenish, firm, acid. Eye, closed, in a deepish, wrinkled basin. Stem, moderate length, in a wide open cavity, generally free from russet. Growth, very dwarf and resembling Lane's Prince Albert ; fertility, good. Leaf, pale green, shining, upcupped, regularly crenate. Origin, unknown. Recorded by Forsyth, in 1803.

Yorkshire Queen : *see Hambledon deux Ans.*

Young's Long Keeper : *see French Crab.*

DESCRIPTIONS OF PEARS.

THE terms used for describing Apples will apply in a great measure to Pears. The only new term is that applied to the stem, which, when it gradually swells to the fruit at its point of insertion is called continued. An example of this is Beurre Superfin.

The autumnal colour of the leaves is noted in many cases, as this will be found to be of great value in determining the names of some varieties.

KEY TO CLASSIFICATION OF PEARS.

IN attempting to classify Pears, great difficulty has always been found in that they are not so constant in form and colour as Apples. I have therefore made my main divisions here those of seasons, Summer—July, August, September; Autumn—October, November; and Winter—December and onwards. It will be evident that there will be some which do not exactly fit in this grouping, but they are fortunately few, and it is a little surprising how many Pears do fall in three such groups. In any case where a variety is at the end of any of these periods it will be well to look also at the following group. The grouping otherwise follows that of the Apples, each fruit being placed as nearly as possible in the middle of its season. There are sub-divisions; such as fruits having a bright red flush, as Clapp's Favourite, fruits which are a smooth green, as Glou Morceau; and those which are entirely covered with russet, such as Calebasse Bosc. These are denoted by certain signs, which will enable them to be picked out at once, without going through the whole series of names. Thus a Summer Pear of large size with a red flush of Calebasse form will be either Marguerite Marillat or Souvenir de Congrès, taking, of course, those described in the following pages.

143

SUMMER PEARS.

July to September.

* Red cheek.
† Smooth green.

	FLAT AND ROUND.	BERGAMOTE.	CONICAL.	PYRIFORM.	OVAL.	CALABASH.

JULY		Oléron des Carmes.† Doyenné d'Été.*				
AUG.	Summer Rose.	Chalk.†	Beacon.* Lammas.* Petite Marguerite.* English Caillot Rosa.†*	St. Swithin. Beurré Giffard.* Windsor.*	Gregoire Bourdillon.	Jargonelle.
SEPT.	Sanguinole. Aspasie Aucourt.		BEURRE MORTILLER.*	Mme. Treyve.† MONCHALLARD.*	BROOKWORTH PARK.* MARGUERITE MARILLAT* SOUVENIR DE CONGRÈS*	
OCT.	Colmar d'Été. Rousselet de Rheims.* Summer Beurré d'Arenberg. Michaelmas Nelis.		Foudant de Cuerne. André Desportes.* Triomphe de Vienne.	Clapp's Favourite.* Beurré d'Amanlis.† Dr. Jules Guyot.* Duchess d'Orleans.* William's Bon Chrétien.		

AUTUMN PEARS.
October and November.

	FLAT TO ROUND.	BERGAMOTTE.	CONICAL.	PYRIFORM.	OVAL.	CALABASH.
		DOYENNE BLANC.† DOYENNE BUSSOCK.* Fondante d'Automne.† FONDANTE DE THIRRIOTT.*	Beurré Caplaumont.*† Jersey Gratioli	King Edward.		CALABASSE BOSC.‡
OCT.	Oignon. Swan's Egg. Aston Town. Achan. La France. Seckle.* Byewood Bergamotte.	BRITISH QUEEN. Hessle. Comte de Lamy. Achan. Alexambre Lambre.‡ Althorpe Crasanne. Dansa Hovey.	Baronne de Mello.‡ BEURRE HARDY.* Beuré Superfin. Fertility.‡ Bergamotte d'Heimberg Beuré Jean Van Geert.*	Marie Louise d'Uccle. Louise Bonne of Jersey.* Directeur Hardy.* BEURRE BALTET PERE.† BEURRE FOUQUERAY.† CHARLES ERNEST.* Magnate. Marechal de la Cour. Napoleon. PITMASTON DUCHESS. Princess.* Thompson's. VAN MONS LEON LE CLERC.	Urbaniste. Sucrée de Montlucon. BELLE GUERANDAISE. Beurré Brown.‡ President d'Osmonville. Belle Julie.‡ Emile d'Heyst. FLEMISH BEAUTY.† Marie Louise.* BOOKWELL.*	Le Brun.† BISHOP'S THUMB.* CONFERENCE.* DURONDEAU.*
NOV.	Bergamotte d'Automne	Gansell's Seckle.	BEURRE DIEL. DUCHESS D'ANGOULEME.	DOYENNE DU COMICE. Winter Windsor.* Soldat Laboreux.	Nouveau Poiteau. Gansell's Bergamotte.	

WINTER PEARS.
December and Onwards.

	FLAT TO ROUND.	BERGAMOTTE.	CONICAL.	PYRIFORM.	OVAL.	CALEBASH.
					Gansell's Bergamotte.	Beurré Clairgeau.*‡
DEC.	Blicking; *Bacon's Incomparable.*	Beurré Sterckmans.*	Beurré Bachelier.‡ Beurré Dumont.‡ *Huyshe's Princess of Wales*	Soldat Laboureur. Beurré Six.† Chaumontel. Nouvelle Fulvie.		
		Winter Nelis, Zephirin Gregoire.	Beurré Alex. Lucas,† Beurré d'Arenberg.	Santa Claus. General Todtleben.†	Beurré d'Anjou.†	St. Germain.† Vicar of Winkfield.†
			Forelle.*	La Lectier.† Triomphe de Jodoigne.		
JAN.	Mme. Lye Baltet.			Glou Morceau.† Huyshe's Victoria. Huyshe's Prince Consort.		
	Girogle.*	Broompark. Monarch. *Josephine de Malines.†*		Double de Guerre.‡ Doyenné d'Alençon. Ramillies.	Admiral Gervais.	
FEB.	Duchess de Bordeaux.‡ *Née Plus Meurie.* Olivier de Serres.	*Marie Benoist.* Bergamotte d'Esperen. President Barabe.		Beurré Rance.†	Rousse Lench. Beurré Dubuisson.	
	Passe Crassane.			President Drouard. Doyenné Georges Bouchés Leon le Clerc de Laval.	Beurré de Jonghe. Easter Beurré. Bergamotte d'Hiver.*	
				Belle des Arbres.†‡		Uvedale's St. Germain.†

PEARS.

ACHAN. (Black Achan, Red Achan.) Dessert, October to November (till December in Scotland), small, round conical, even. Skin, fairly smooth with a little russet. Colour, pale yellow-green with brown red flush. Flesh, pale yellow, juicy and sweet. Eye, open, nearly on surface. Stem, ¾ inch, moderately stout. Growth, vigorous; fertility, regular. Origin, probably Scotch; there are places of this name in Sutherlandshire. An old variety, seldom seen south of the Tweed, but valued in its own country.

ADMIRAL GERVAIS. Dessert, till February, medium, 2¾ by 2¾, round oval, uneven. Skin, a little rough. Colour, dark green with russet dots and patches fading to slight yellow. Flesh, pale yellow, with salmon tinge, very juicy, melting and deliciously flavoured. Stem, rather short and stout, in a narrow cavity. Fertility, good. A very fine late pear.

Albertine: *see Doyenné Bussoch.*

Alexandre Helie: *see Belle Julie.*

ALEXANDRE LAMBRE. *Bivort* I., 31. Dessert, October to November, medium, 2¼ by 3, short conical, even. Skin, smooth with russet patches around stem and large dots. Colour, pale yellow-green with cinnamon russet. Flesh, white, melting, not gritty. Eye, large, a little open in a shallow rounded basin. Stem, generally long and woody. Growth, moderate, makes a good standard; fertility, excellent. Leaf, rather

145

small, held nearly flat, finely serrate, turns dull brownish-red. Origin, raised by Van Mons, and fruited by Bivort, in 1844. This is a very valuable fruit and is in appearance as a larger and earlier Josephine de Malines.

ALTHORP CRASANNE. *Her. Pom.* I., 4. Dessert, October to November, medium, round, tapering to stem, even. Skin, rough. Colour, greenish, yellow covered with fine russet. Flesh, white, melting, juicy and pleasantly flavoured. Eye, rather large, open, in a shallow basin. Stem, moderate, curved, rather slender, continued. Growth, vigorous; fertility, regular. Origin, raised by T. A. Knight, and first fruited in 1830. This was considered by Knight to be one of the hardiest of his seedlings and to succeed in soils unfavourable to the majority of Pears.

ANDRE DESPORTES. Dessert, September, medium, 2½ by 3½, conical, even. Colour, pale yellow green with dull brown red flush. Skin, smooth with numerous large white dots. Flesh, white, juicy, sweet, fair flavour. Eye, small open in a shallow very even basin. Stem, medium, ½in. usually a little to one side. Growth, moderate, erect; fertility very great. Leaf, long oval, a little twisted, upfolded, entire. Origin, raised by André Leroy at Angers in 1854. A nice early fruit coming in just before Williams and of better flavour than Dr. Jules Guyot.

ASPASIE AUCOURT. Dessert, end August, medium 2½ by 2½, round, conical, even. Colour, straw yellow with russet specks and dots. Skin, slightly rough. Flesh, melting, whitish, very juicy and sweet. Eye, small, nearly closed in an even medium basin. Stem, stout, rather long at an angle. Growth, very weak; fertility moderate. Origin, raised by M. Rollet at Villefranche, Rhone, France, and introduced in 1885. A good pear, but so poor in growth as to be hardly worth retention.

ASTON TOWN. *Lind. Pom. Brit*. III., 139. Dessert, October to November, small, 2 by 2, quite round, even. Colour, yellow green with russet dots and markings. Flesh, pale yellow, melting, sweet, highly perfumed. Eye, small, a little open. Stem, long and woody. Growth, strong, makes long straggling shoots ; fertility, very good. Leaf, small oval, little upfolded, hold out, serrate at tip, entire at base. Origin, raised at Aston in Cheshire and known early in the 19th century. First described by Lindley in his " Guide to the Fruit and Kitchen Garden."

Aurore : *see Beurré Capiaumont.*

Autumn Bergamotte : *see English Bergamotte.*

BARONNE DE MELLO (G. Baronin von Mello. *His. Phillipe Goes.*) Dessert, October, small to medium, 2¾ by 3¼, oval conical, even. Colour, golden brown, russet covers the whole fruit. Flesh, greenish white, very melting and deliciously perfumed. Eye, open in a very shallow depression. Stem, medium, woody. Growth, upright spreading ; fertility good. Leaf, long oval, held out, little upfolded, shallow serrate, turning yellow red, rather pale. Origin, raised by Van Mons. It does well either on the Quince or Pear.

Bancrief : *see Chalk.*

BEACON. Dessert, mid to end August, medium, long conical, Skin, fairly smooth, occasional patches of russet. Colour, pale golden yellow with faint brick red flush. Flesh, pale yellow, crisp, juicy, with a pleasant aroma. Stem, very short, fleshy and unusually lipped. Growth, stout, compact, very upright ; fertility fair. Leaf, very long and narrow, upfolded, down hanging, regularly serrate, almost crenate. Origin, raised by Mr. Rivers from Grosse Calebasse. Is only of ordinary merit and in its season is much surpassed by Dr. Jules Guyot.

Bedminster Gratioli : *see Jersey Gratioli.*

Belle Angevine : *see Uvedales St. Germain.*

BELLE DES ARBRES. Culinary, till June, very large, 3½ by 5, irregular oval, flat sided and much bossed. Skin, smooth. Colour, grass green with slight russet. Flesh, breaking, firm, white, very juicy. Eye, closed or open in an irregular basin. Stem, very long, generally curved with always a fleshy ring at base. Growth, vigorous; fertility good. Origin, introduced by M. Houdin of Chateandun, France, about 1880. This fruit which resembles Uvedales St. Germain is a fine late cooking fruit. As it always has the accent on the " e " in French works I presume " Arbrés " is a place name and not as usually written " arbres " (trees).

Belle des Bois : *see Flemish Beauty.*

Belle de Flandres : *see Flemish Beauty.*

BELLE GUERANDAISE. Dessert, large, 3¾ by 4, round oval, even. Colour, pale yellow almost covered with brown smooth russet. Flesh, white, melting, perfumed, of excellent quality. Eye, open in a shallow depression or often on level. Stem, medium, stout, in a slight uneven cavity. Growth, upright spreading; fertility, fair. Leaf, small, pointed oval, slightly up upfolded, entire, turning very pale yellow, falling early. Origin, raised by M. Dion near Guerande (Loire), from a seed of Doyenne du Comice and introduced by M. Bruant of Poitiers in 1895. This is a large and fine fruit and if sufficiently fertile in this country it should be widely grown.

BELLE JULIE. *Fl. and Pom.* 1863, 128. (Alexandre Hélie.) Dessert, October to November, medium, 2½ by 3¼, oval, even. Colour, entirely covered with golden brown russet with a slight flush. Flesh, pale yellow green, very melting and delicious. Eye, wide open and clove like in a shallow depression. Stem, stout, medium length, often oblique. Growth, moderate, upright spreading; fertility good. Leaf, rather small, oval, regularly serrate, turns dull brown red, hangs late. Origin, raised by Van Mons and named after his granddaughter Mlle. Julie Van Mons. It first fruited in 1842.

A delicious fruit which deserves cultivation as it does not go soft at the core as do so many of its season. It can be distinguished from Baronne de Mello by its clove like eye.

Belle Magnifique : *see Beurré Diel.*

BELLISIME D'HIVER. *Her. Pom.* I., 15. G. Schönster Winterbirn. Culinary, till March, large, 3¼ by 4, oval to oval conical, even. Skin, smooth, shining. Colour, green to palish yellow with red flush and marked with conspicuous dots. Flesh, white, tender, free from grit. Eye, open, rather large in an even shallow basin. Stem, medium, slender, woody, in a slight cavity. Growth, vigorous, upright, makes a well spurred tree ; fertility very good. Leaf, narrow oval, slightly undulating, shallow crenate, turns pale yellow red. Origin, an old variety known in France since the 17th century. Undoubtedly one of the very best culinary pears ; it does not turn dark in cooking like Catillac but is superior in every other respect : it does well as a standard.

BERGAMOTTE D'AUTOMNE. *Verger* III., 41. G. Roter Bergamotte. Dessert, October to December, medium, 2¾ by 2, flattened round, even. Skin, a little rough. Colour, yellowish green dotted and striped with russet and a little red flush. Flesh, white, melting, juicy, pleasantly flavoured. Eye, small, open in a broad basin. Stem, slender in a small cavity. Growth, very vigorous ; fertility, excellent. Leaf, long oval, undulating, entire, down hanging. Origin, this is of great antiquity going back to the middle ages and quite possibly to Roman times and is probably the original Bergamotte. This is now seldom met with in England but can be easily distinguished from the English Bergamotte by its later season.

BERGAMOTTE D'ESPEREN. *Her. Pom.* II., 70. (Poire d'Esperen.) G. Esperen's Bergamotte. Dessert, till March, medium, 3 by 3, round conical tapering evenly to eye, a little uneven. Colour, dull green with dusky russet in patches, changing to pale yellow. Flesh, yellowish, tender, melting and deliciously perfumed. Eye, nearly closed in a slight, ribbed basin. Stem, short, stout, woody, almost on surface. Growth, vigorous, upright, spreading; fertility moderate. Leaf, long oval, little upfolded, down hanging, regularly shallow serrate, turns pale yellow. Origin, raised by Major Esperen at Malines about 1830. A valuable late variety, deserving a wall. It is ready for use when it turns yellow in March. It makes a largish tree.

BERGAMOTTE D'HEIMBOURG. *Verger* III., 159.

G. Heimbourg's Bergamotte. Dessert, October, small, to medium, 2½ by 3, conical, even. Skin, smooth. Colour, yellowish green with a little russet especially round eye. Flesh, white, melting, very juicy, very sweet, delightfully perfumed. Eye large, open but very irregular, almost on level. Stem, rather long and slender in a slight cavity generally on one side of fruit. Growth, medium; fertility moderate. Leaf, oval, upfolded, deeply serrate, down hanging. Origin, raised by Vans Mons and first fruited in 1847, and was dedicated by Bivort to M. Heimbourg, president of the Philharmonic Society of Brussels. This fruit is quite of first quality, but its cropping in this country leaves something to be desired.

Bergamotte de Paques : *see Easter Beurré.*

Besi de Chaumontel : *see Chaumontel.*

BEURRE ALEXANDRE LUCAS. *Rev. Hort.* 1875,

150. Exhibition and Dessert, November to January, large, 3¼ by 4, round conical, even. Colour, pale green changing to yellow, marked with distinct russet dots, taking a red flush in favourable seasons. Flesh, white, melting, very highly perfumed. Eye, small, open in a slightly irregular basin. Stem, medium, stout in a narrow russet cavity. Growth, vigorous, with long arched shoots, fertility moderate. Leaf, upfolded, long

oval, down hanging, faintly serrate, turns dark red.
Origin, found in a wood in the Department of Loire
et Cher, France. Imported to England in 1892. It
grows well on the pear or quince. A fine fruit when
well ripened. It becomes strongly scented at maturity.

Beurré D'Arenberg : *see Glou Morceau.*

BEURRE BACHELIER. *Her. Pom.* I. 24. G.
Bachelier's Butterbirne. (Chevalier.) Dessert, November
to December, medium, 3 by 3½, round conical, flattened
at stem, even. Skin, smooth. Colour, green to pale
yellow green, with small russet dots. Flesh, yellowish,
fine, melting, juicy and pleasantly flavoured with a
slight acidity. Eye, large, nearly closed in a slight
basin. Stem, short, woody, often in a deepish cavity.
Growth, medium, upright spreading; fertility good.
Leaf, small, round, flat or a little folded, finely serrate.
Origin, obtained by M. Bachelier of Capelle-Brouck in
the North of France, and first fruited in 1845. This is
a valuable fruit but suffers from being in at the same
season as Doyenne du Comice. A little subject to
scab. It should be gathered a little before it is ready
to part from the tree.

BEURRE BALTET PERE. *Arbor Belge.* 1885, 353.
G. Baltet Senior. Dessert, October to November, large,
3½ by 4, pyramidal, even. Skin, smooth. Colour, green
to greenish yellow, occasionally with a brown red flush.
Flesh, yellowish white, fine grained, melting, with a
good flavour. Eye, closed, woody in a broad even and
shallow basin. Stem, short and fleshy, generally at
an angle. Growth, strong, rather upright; fertility
fair. Leaf, rather large, nearly flat, down curved, very
faintly serrate. Origin, raised and introduced by
Messrs. Baltet Frères of Troyes, France.

BEURRE D'AMANLIS. *Her. Pom.* I., 9. G. Amanlis
Butterbirne. (Hubard, Wilhelmine, Delbart.) Dessert
early to mid September, medium, 3½ by 3, round
pryiform, fairly even. Colour, pea green changing to

yellowish green with occasional red brown flush. Skin, slightly rough with thin brown russet. Flesh, melting, yellowish white, very juicy and pleasantly sweet. Eye, open in a very slight basin. Stem, slender, woody. Growth, vigorous and very straggling. Leaf, rather large, oval pointed, sharply curved serrate, flat, down hanging, turning yellow then black. Origin, raised at Amanlis near Rennes, France, before 1800, and introduced to notice in 1826. This pear does well as a standard and in all forms. It thrives well in Scotland and is in all ways a cosmopolitan fruit.

BEURRE D'ANJOU. F. Nec Plus Meuris. G. Winter Meuris. Dessert, November to January, fairly large, 4 by 3, round oval, very even. Skin, smooth with a few feathery russet patches. Colour, pale yellow with occasional slight brown flush. Flesh, white, melting, flavour most delicious. Eye, open, laid back, almost on level. Stem, short and stout, fleshy. Growth, moderate; fertility, fair. Leaf, narrow oval, upfolded, down hanging, undulated, regularly serrate, light green turning pale yellow, occasionally red. Origin, a seedling of Van Mons; the name Beurré d'Anjou, though wrong, is now so firmly rooted in this country that it must remain.

BEURRE D'ARENBERG. *Her*. *Pom*. II., 70. G. Die Arenberg. (Orpheline d'Enghien, Colmar Deschamps.) Dessert, November to January, 4 by 3½ or larger, round conical, uneven, a little ribbed round eye and generally bossed. Skin, fairly smooth. Colour, yellow with small patches of russet all over and brown red flush. Flesh, nearly white, juicy and sweet with a characteristic aroma, sometimes a little gritty. Eye, open. Stem, ⅝ in., very stout, woody, obliquely inserted under a small protuberance. Growth, very stout, moderate; fertility variable. Leaf, large, upfolded, finely serrate. Origin, according to Van Mons this was obtained at Enghien by Abbe Deschamps in a garden of the Orphanage of this town. A good fruit doing well on quince but it does not thrive in all soils.

Beurré Bosc : *see Calebasse Bosc.*

BEURRE BROWN. *Her. Pom.* II., 36. G. Graue Herbst Butterbirne. (Beurre Gris, etc., etc.) Dessert, October, medium, 3 by 4, round oval tapering to stem even. Skin, smooth. Colour, greenish yellow with golden russet and often a red flush, variable in this respect. Flesh, greenish white, very buttery, juicy and well flavoured, often a little gritty. Eye, open in a shallow basin which is faintly ribbed. Stem, rather long, stout, fleshy, continued. Growth, very spreading, stout branches; fertility moderate. Leaf, upfolded down curved, markedly crenate. Origin, this is one of our oldest pears. It was the first variety to be called Beurre and was mentioned by Olivier de Serres in 1608 as Isambart " now called Beurre." A fine fruit but subject to scab. Its variable colour led several to split the variety into grey, red and gold varieties, but all such variations may often be observed on one tree as de la Quintinye first pointed out. It has 58 synonyms.

BEURRE CAPIAUMONT. *Her Pom.* II., 59. G. Die Capiaumont. (Aurore, Calebasse Vasse.) Culinary or dessert, Sepember to October, small to medium, 2¼ by 3¼, oval conical, even. Skin, rough. Colour, brownish red almost covered with fine russet and a red flush. Flesh, pale yellow, melting with a sweet and perfumed flavour. Eye, large, open in a very shallow basin or on surface. Stem, quite short, thick and fleshy, generally placed obliquely. Growth, moderate; fertility good. Leaf, large, long oval, upfolded, sharply but shallow serrate, down hanging, Origin, raised by M. Capiaumont a chemist at Mons, Belgium, from a seed of Beurre Gris, and first fruited in 1787. An excellent fruit in some seasons, and always specially good when cooked. On dry soils it often attains a wonderful colour and justifies its synonym " Aurore." It must be carefully watched or it will decay internally if left in the fruit room too late.

BEURRE CLAIRGEAU. *Her. Pom.* II., 32. G. Clairgeaus Butterbirne. Culinary, November to December, large, 3¼ by 4¼, long oval, even. Skin, rough. Colour, golden brown, often red flushed. Flesh, firm, not melting, white, faint musky flavour. Eye, large. open in a narrow shallow basin which is often a little ribbed. Stem, short, fleshy and thick, continued, Growth, vigorous, extremely upright; fertility good, Leaf, round oval, flat or a little folded, finely serrate. Origin, raised by Pierre Clairgeau, a gardener at Nantes, France, in 1848. A vigorous healthy tree, the quality of the fruit is variable but it is seldom better than second class. It makes a good erect standard.

Beurré D'Hiver : *see Chaumontel.*

BEURRE DIEL. *Her. Pom.* II., 66. G. Diel's Butterbirne. (Belle Magnifique, Beurré des Trois Tours.) Dessert, October to December, large, round oval, tapering to stem, even, always, however, showing a certain flattening at the sides. Skin, rough, covered with large russet dots and slight russet. Colour, dull yellow with a slight red brown flush in favourable seasons. Flesh, white, melting, a little gritty at core with a delicious flavour when well ripened. Eye, open, segments erect, in a small irregular basin. Stem, very stout, ¾ in., nearly always curved, in a very slight depression. Growth, very vigorous; fertility, great. Leaf, large, round pointed, irregularly serrate, sometimes finely, sometimes very coarsely. Origin, found by Meuris, Van Mons' gardener, about 1800, at the Chateau of Perck near Vilvorde, which once belonged to the painter, David Teniers. It was named after Diel, the great German pomologist. A pear which is still very largely grown despite many detractors. As well finished in France it is delicious, but in a cold season it is only fit for stewing.

Beurré Drapiez : *see Urbaniste.*

BEURRE DUBUISSON. *Arbor Belge.* 1872. 271. G. Dubuisson's Butterbirne. Dessert, December to

March, fairly large, 2¼ by 3½, long oval, even. Skin, fairly smooth. Colour, pale yellow, almost covered with fine golden russet and occasional flush. Flesh nearly white, very melting, not gritty, deliciously sweet and perfumed. Eye, closed in a shallow uneven basin. Stem, medium, stout and woody, generally inserted at an angle. Growth, very dwarf on quince, moderate on pear; fertility good. Leaf, upfolded, down curved, finely serrate. Origin, raised by M. Isidore Dubuisson, a nurseryman, at Jolain, near Tournai, Belgium, about 1829. First fruited in 1834. It is valuable for keeping several months in condition, the hard skin also keeps it from damage.

BEURRE DUMONT. *Pom. Belg.* 1857. Dessert, November to December, large, 3 by 3, round conical tapering to stem where it is abruptly flattened, even or a very little angular. Colour, cinnamon brown, the russet being smooth and fine. Flesh, white, very fine grained, very melting, deliciously sweet and perfumed flavour. Eye, open in a deep even basin. Stem, very short and stout in a deepish cavity. Growth, very spreading, rather dwarfish on quince; fertility moderate Leaf, medium, narrow oval, nearly flat, almost entire, turning faint red. Origin, a seedling found by M. Joseph Dumont, gardener to the Baron de Joigny, à Esquelines, near Pecq. First fruited in 1833. This most delicious fruit keeps a few weeks longer than Doyenné du Comice and is thus of great value.

Beurré d'Esperen : *see Emile d'Heyst.*

BEURRE FOUQUERAY. *Rev. Hort.* 1885, 444. Dessert, October to November, very large, 3¾ by 4¼, oblong oval, a little uneven. Skin, smooth. Colour, green with russet dots and occasional patches and often slight flush. Flesh, white, fine grained, very juicy and agreeably perfumed. Eye, large, a little open in a shallow basin. Stem, very stout, rather short, generally curved in a shallow cavity. Growth, very vigorous and erect; fertility, good. Leaf, large, oval, little undulating, nearly entire. Origin, obtained by M. Fouqueray-Gautron, a nurseryman at Sangey, France. It first fruited in 1880. This is not often met with in this country, but it is very good when well grown.

Beurré Gellert : *see Beurré Hardy.*

BEURRE GIFFARD. *Her. Pom.* I., 26. G. Giffard's Butterbirne. Dessert, August, medium, pyriform tapering much to stem, a little even. Colour, pale yellow with brownish red flush, skin smooth. Flesh, white, melting, very juicy, fair sweet flavour. Eye, open on level. Stem, rather long and slender in a flat cavity surrounded with russet. Growth, rather weak, very straggling; fertility good. Leaf, small pointed, oval, upfolded, down hanging, margin entire or only faintly serrate. Origin, found wild by M. Nicolas Giffard, near Angers, France, in 1825. An excellent early fruit, keeping better than most of its season. It is extremely hardy and is successfully cultivated up to 1,200 metres in Switzerland. It succeeds as a standard.

Beurré Gris : *see Beurré Brown.*

Beurré d'Hardenpont : *see Glou Morceau.*

BEURRE HARDY. *Her. Pom.* I., 13. G. Gellert's Butterbirne. (Hardy, Beurré Gellert.) Dessert, mid to end October, large round conical, uneven. Skin, rough. Colour, russet bronze with faint red cheek. Flesh, white, faint pink tinge, very tender, transparent with a rose water flavour. Eye, open or nearly closed in a shallow even basin. Stem, stout, fairly long, in a very shallow cavity. Growth, very vigorous; fertility excellent. Leaf, large, round, much down curved, upfolded, nearly entire, turns orange red. Origin, raised by M. Bonnet, a friend of Van Mons at Boulogne, about 1820. Named after M. Hardy, the director of the Luxembourg gardens. Introduced about 1840. Quite one of the best and hardiest pears, in season just before Marie Louise. It should be gathered a little before it parts readily from the tree to have it in the best condition. Does well on quince or pear.

BEURRE DE JONGHE. *Le Verger*, I., 43. G. Jonghes Butterbirne. Dessert, December to January, medium, 2¾ by 2¼, oval tapering most to stem, a little uneven. Skin, a little rough. Colour, pale green fading to pale yellow. covered with patches of dull brown russet. Flesh, yellowish, melting, transparent, with pleasant flavour rather like Marie Louise. Eye, open in a shallow slightly ribbed basin. Stem, short, woody, continued, often inserted under a fleshy lip. Growth upright, a little spreading and rather weak ; fertility good. Leaf, medium, oval, nearly flat, held out, nearly entire. Origin, raised by M. Gambier, of Rhode St. Genêse, near Brussels, before 1865, and dedicated to M. de Jonghe, the Belgian pomologist. It makes a moderate tree on the quince. Dr. Hogg considered this pear as "equal if not superior to Marie Louise," but though good I hardly rate it so high.

BEURRE JEAN VAN GEERT. *Ill. Hort.* 1864, 416. G. Van Geert's Butterbirn. Dessert and market, October to November, medium, 2½ by 3½, round conical tapering slightly to stem, even. Skin, smooth. Colour, golden yellow with brilliant scarlet flush. Flesh, white, half melting, sweet with a brisk flavour, extremely juicy. Eye, a little open in a rather deep basin. Stem, rather short, woody, generally oblique. Growth, dwarf, and compact, fertility remarkable. Leaf, long oval nearly flat, regularly shallow, crenate, turns brilliant crimson and hangs late in this state. Origin, raised by M. Jean Van Geert, of Ghent, Belgium, and introduced in 1864. This is considered to be of the first quality by Leroy, but it is hardly that in my experience. A most attractive fruit for selling, but connoisseurs would probably sell.

Beurré de Merode : *see Doyenne Bussoch.*

BEURRE MORTILLET. *Bull. d'Arb.* 1891, 289. Dessert, end of August, early September, large 3¼ by 3, oval conical. Colour, creamy yellow with brick red flush and faint broad stripes. Skin, smooth. Flesh, firm, pale yellow, juicy and sweet but not of a remarkable flavour. Eye, small, closed, in a shallow boldly ribbed basin. Stem, very short and thick, obliquely inserted. Growth, very upright. Leaf, long oval, rather large, pea green, markedly upfolded, regularly shallow crenate, turning pale yellow. Fertility remarkably good. Origin raised by M. Fougere at St. Priest (Isère) France from a seed of Bon Chretien, and named after the famous French pomologist of Grenoble before 1875. This is beginning to be noted by market growers and it is certainly one of the best cropping varieties we have.

Beurré Perrault : *see Duchesse de Bordeaux.*

BEURRE RANCE. *Her. Pom.* II., 68. (Hardenpont de Printemps, Bon Chretien de Rance, Beurré de Rance.) Culinary or dessert, December to March, large, 3 by 4, oval pyriform, ending squarely at stem, uneven. Skin, a little rough. Colour, dark green fading to yellowish green, covered with many dots of russet and patches. Flesh, greenish white. Eye, medium, a little open in a rather wide and deep basin. Stem, very long and stout in a shallow cavity. Growth, dwarf, makes a small stubby tree inclined to weep ; fertility good. Leaf, flat, held up, entire, turns black. Origin, raised by the Abbe Hardenpont of Mons, Belgium, about 1762. In its young vigour the fruit has a slightly rancid taste, but advancing years have corrected this fault. The origin of the name from a village named Rans is incorrect. For full details see Du Mortiers " Pomone Tournaisienne." With good cultivation and a warm wall this variety is quite first class. It is rather apt to blow off in an exposed position.

BEURRE SIX. *Decaisne* III. G. Six Butterbirne. Dessert, November to December, large, 3 by 3¾, pyriform tapering markedly to stem and eye, surface ribbed and bossed, distinctly five sided, resembling a pear-shaped quince. Skin, smooth with small dark dots. Colour, grass green hardly turning yellow at all. Flesh, very tender, melting pale yellow, not gritty, sweet and deliciously flavoured. Eye, open, segments upright and separate in a very shallow ribbed basin or often on surface of fruit. Stem, long, continued, fleshy at base. Growth, vigorous; fertility, good. Leaf, small, round oval, very faintly serrate or entire. Origin, raised by M. Six, a nurseryman, at Courtrai, and first described by Bivort in 1845. A very good fruit which deserves to be better known. It crops regularly with me and is of very good quality.

Beurré Spence : *see Flemish Beauty.*

BEURRE STERCKMANS. *Her. Pom.* II., 62. G. Sterckmans' Butterbirne. Dessert, November to January, medium, flattened conical. Skin, rough. Colour, pale green to yellow with a red flush. Flesh, yellowish white, nearly transparent when ripe, very juicy, sweet and highly perfumed. Eye, closed or nearly so. Stem, rather long, woody, generally obliquely inserted in a small ribbed cavity. Growth, upright, rather spreading, fertility good. Leaf, long oval, nearly flat, faintly serrate. Origin, raised by M. Sterckmans at Louvain, and introduced to notice by Van Mons.

BEURRE SUPERFIN. *Her. Pom.* II., 22. Dessert, October, medium, round conical, tapering to stem, a little uneven on surface. Skin, a little rough. Colour, yellow with many patches of fine russet. Flesh, pale yellow, very melting, sweet and deliciously perfumed. Eye, small, closed, or a little open, in a deep round basin. Stem, short, very stout and fleshy, always with some fleshy wrinkles at base. Growth, moderate; fertility, moderate to good. Leaf, oval, pale green, held nearly flat, a little twisted, irregularly crenate. Origin, raised by M. Goubalt at Mille Pieds, near Angers, France. First fruited in 1844. One of the best half-dozen pears, by some preferred to Doyenne du Comice. Does well on quince. Should be gathered before it parts readily and carefully watched in the fruit room. Requires to be eaten when the skin seems fairly firm as it begins to ripen at the core.

Beurré des Trois Tours : *see Beurré Diel*.

BISHOP'S THUMB. *Her. Pom*. II., 42. F. Pousse de l'Evêque. Dessert, October to November, variable 2¾ by 5, long calebasse form, even. Skin, a little rough. Colour, pale yellow with bright scarlet flush. Flesh, palest yellow, fine grained, a little melting, slightly perfumed, very juicy. Eye, wide open almost on level. Stem, long and woody, continued, generally at angle the flesh growing higher up |the stem one side. Growth, vigorous, makes a good standard ; fertility good. Leaf, elliptical, nearly flat, finely serrate. Origin, this has been known in England for many years and is generally considered to be a native. First described by Diel in 1804. An old variety often found in orchards but of no special merit. The curious growth of flesh up one side of the stem is, I suppose, the origin of its name.

Black Achan : *see Achan*.

Black Worcester.

BLACK WORCESTER. *Her. Pom*. II., 60. F. de Livre G. Konigsgeschenk von Neaple. Culinary, till April, large, 3½ by 4. Shape round Bergamotte, uneven. Skin, rough, entirely covered with dark coppery brown russet. Flesh, pale yellow, crisp, flavourless and rather gritty. Stem, 1 inch, very stout and woody. Growth moderate. Fertility moderate. Eye nearly closed in a deepish uneven basin. · This has been known in Worcester since the 16th century, where according to legend Queen Elizabeth saw it at Whystone Farm. It is, I think, almost certainly the Poire de Livre of Leroy, which has been known in France for several centuries, and which may even go back to Roman days. A good cooking pear, but not equal to Catillac, Double de Guerre and Bellissime d'Hiver.

BLICKLING. Dessert, December to January, smallish 2¼ by 2, round, tapering most to stem, even. Skin, smooth. Colour, pale greenish yellow with russet round eye and prominent dots. Flesh, white, coarse grained, extremely sweet and juicy, a little gritty. Eye, closed in a round shallow even basin. Stem, medium, woody, curved in a small narrow cavity. Growth, moderate; fertility good. Origin, this is said to have been introduced from Belgium by a monastic order. A delicious fruit, rather like a later Comte de Lamy. It deserves a wall and careful thinning when a good crop is set.

Bonne de Malines : *see Winter Nelis.*

Bonne Rouge : *see Gansels Bergamotte.*

BRITISH QUEEN. *Fl. and Pom.* 1863. 80. F. Reine d'Angleterre. G. Britische Königin. Dessert, October, rather large, 4 by 3, round conical, even. Skin, covered very smooth russet. Colour, pale brownish yellow with occasional slight flush. Flesh, pale yellow, very fine texture, flavour sweet and brisk. Eye, very small, closed in an even rather deep basin. Stem, 1 inch, stout, in a narrow cavity. Growth, vigorous; fertility moderate. Leaf, medium, eliptical, down hanging. Origin, raised by M. Ingram of the Royal Gardens, Windsor, and naturally considered by the Prince Consort to be the best of all pears. This old variety is occasionally met with.

Brocas Bergamotte : *see Gansel's Bergamotte.*

BROCKWORTH PARK. *Her. Pom.* II., 66. F. Bonne d'Ezée. G. Gute von Ezée. Dessert, early September, rather large, 3¼ by 2¼, long oval, flattened at stem, even. Skin, rather thick, a little rough, covered with russet dots. Colour, greenish yellow with very faint flush and stripes. Flesh, yellowish white. Eye, in a very shallow basin. Stem, very stout, fleshy, 1 inch, obliquely inserted. Growth, upright spreading, making a large tree. Leaf, medium, oval, regularly serrate. Origin, discovered at Ezée near Loches, France, in 1838, by M. Jamain, of Paris. A pear of quite good quality and rather undeservedly in the background. The British name is correctly a synonym.

BROOMPARK. *Her. Pom.* II., 51. Dessert January medium, 2¼ by 2¼, Bergamotte shape, flattened, uneven. Skin, rough. Colour, orange yellow, almost covered with very fine golden russet. Flesh, pale yellow, slightly transparent, half melting, extremely sweet with vinous flavour. Eye, closed in a moderately deep basin. Stem, rather long, woody, in a slight cavity. Growth, rather staggling, moderate; fertility, good. Leaf, large, oval little upfolded, entire or irregularly serrate. Origin, raised by Thos. Andrew Knight, first fruited in 1830, and named after Broompark, near Canterbury. This is now seldom grown as it is rather small for modern tastes, but on a good soil it is excellent.

Caillot Rose : *see Summer Rose.*

CALEBASSE BOSC. *Verger* III., 138. Dessert, September to October, large, 2¾ by 4¼, very long calebasse form, uneven. Skin, smooth, with fine russet. Colour, rich golden brown entirely covered with russet. Flesh, yellowish, very tender, juicy, perfumed. Eye, wide open like a clove. Stem, slender, rather long, woody. Growth poor and straggling, not spurring well ; fertility good. Leaf, rather large, round oval, almost entire, little upfolded, turns dull crimson red. Origin, a seedling found by Van Mons in the garden of M. Swates, at Linkebeeke. An excellent fruit doing well as a standard, but has the great fault of being too liable to scab. This pear is often wrongly called Beurré Bosc.

Calebasse Vasse : *see Beurré Capiaumont.*

CATILLAC. *Her. Pom.* I., 15. (Pound pear.) G. Katzenkopf. Culinary, till April, 3½ by 3¼. Shape, Bergamotte, nearly even. Skin smooth, colour dull green, brown red flush. Stem, stout, moderately long in a slight cavity. Eye open in a slight ribbed basin. Growth, stout and vigorous; fertility, good. Leaf large round, downy, regularly serrate, turns clear yellow, no red. Generally supposed to have been found near Cadillac in the Gironde. It was first described under this name by Bonnefond in the " Jardinier François," 1665. One of the very best of all stewing pears, cooking a deep red. Makes a fine large spreading standard.

CHALK. (Crawford, Bancrief.) Dessert, early August, small, 2 by 1⅛, round conical, even. Skin, nearly smooth, a little fine russet. Colour, very pale green with the faintest red flush. Flesh, nearly white, mealy, sweet and juicy, flavour nil. Eye open in a shallow basin. Stem, ½ inch, stout, fleshy. Growth, stout, weeping; fertility remarkable. Leaf, broad, dark green, very downy below. Origin, probably Scotch. It is similar to Citron des Carmes but not identical. A fruit much grown in Kent for London markets, and greatly appreciated at Hampstead Heath on August Bank Holiday.

CHARLES ERNEST. *Rev. Hort.* 1879, 410. Dessert, October to November, very large, oval pyriform, flat at eye, a little uneven. Skin, smooth. Colour, pale golden yellow generally wih a scarlet flush. Flesh, white, tender, juicy, with a delicate aroma. Eye, nearly closed. Stem, long and rather slender. Growth, remarkably upright, makes a large tree; fertility, excellent. Leaf, large, round. flat, shallow serrate, little down hanging, turns chocolate brown. Origin raised by Mm. Baltet Frères of Troyes, France, and introduced in 1879. It does well on quince or pear.

CHAUMONTEL. *Her. Pom.* II., 38. (Bési de Chaumontel, Beurré d'Hiver.) Dessert, November December, large, 3¼ by 4, oblong pyriform, uneven. Skin, very rough. Colour, greenish yellow nearly covered with curious purplish russet and red flush. Flesh, white, fine, melting, little gritty, very sweet and

163

vinous flavour. Eye, open in a deep broad, uneven basin. Stem, stout, rather long, generally inserted straight. Growth, long and straggling ; fertility good. Leaf, rather large, held flat, undulating, much twisted, coarsely serrate, turns black. Origin, raised at Chaumontel, France, about 1660. Du Hamel saw the original tree in 1775, and it is said to have died in the cold winter of 1789. It makes a rather large straggling tree, not very much dwarfed by quince. This fruit is good when thoroughly well ripened and grown. It is rather subject to scab and does best on a wall.

Chevalier : *see Beurré Bachelier.*

Choix de l'Amateur : *see Nouveau Poiteau.*

Citron : *see Doyenne Blanc.*

CITRON DES CARMES. *Her. Pom.* II., 44. (Madeleine.) Dessert, end July, small, 2 by 1¾, round conical, even. Skin, smooth, thin. Colour, pea green with occasional slight brown red flush. Flesh, tender, greenish white, a little sweet, no flavour. Eye, wide open on level. Stem, stout, 1¼ inches, obliquely inserted level. Growth, rather small ; fertility good. Leaf, oval pointed, flat, down held, coarsely serrate. This is often met with in old orchards where it makes a good standard. Rather similar to, but quite distinct from, the Chalk or Crawford Pear of Kent. It should be eaten before the green colour changes.

CLAPP'S FAVOURITE. *Verger* II., 102. Dessert, early September, medium, 3¼ by 2¼, pyriform, tapering to eye, fairly even. Skin, thin, smooth. Colour, pale milky yellow with a bright scarlet flush and stripes. Flesh, pale yellow, melting, very juicy with slight aroma. Eye, open in a shallow basin. Stem, stout, 1 inch long, slightly lipped. Growth, vigorous, upright ; fertility, excellent. Leaf, moderate, oval, long, held out, finely and regularly serrate, turns muddy brown yellow.

Origin, raised by Thaddeus Clapp, of Dorchester, Mass., U.S.A. A pear of fair quality, esteemed for market growth, but rather too gritty and glassy in texture.

Colmar Deschamps : *see Beurré d'Arenberg.*

COLMAR D'ETE. *Her. Pom.* II., 44. G. Sommer Colmar. Dessert, early September, small to medium, 2¼ by 2¼, short conical, very even. Skin, smooth, becoming a little greasy when ripe, covered with conspicuous dots. Colour, pale greenish yellow with occasional brown red flush. Flesh, yellowish white, very melting, juicy and with a strong musky flavour. Eye, open in a shallow basin. Stem, ⅜ inch, slender in a shallow cavity. Growth, rather dwarf; fertility excellent. Leaf, large, upfolded, down hanging and down curved, very faintly serrate, turns a fine " sang de boeuf " red. Origin, raised by Van Mons at Louvain about 1825, and brought to notice principally by Louis Vilmorin of Paris. It makes a good standard or pyramid. Dr. Hogg's advice to eat it before it becomes yellow is quite sound in a warm year, but in a cold summer it turns yellow on the tree while still unripe.

Coloma : *see Urbaniste.*

COMTE DE LAMY. *Her. Pom.* II., 70. F. Beurre Curtet, G. Curtet's Butterbirne. Dessert, October to November, small, short conical or peg top, a little uneven, generally lop-sided. Skin, smooth. Colour, pale green changing to yellow and often a little russet with many small russet dots. Flesh, white, very melting, most delicious, quite first class. Eye, open in a wide shallow basin often russeted. Stem, ½ inch, woody, usually inserted by a small bump on the surface. Growth, moderate, low spreading tree; fertility good. Leaf, flat, edges undulated, irregularly serrate or entire, turns orange yellow. Origin, raised by M. Bouvier, of Joidoigne, in 1828, and dedicated to Curtet, professor at Brussels. The correct name is Beurre Curtet. A most delicious fruit which deserves wider culture and which forms a worthy predecessor to Doyenne du Comice.

CONFERENCE. Dessert, October to November, medium, long calebasse form, even. Skin, a little rough. Colour, dark green fading to pale yellow with much russet spotting. Flesh, pale yellow, slight pinkish tinge, melting, very juicy, and sweet. Eye, open, segments upright, in a shallow basin. Stem, long, woody, little curved. Growth, moderate, not making a large tree when on quince ; fertility very good. Leaf, rather large, round oval, very irregularly serrate, down hanging, little twisted, turns orange yellow and slight red, hanging late. Origin, raised by Messrs. Rivers, and introduced in 1894. This pear is now grown in enormous quantities for market purposes, and is one of the most regular cropping varieties we have, and though not quite first class is indispensable.

Conseilleur de la Cour : *see Maréchal de la Cour*.

Crawford : *see Chalk*.

DANAS' HOVEY. *Her. Pom.* 70. F. Hovey de Danas. Dessert, October to November, small to medium, $2\frac{1}{4}$ by $2\frac{1}{4}$, round conical, even. Skin, a little rough. Colour, golden yellow almost covered with fine cinnamon russet which is thickest round eye. Flesh, white, very melting, extremely sweet and musky. Eye, medium, a little open almost on level. Stem, rather long, woody, with fleshy lip at base. Growth, very upright, makes a moderate sized tree ; fertility good. Leaf, a little upfolded, down curved, rather boldly serrate, rather large, held out, turning a deep claret. Origin, raised at Roxbury, U.S.A. by Mr. Francis Danas, and named after Mr. C. M. Hovey a well known American pomologist. Lovers of Sparkling Muscatelle will appreciate this fruit.

Delbart : *see Beurré d'Amanlis*.

Des Eparonnais : *see Duchesse d'Angoulême.*

DIRECTEUR HARDY. Dessert, September to November, medium, 3 by 4, oval pyriform, uneven. Skin, a little rough. Colour, pale yellow almost covered with fine russet and slight red flush. Flesh, yellowish white, melting, extremely juicy, finely perfumed. Eye, open, small, in a fairly deep basin. Stem, rather long, and stout in a slight cavity. Growth, very upright, moderate ; fertility, good. Leaf, long oval, undulating, upfolded, shining, pea green, neatly serrate, upheld, turns very pale yellow then black. Origin, raised by M. Tourasse and introduced by Mm. Baltet Frères of Troyes, in 1893. Makes a rather small tree either on quince or pear.

DR. JULES GUYOT. *Lauche* II., 71. Dessert, early September, rather large, 3¼ by 4¼, oval pyriform, a little uneven. Skin, a little rough. Colour, pale yellow with russet patches and slight red flush. Flesh, pale yellow, very juicy and melting, with slight musky flavour. Eye, open, almost level. Stem, short, rather stout, generally inserted obliquely. Growth, moderate, upright ; fertility, very good. Leaf, medium, round oval, upfolded and down curved, finely crenate, turns dull yellow brown. Origin, raised by M. Ernest Baltet of Troyes, in 1870. This much resembles Williams, but has less of the musky flavour. It is grown in large quantities for market but is only second class in flavour. It should be gathered in good time and stored in a cool place.

DOUBLE DE GUERRE. *Trans. R.H.S.*, Series II., Vol. I., 328. Culinary, December to February, fairly large, 3 by 4¼, oval pyriform, even. Skin, rough. Colour, yellow brown, nearly covered with a dark purplish red flush. Flesh, yellow, firm, slightly acid. Eye, open nearly on surface. Stem, short, stout, generally obliquely inserted. Growth, very stout, compact ; fertility, excellent. Leaf, large, pale green, edges undulating, irregularly serrate, down hanging.

Origin, introduced to England from Mr. Stoeffels, of Mechlin, about 1835. I have not been able to find it in any foreign work. According to Thompson, the Dutch name is Doppelte Krieges. This hardy and excellent variety can be strongly recommended. It is quite one of the best cooking pears we grow.

Downham Seedling : *see Hacons Incomparable*.

Doyenné : *see Doyenné Blanc*.

DOYENNE D'ALENCON. *Her. Pom*. II. 40. G. Dechants Birne von Alençon. Dessert, December to February, 3 by 3⅓, pyriform, very even. Skin, a little rough. Colour, pale yellow with many russet dots and patches, sometimes a little flushed. Flesh, white, melting, juicy, very good flavour, with a little astringency. Eye, small, nearly closed in a wide, shallow basin. Stem, 1 in., in a small cavity, often at an angle. Growth, very slow ; fertility good. Leaf, long, oval, down hanging, upfolded, crenate, turns pale yellow-brown. Origin, generally considered to have been discovered in a hedge by M. Thuillier of Alençon, and introduced about 1839. There was, however, a pear of the same name and season cited by Le Lectier in 1628. A very valuable fruit, but a poor grower on hot soils. It makes a large spreading tree, branches well spurred.

DOYENNE BLANC. *Lind. Pom. Brit*. II., 60. G. Weisse Herbst Butterbirne. (Doyenné, St. Michel, Citron, White Doyenné, etc., etc.) Dessert, September to October, large, 3⅓ by 3¾, round, tapering a little to stem, even. Skin, smooth. Colour, pale green fading to pale yellow, with a little cinammon russet. Flesh, white, very melting, juicy, not gritty, of delicious flavour. Eye, half open, tips of sepals reflexed, in a moderately deep basin. Stem, short, very stout, in a rather deep cavity. Growth rather spreading ; fertility good. Leaf, narrow oval, lanceolate, upfolded, down curved, regularly serrate. Origin, an old variety which is possibly Italian, but has been recorded in the seventeenth century by Merlet. It is now seldom grown, but in good seasons it is quite first class.

DOYENNE BUSSOCH. *Her. Pom.*, II., 42. G. Doppelte Philipps Birne. (Doyenne de Merode, Albertine, etc.) Dessert, September to October, large, 3¼ by 3, flattened round, even. Skin, a little rough. Colour, bright yellow with russet patches and often a brilliant red cheek. Flesh, white, a little coarse, poor flavour. Eye, small, segments fleshy, upright in a round even basin. Stem, short and stout in a rather deep cavity. Growth, sturdy, makes a low spreading tree; fertility very good. Leaf, large, oval, down curved, held nearly flat, irregularly serrate. Origin, this is an old Belgian variety originally known as Double Philippe. This name was changed by Van Mons to B. Merode, in honour of Count Merode of Waterloo. The origin of Bussoch is doubtful. This pear is grown for market in some quantity, but is only third rate.

DOYENNE DU COMICE. *Her. Pom.*, I., 13. G. Vereins Dechants Birn. Dessert, November, large, 3¼ by 4, oval pyriform, nearly even. Skin, slightly rough. Colour, pale yellow, with very fine russet over most of fruit and occasional red flush. Flesh, pale yellow, extremely melting and delicate, most deliciously flavoured. Eye, closed in a deep round basin. Stem, medium, stout, little fleshy, on level. Growth moderate, upright spreading; fertility irregular. Leaf, medium, long oval, upfolded, down curved, regularly shallow serrate. Origin, raised at Angers, France, by the Hort. Soc. of Maine et Loire. First fruited in 1849. Introduced into England by Sir Thomas Dyke Acland in 1858. This delicious fruit can hardly be too highly praised and should be grown in different forms and positions so that its season may be extended. On rich brick earth I have seen it doing well as a standard.

DOYENNE D'ETE. *Her. Pom.*, I., 26. F. Doyenné de Juillet. G. Juli Dechants Birn. (Summer Doyenné,

Jolimont Precoce, Poire de Juillet.) Dessert, mid July to August, small 1⅝ by 1¼, round, conical, tapering to stem, even. Skin, thin, smooth. Colour pale yellow with brownish-red flush. Flesh, melting, very juicy, white, sweet. Eye, closed almost on surface. Stem, 1 in., thick, inserted straight on level. Growth, weak, upright spreading; fertility excellent. Leaf, pointed oval, small, flat, down hanging, very coarsely serrate. Origin, raised by the Capucin Monks at Mons about 1700. Hogg attributes this wrongly. The words " par nous " used by Van Mons are by no means always applied to his own seedlings. Beurré Diel, for example is thus noted, meaning that it was named by him. For its earliness and fertility it should be included in every garden. It does well as a standard, but is apt to die out on the Quince on light soils, and is not too vigorous on the Pear.

DOYENNE GEORGES BOUCHER. *Rev. Hort.*, 1906, 496. Dessert, till March, large, 4 by 4¼, round pyriform, a little uneven. Skin, slightly rough. Colour, palest yellow covered with grey brown russet. Flesh, nearly white, very juicy, good flavour. Eye, nearly closed in a narrow, rather deep basin. Stem, rather short, woody and stout in a slight cavity. Growth, vigorous, upright; fertility good. Leaf, long oval, much undulating, broadly serrate. Origin, raised by M. Pinguet-Guindon, and first fruited in 1894. Dedicated to M. Georges Boucher, the Parisian horticulturist. This fruit has received the highest awards in France, and is considered to be a late Comice. I have not grown it long enough to confirm this opinion. It should be noted that this fruit turns yellow some time before it is ripe.

Doyenné d'Hiver : *see Easter Beurré.*

Doyenné de Merode : *see Doyenné Bussoch.*

Duchess : *see Duchess d'Angoulême.*

DUCHESS D'ANGOULEME. *Her. Pom.*, II., 66.
G. Herzogin d'Angoulême. (Des Eparonnais, Duchess.)
Dessert, October to December, large, often enormous,
4 by 4, round conical, uneven. Skin, rough. Colour,
yellowish green marked with conspicuous russet dots
and patches. Flesh, nearly white, very melting, juicy
fine aromatic aroma, extremely sweet. Eye, open in
a deep, uneven basin. Stem, very stout and fleshy in
a slight cavity or on level. Growth, moderate, upright, spreading ; fertility great. Leaf, small, oval,
entire or very shallowly and widely crenate. Origin,
a seedling found wild near Chateau Neuf, France, about
1808. It was introduced by M. Audusson, a nurseryman
of Angers, as Poire des Eparonnais, but renamed in 1819
in honour of the Duchess d'Angoulême, daughter of
Louis XVI. This fruit is rather uncertain in quality,
but when all conditions are favourable is often of the
highest merit. It makes a small, compact and upright
tree.

DUCHESSE DE BORDEAUX. *Verger*, I., 65.
F. Beure Perrault, G. Herzögin von Bordeaux. (Beurrê
Perrault.) Dessert, January to March, medium, 2¾ by
2¼, round, sometimes tapering a little to stem, even or
slightly uneven. Skin, rough. Colour, dull yellow,
almost entirely covered with rough brown red russet.
Flesh, pale yellow, melting, buttery, extremely juicy and
richly flavoured. Eye, small, half open, in a shallow
basin. Stem, short and stout, generally on level with
fruit, often curved. Growth, slow, upright, makes a
large tree ; fertility moderate. Leaf, long, narrow oval,
down hanging, little twisted, very shallow serrate,
turns black. Origin, raised from some seedlings sold
by M. Perrault of Montjean, France, to M. Secher about
1850. This fruit was first called Beurré Perrault but
was later changed to Duchesse de Bordeaux. A very
valuable late fruit worthy of a place in every collection.

DUCHESSE D'ORLEANS. *Her. Pom.* II., 32.
F. Beurré St. Nicholas. G. Butterbirn von St. Nicholas.
Dessert, early to mid September, medium to large,

3¼ by 2¾, long pyriform, tapering to eye, uneven. Skin, fairly smooth. Colour, pale yellow green with dull red flush and a little russet streaking. Flesh, white, melting, very sweet and juicy. Eye, closed, on surface. Stem, long and thin, rather fleshy and often lipped at base. Growth, moderate; fertility moderate. Origin, a chance seedling found near Angers, France, in 1839. Decribed and generally known in England as Duchesse d'Orleans, but the French name is the correct one.

DURONDEAU. *Her. Pom.*, II., 32. G. Birne von Tongre. (De Tongre.) Dessert, October to November, fairly large, 3¼ by 4¼, long pyramidal, almost calebash, uneven, much bossed. Skin, rough. Colour, golden yellow, nearly covered with red gold russet with red cheek. Flesh, white, melting, sweet, juicy, well flavoured. Eye, open in a shallow basin generally a little ribbed. Stem, short, fleshy, continued, often obliquely inserted. Growth, moderate, compact; fertility excellent. Leaf, medium, oval, shallow crenate, remarkably upfolded, turns dark brown red. Origin, raised by M. Durondeau of Tongre, near Tournai, Belgium, in 1811. Grows well on Quince unless the soil is very dry. It makes a good standard. Largely grown for market, but if well manured and watered is of good flavour.

EASTER BEURRE. *Her. Pom.*, II., 70. F. Doyenné d'Hiver, G. Winter Deschants Birne. (Bergamotte de Paques, Poire de Pentecote, Doyenné d'Hiver.) Dessert, February to April, medium, round oval, even. Skin, rough. Colour, pea green fading to yellow green with russet dots and patches. Flesh, white, melting, with a rich sweet musky flavour. Eye, closed, fleshy segments folded over each other. Stem, very short and stout in a narrow cavity. Growth, strong, making a wide spreading tree; fertility, moderate. Leaf, very small, oval, upfolded, very faintly crenate, held out, turns yellow with faintest brown. Origin, raised by M. Vilain, a solicitor of Mons, about 1804. One of the best of late pears, often a little feeble on Quince and rather subject to scab.

Emile : *see Emile d'Heyst.*

EMILE D'HEYST. *Her. Pom.*, II., 32. G. Heysts Zuckerbirne. (Emile, Beurré d'Esperen.) Dessert, October to November, medium, 2¾ by 4½, long oval even. Skin, a little rough. Colour, pale yellow marbled with brown russet, especially around stem. Flesh, yellowish green, melting, sub-acid and pleasantly perfumed. Eye, very small, a little open in a slightly ribbed shallow basin. Stem, rather long, slender, woody, set on level. Growth, rather dwarf, becoming weeping as a standard ; fertility, very good. Leaf, long, pointed, very finely and regularly serrate, very much upfolded, turns a distinct claret red, then vermilion. Origin, raised by Major Esperen and named after M. Emile d'Heyst, of Heyst-op-den-Berg. First fruited in 1847. It does well on nearly all soils, in all forms, and in Scotland. A most reliable variety which for hardiness and regular crop cannot be bettered at its season.

English Bergamotte.

ENGLISH CAILLOT ROSAT. (King's Pear.) Dessert, August, medium, obtusely pyriform, even. Skin, a little rough. Colour, yellowish green, sprinkled with russet spots on shaded sides, dark brownish red, interspersed with some grey specks on sunny side. Flesh, yellowish white, juicy, rich, aromatic. Eye, open in a shallow basin. Stem, long, woody, in a shallow cavity. Growth, vigorous, makes a good standard ; fertility good. Leaf, medium, oval, finely and sharply serrate. I have been unable to find the origin of this fruit, and many varieties bear this name. I give above Thompson's description from the *Gardener's Assistant,* as I have not been able to secure good specimens of this fruit.

Epine d'Eté : *see Monchallard.*

Epine Rose : *see Monchallard.*

Epine Rose : *see Summer Rose.*

EYEWOOD BERGAMOTTE. *Her. Pom.*, II., 51.
G. Augenwald. Dessert, October to November, medium,
2¼ by 2¼, flattened round, even. Skin, rough. Colour,
yellowish green, largely covered with russet dots and
markings. Flesh, white, extremely juicy, sweet and
very aromatic. Eye, open, woody, and all united in
one piece, in a shallow even basin. Stem, very long and
slender in a shallow, small cavity. Growth, very
vigorous, spreading ; fertility good. Leaf, round
tapering sharply to point, very irregularly serrate, held
out, flat, turns clear yellow. Origin, raised by Thomas
Andrew Knight, and named after Eyewood, near
Kington, Hereford. It bears well as a standard, and
makes a good pyramid on Quince.

FERTILITY. *Her. Pom.*, II., 64. Market and
dessert. October, small, 2 by 3, round conical. Skin,
rough. Colour, dull yellow, almost covered with brown
russet. Flesh, yellowish, crisp, juicy, poor or no
flavour. Eye, open on surface of fruit. Stem, woody,
moderately long, rather stout. Growth, moderate,
upright spreading ; fertility great. Leaf, very variable,
round to long oval, very sharply and finely serrate,
turns fine crimson red. Origin, raised by Mr. Rivers
about 1875, from a seed of Beurre Goubalt. A poor
fruit, but grown in large quantities for market. On
Quince it attains a medium size, but with no improve-
ment in quality. Dr. Hogg finds the flavour like
Williams " much subdued." Very much ! Makes a
spire-like tree.

FLEMISH BEAUTY. *Her. Pom.*, I., 9. F. Belle
des Bois. G. Holzfarbige Butterbirne. (Belle des
Bois, Beurré Spence, Belle de Flandres, etc.) Dessert,
October to November, large, 3¼ by 3¼, oval, a little
flattened each end, a little uneven. Skin, smooth.
Colour, dull greenish yellow with dull red brown flush,
russeted around eye. Flesh, white, juicy, a little gritty,
pleasantly flavoured. Eye, open or closed in a deep,

irregular basin. Stem, medium, stout, in a slight cavity. Growth, strong, vigorous; fertility great. Origin, found by M. Chatillon, of Alost, Belgium, in a wood, and introduced to notice by Van Mons about 1818. A hardy and vigorous variety making a good standard. It must be gathered before it parts readily from the tree.

FONDANTE D'AUTOMNE. *Her. Pom.*, II., 34. F. Bergamotte Lucrative. G. Esperen's Herrenbirn. Dessert, September to October, medium, 2½ by 2¼. Shape, Bergamotte, very even. Skin, green fading to yellow, partly covered with brownish russet. Eye, open, segments upright, claw-like. Stem, short and stout on a slight cavity. Growth, rather dwarfish, a little spreading; fertility excellent. Leaf, narrow oval, undulated at edge, irregularly shallow crenate, sharply pointed, down curved, turns dull crimson red. Origin, raised by M. Fiévée at Maubeuge before 1825. One of the most reliable of Autumn pears, doing well in any form.

FONDANTE DE CUERNE. *Her. Pom.*, II., 42. Dessert, mid September, medium to large, 2¾ by 3¼, round conical, even. Skin, fairly smooth, thin. Colour, greenish yellow, thin brown russet round eye, covered with russet dots. Flesh, pale yellow, melting, sweet and pleasantly flavoured. Eye, open in a rather deep, irregular basin. Stem, long and stout, fleshy. Growth, strong, making a large, spreading tree; fertility moderate. Leaf, medium, upfolded, very regularly and finely serrate. Origin, found at Cuerne, near Courtrai, by M. Reynaert Bernard. First described by Bivort in the *Annales de Pomologie*. An excellent fruit in warm seasons. The variety described by Hogg is evidently not the true variety.

FONDANTE DE THIRRIOTT. *Bull. d'Arbor*, 1883, 5. G. Schmelzen de von Thirriott. Dessert, September to October, large, 3¼ by 3½, round conical. Skin, smooth. Colour, light yellow with brown-red flush and prominent dots. Flesh, white, fine grained, melting, sweet and of fair flavour. Eye, closed or a little open in a deep regular basin. Stem, long, slender, a little fleshy, often curved. Growth, vigorous, upright; fertility remarkable. Leaf, medium, oval, pale green, little upfolded, down curved, faintly serrate, dies off pale yellow-red. Origin, raised by M. Thirriott, a nurseryman of Ardennes, Charleville, France, in 1858. First fruited in 1862. Remarkable for its fertility and of quite good flavour in warm soils. The fruit is rather apt to fall on standard trees.

FORELLE. *Her. Pom.*, I., 9. F. Truitée. G. Forellenbirne. (Trout Pear, Corail.) Dessert, November to January, medium, shortened pyriform, even. Skin, smooth. Colour, lemon yellow with brilliant scarlet cheeks and many conspicuous large dots. Flesh, white, melting, with a delicate and sweet taste. Eye, open in a shallow basin. Stem, long, slender, in a shallow cavity. Growth, vigorous, outward spreading; fertility moderate. Leaf, flat, much down curved, margin nearly entire. Origin, known since 1670, and named for its bold spots resembling those of the trout. Best on Pear; it is too much dwarfed on Quince.

GANSELL'S BERGAMOTTE. *Her. Pom.*, II., 53. G. Rote Dechantsbirne. (Brocas Bergamotte, Bonne Rouge.) Dessert, November to December, fairly large, 2¾ by 2¼, flattened round. Skin, a little rough. Colour, pale yellowish-green with red-brown flush and russet flecks. Flesh, white, melting, remarkably sweet and richly flavoured; a little gritty. Eye, open in a shallow basin. Stem, medium, fleshy in a moderate deep cavity. Growth, weak, straggling; fertility moderate. Leaf, round oval, entire, undulating. Origin, according to Lindley this was raised by Lt.-Gen. Gansel at Donneland Hill, Colchester, from a seed of Autumn Bergamotte, about 1768. A weak grower, doing best when double grafted. It requires a wall to bring its fruits to perfection.

GANSEL-SECKLE. *Her. Pom.*, II. 70. F. Seckle de Gansel. Dessert, November, small, flattened round, even. Skin, a little rough. Colour, lemon yellow with a red flush and dark brown russet, very much like Seckle. Flesh, pale yellow, little gritty, very sweet. Eye, closed in a fairly deep basin. Stem, rather short and stout in a narrow cavity. Growth, medium ; fertility, moderate. Origin, raised by Mr. Williams, of Pitmaston, about 1820 (Seckle × Gansel's Bergamotte).

GENERAL TODLEBEN. *Her. Pom.*, I., 24. Dessert (in a warm season), November to January, very large, long pyriform, uneven. Skin, slightly rough. Colour greenish-yellow, with russet patches and faint flush. Flesh, slightly rose tinted, melting, juicy, perfumed. Eye, open, in a moderately deep basin. Stem, moderate, stout, woody. Growth, moderate, upright, a little spreading ; fertility good. Leaf, rather large, oval, upfolded, very faintly serrate or entire, turning pale orange-yellow. Origin, raised by M. Fontaine de Gheling, of Mons, in 1839, and named after the famous defender of Sebastopol. It makes a medium sized tree. The fruits hang late and in a cool season hardly mature.

GIROGILE. *Her. Pom.*, II., 60. (Gilogil, Gilles-ô-Gilles, Girogile.) Culinary, flattened round, December to February, large 3¼ by 3¼. Skin a little rough, golden yellow with some rough russet and brown-red flush. Stem, rather short in a rather narrow cavity. Eye, large, a little open, in a wide, even basin. Flesh, white, a little breaking, cooking a rich red. Growth, sturdy, making a large, spreading standard ; fertility good. Leaf round, very large, down curved, boldly, and irregularly serrate, hangs late, turning dull crimson red. Origin, of great antiquity, has been grown for four centuries. The curious name of this fruit has been the subject of much discussion, but I think the most reasonable origin is that suggested by M. Messager. He points out that many places where the monasteries of the order of St. Denis were established had the

177

termination " ogile." Thus altum-ogile became in French
Altogile, finally Auteuil; Argentogile-Argenteuil. In
the same way Girum-ogilium gave Girogile, which is the
oldest spelling of Gilogil, and which I, therefore, adopt.

Giroflé : *see Rousselet de Rheims.*

GLOU MORCEAU. *Her. Pom.,* II., 55. F. Beurré
d'Hardenpont. G. Hardenponts Winter Butterbirne.
(Beurré d'Hardenpont, Beurré d'Arenberg.) Dessert,
December to January, fairly large, oval pyriform, often
snout-like at eye, uneven. Skin, smooth. Colour, pea
green till it approaches ripeness, when it changes slowly
to a pale greenish yellow. Flesh, very smooth, very
melting, nearly white, flavour first rate. Eye, wide
open in a wide basin, which is a little uneven. Stem,
long, fairly stout, woody, generally inserted at an angle.
Growth, moderate, rather spreading ; fertility good.
Leaf, flat and undulating, down curved, finely and
regularly crenate, turns dark brown. Origin, raised
by the Abbe Hardenpont in the eighteenth century.
It is known as Beurré d'Hardenpont, or Beurré d'Arenberg in France ; our Beurré d'Arenberg being the
Orphelin d'Enghien of Belgium. It is regrettable
that the memory of the pioneer of Pear raising, l'Abbe
Hardenpont, is not commemorated in this fruit. One
of the finest of winter pears, ripening successively and
lasting in good condition for some time. On a South
or West wall it crops regularly and ripens its fruits
splendidly. In France it is said to benefit by a shade
over the tree to protect it from spring frosts.

Gratioli of Jersey : *see Jersey Gratioli.*

GREGOIRE BOURDILLION. Dessert, August,
medium, 3 by 3¼, round oval, tapering most to stem,
even. Skin rough. Colour, pale yellow, abundantly
marbled with brown russet and occasional flush. Flesh,
pale yellow, very tender and juicy, sweet, a little
gritty at the core, very agreeably flavoured. Eye, open
is a shallow basin. Stem, extremely short and thick,

and spreading; fertility great. Leaf, rather small, upfolded, curved, regularly and finely serrate. Origin, raised by Andre Leroy from a seed of the Pear Graslin. It first fruited in 1866. A very good early pear, considered by some authorities as equal to Williams.

GROSSE CALEBASSE. *Verger* III., 30. F. Van Marum. Exhibition or dessert. October, enormous, 4½ by 7, long calebasse, uneven. Skin, rough. Colour, entirely covered with a fine dark brown russet with an occasional red flush. Flesh, greenish, white melting, of good flavour in a warm season, extremely juicy. Eye, large, open, in a regular shallow basin. Stem, moderately long, very stout and fleshy, continued. Growth, moderate, rather upright; fertility, fair. Leaf, elliptical, little up-folded, twisted, shallow, serrate. Origin, a seedling of the Van Mons and first fruited at Louvain in 1820. Named after the chemist, Van Marum. The name Grosse Calebasse is now so firmly established in this country that it is probably impossible to revert to its correct original name.

HACON'S INCOMPARABLE. *Her. Pom.*, II., 38. F. Poire d'Hacon. G. Hacon's Onvergleichliche. (Downham Seedling.) Dessert, December to January, medium, 2¾ by 2¾, flattened round, tapering a little to stem, even. Skin, nearly smooth. Colour, palest yellow with flecks and dots of russet. Flesh, palest yellow, melting and deliciously flavoured. Eye, wide open in a shallow basin or on level. Stem, slender, rather long in a marked cavity. Growth, very spreading, moderately vigorous; fertility moderate. Leaf, nearly flat, long oval, regularly shallow serrate. Origin, uncertain. One account attributes it to Mr. Hacon, of Downham Market, Norfolk, as a seedling raised in 1815. Another says it was raised in 1792 by a Mrs. Raynor of the same town.

Hardenpont de Printemps: *see Beurré Rance*.

Hardy: *see Beurré Hardy*.

HESSLE. *Her. Pom.*, I., 28. (Hasel.) Market October, small, round, conical, even. Skin, fairly smooth, covered with small russet dots. Colour, pale yellow-brown. Flesh, pale yellow, juicy, a little sweet. Eye, open in a shallow basin. Stem, ¼ in., stout, obliquely inserted. Growth, good, upright spreading ; fertility excellent. Leaf, long, oval, nearly flat, entire, Origin, found at the village of Hessle, Yorks. A hardy prolific variety, thriving in the North and making a good standard but of very poor quality. Hogg speaks of another variety of the same name, but I have never seen this.

His : *see Baronne de Mello.*

Hubard : *see Beurré d'Amanlis.*

HUYSHE'S PRINCE CONSORT. *Her. Pom.*, II., 68. Dessert, December to January, large, 3 by 4¼, long pyriform, uneven. Skin, rough. Colour, pale yellow-green, very much netted with thin russet. Flesh, yellow, melting, with a delicious aroma and flavour. Eye, small, open, in a deep wide basin. Stem, long, very stout, generally obliquely inserted. Growth. moderate ; fertility fair. Origin, raised by the Rev. J. Huyshe, of Clyst Hydon (Beurré d'Arenberg × Passe Colmar). First fruited in 1864. Quite distinct from Prince Albert, a seedling of Van Mons. This is now seldom met with, but is quite worthy of a place in collections.

HUYSHE'S PRINCESS OF WALES. *Fl. and Pom.*, 1867, 93. Dessert, December, medium, 3¼ by 2¼, oblong conical or round oval, flattened at stem, even. Colour, pale yellow covered with cinnamon russet. Flesh, yellow, melting, juicy, very rich flavour. Eye open in a slight depression or on level. Stem, very short and stout in a deep cavity. Growth, very upright, compact ; fertility moderate. Leaf, flat, down curved, very faintly serrate or entire. Origin, raised by the Rev. John Huyshe, of Clyst Hydon, Exeter, in 1830. (Gansel's Bergamotte × Marie Louise.)

HUYSHE'S VICTORIA. *Fl. and Pom.*, 1867, 237.
Dessert, December to January, medium or large,
pyriform, ribbed round eye. Skin, russet in veins and
patches. Colour, deep yellow with cinnamon russet.
Flesh, melting, little gritty, very rich and sweet flavour,
Eye, open in a very shallow basin. Stem, very short and
stout, obliquely inserted. Growth, rather dwarf,
upright, spreading; fertility good. Leaf, much upfolded, held upright, dies off scarlet-red. Origin, raised
by the Rev. John Huyshe, of Clyst Hydon, Exeter, in
1830. (Gansel's Bergamotte × Marie Louise.) A very
delicious pear, now seldom met with. It has many good
points; its only bad one being its grittiness at the core.

IDAHO. (Lindsey.) Dessert, November to December, large, 3¼ by 3, flattened round, quite apple like,
uneven. Skin, rough. Colour, light yellow, largely
marked and marbled with rough russet. Flesh, fine
grained, juicy, sweet, with a curious flavour not very
attractive. Eye closed, twisted in a deep basin. Stem,
very stout in a deep cavity. Growth, very vigorous;
fertility good. Origin, raised at Idaho, and introduced
in 1889.

Jackman's Melting : *see King Edward.*

JARGONELLE. *Her. Pom.*, I., 26. F. Epargne.
G. Sparbirne. (Synonyms are very numerous; it is
often known as English Jargonelle.) Dessert, August,
medium, very long conical, even. Skin, smooth. Colour,
greenish yellow, with a faint brownish-red flush. Flesh,
pale yellow, very tender and juicy, sweet with a touch
of musky flavour. Eye, open in a shallow basin. Stem,
long and slender. Growth, straggly, long spreading
branches; fertility excellent. Leaf, large, pale green,
little upfolded, coarsely serrate, down hanging, turns
lemon yellow with very faint red. Origin, known in
France before 1600. The French Jargonelle is quite
distinct and must not be confused with this. A very
valuable early variety, doing well as a standard, but
rather too straggling to form a nice pyramid. Does well
on a North wall, and succeeds in Scotland.

JERSEY GRATIOLI. *Her. Pom.*, II., 55. (Gratioli of Jersey, Bedminster Gratioli.) Dessert, September to October, medium, 2¼ by 2¼, round conical to short pyriform, even. Skin, very rough. Colour, pale yellow covered with greyish dots and russet patches. Flesh, very fine, melting, very sweet and perfumed, nearly first class. Eye, large, open in a rather deep even basin. Stem, very short and stout, continued. Growth, vigorous and compact; fertility extra good. Leaf, medium, oval, much upfolded, boldly serrate. Origin, this has been known in England for some hundred years and was originally from Jersey, where it was probably raised. A hardy and very fertile variety, making a good standard. It must be gathered rather early or it will rot at the centre.

JOSEPHINE DE MALINES. *Her. Pom.*, II., 70. Dessert, December to January, rather small, short conical. Skin, smooth. Colour, pale green, fading to pale yellow, with a russet patch round stem. Flesh, slightly pinkish, very melting, sweet and deliciously perfumed. Eye, open in a slight basin, upright segments. Stem, rather short and woody. Growth, moderate, rather weeping; fertility good. Leaf, small, very long petiole, very finely crenate, narrow oval, sharply pointed, held flat, down hanging, turns pale yellow. Origin, raised by Major Esperen in 1830, and named after his wife. Quite the most reliable fruit of its season, ripening successively in the fruit room. If one winter pear only can be grown this should be selected.

Jolimont Précoce : *see Doyenné d'Eté.*

King Pear : *see English Caillot Rosa.*

KING EDWARD. F. du Roi Edouard. G. König Eduard. (Jackman's Melting.) Culinary, September to October, enormous, long pyriform, uneven. Skin, a little russset in dots and at base of fruit. Colour, greenish yellow, with orange flush. Flesh, pale yellow, a little melting, sweet, juicy. Eye, a little open in a very shallow basin. Stem, very short, stout, fleshy, continued. Growth, strong upright, spreading, well spurred. fertility moderate. Leaf, roundish, held up flat, very shallow serrate. Origin, first mentioned by Thompson in *Catg. Hort. Soc.*, 1842. Origin undiscovered. An immense fruit resembling Uvedales St. Germain, but unlike that sort stewing very well.

LA FRANCE. Dessert, October to November, small, 2¾ by 2¾, roundish, very uneven. Skin, rough. Colour, greenish-yellow, much covered with grey russet and often a little bronzed on the sunny side. Flesh, white, melting, juicy and very perfumed in flavour. Eye, open in an uneven basin. Stem, short and thick in a deep irregular cavity. Growth, weak and dwarfish; fertility good. Leaf, small, oval, petiole long, little upcupped, held out, entire. Origin, raised about 1864, by M. Claude Blanchet, a nurseryman at Vienne, France. A delicious fruit, rather too weak on Quince, best double grafted.

LAMMAS. Dessert. August, small to medium, 2¼ by 2, conical, even. Skin, smooth. Colour, pea green to creamy yellow. Flesh, soft, rather mealy, whitish-yellow, strong pear flavour. Eye, open, segments erect, in a deep basin. Stem, short, stout, generally lipped. Growth, vigorous and hardy; fertility good. Origin, undiscovered. This is much grown around London for market and makes a very large tree.

LE BRUN. Dessert, October, large 3 by 4½, long calebasse, uneven. Skin, smooth. Colour, greenish, yellow, a faint russet patch here and there. Flesh, yellowish-white, fine grained, half melting, a little sweet and perfumed. Eye, half open in a regular and even basin. Stem, short and stout, generally at an angle. Growth, vigorous and upright; fertility great. Leaf, rather small, pointed oval, regularly and finely serrate, turns dull yellow with slight red. Origin, raised at

Troyes in 1856, by M. Gueniot, a nurseryman of that town. This has never been other than second rate with me.

LE LECTIER. Dessert, December to January, rather large, 3¼ by 4½, pyriform, fairly even. Skin, smooth. Colour, green to pale yellow, a little russet round stem and occasionally on sides. Flesh, white, melting, deliciously perfumed. Eye, a little open. Stem, rather long, often continued, fleshy. Growth, very upright, strong; fertility moderate. Origin, raised by M. Auguste Leseur, of Orleans, about 1882, from William's Bon Chretien × Bergamotte Fortunée, introduced by Messrs. Transons in 1888. It is named after the famous Le Lectier, who collected no less than 260 varieties of pears in 1628. A valuable fruit, doing well on all walls except the North, and also on most soils.

Leon le Clerc : *see Leon le Clerc de Laval*.

LEON LE CLERC DE LAVAL. *Her. Pom.*, II., 60. (Leon le Clerc.) Culinary, January to June, very large, 3¼ by 4, long pyriform, uneven. Skin, rough. Colour, greenish yellow with bold russet dots and patches, especially round the stem, and occasionally flushed red. Flesh, white, firm, juicy, breaking, does not turn red in cooking. Eye, large, a little open, in a wide, shallow basin. Stem, unusually long, woody, curved. Growth, stout and compact; fertility good and regular. Leaf, upfolded, down hanging. Origin, raised by Van Mons at Louvain in 1825, and dedicated to his friend and fellow pear raiser Le Clerc, of Laval.

Liart : *see Napoleon*.

Lindsey : *see Idaho*.

LOUISE BONNE OF JERSEY. *Her. Pom.*, I., 9. F. Louise Bonne d'Avranches. G. Gute Louise van Avrauches. Dessert, October, medium, 2¼ by 4½, long conical, oval, even. Skin, smooth. Colour, yellowish-green, with red flush and prominent red spots. Flesh, white, very melting, sweet and delicious. Eye, medium, open, in an even, regular russeted basin. Stem, fairly long, woody, in a slight cavity, or on level with surface. Growth, upright, spreading; fertility great. Leaf, narrow, little upfolded, very boldly crenate, turns very dark yellow-brown. Origin, raised by M. Longueval, of Avranches, France, about 1780. There is another Louise Bonne of older date than this. This is known in France as Louise Bonne d'Avranches. It makes a rather large, well-shaped tree, very highly to be recommended for its quality and regular cropping habits.

MADAME LYE BALTET. Dessert, December to January, medium, 3 by 3, round, uneven. Skin, a little rough. Colour, green or slightly yellow, marbled with greyish russet. Flesh, white, sweet, juicy, delicately perfumed. Eye, open in a wide slightly ribbed basin. Stem, long, curved, woody in an irregular cavity. Growth, moderate; fertility moderate. Leaf, medium, undulated, markedly serrate. Origin, raised by M. Ernest Baltet, of Troyes, France, and introduced in 1877. A very delicious fruit, but a little difficult to grow. A warm corner and a rich soil are necessary to perfect it.

MADAME TREYVE. *Verger*, II., 6. F. Souvenir de Madame Treyve. Dessert, August to September, large, 3 by 3½, oval pyriform, even. Skin, smooth. Colour, pea green to pale yellow with red flush and russet patches. Flesh, greenish white, very melting, sweet and refreshing. Eye, small, nearly closed in a wide uneven basin. Stem, rather long, woody, not sunk. Growth, vigorous at first, then spurring closely, rather upright; fertility good. Leaf, roundish, upfolded finely serrate. Origin, raised by M. Treyve, a nurseryman of Trevoux, France. It first fruited in 1858. A very delicious fruit, well worthy of cultivation. Its flower buds are remarkable pink.

Madeleine : *see Citron des Carmes*.

MAGNATE. Dessert, October to November, large, pyriform, even. Skin, rough. Colour, russet brown on yellow ground, with russet dots. Flesh, yellow, soft, somewhat gritty on some soils. Eye, half open nearly on level. Stem, rather long and stout. Growth, moderate, upright spreading, making a well spurred tree ; fertility moderate. Leaf, remarkably long, oval, slightly upfolded, very finely crenate, turns slight brownish red. Origin, raised by Messrs. Rivers, and introduced about 1888.

MARECHAL DE LA COUR. *Her. Pom.*, II., 42. G. Hofratsbirne. (Conseilleur de la Cour.) Dessert, October to November, large, 3 by 4½, long pyriform, distinctly waisted, even. Skin, slightly rough. Colour, palest yellow, almost covered with a light brown russet. Flesh, white, melting, a little gritty, exceedingly juicy, vinous flavour. Eye, large, open, almost on level. Stem, long and slender, generally curved. Growth, very vigorous ; fertility good. Leaf, large, even, oval, little upcupped, serrate, turns faint orange brown. Origin, raised by Van Mons in 1841. It makes a rather upright tree. The quality varies according to soil, a warm one being best. It makes a good standard.

MARGUERITE MARRILAT. *Rev. Hort.*, 1883, 348. Dessert, September, enormous, 3½ by 5 or larger, long calebasse form, uneven. Skin, a little rough. Colour, golden yellow with brilliant vermilion flush and slight russet. Flesh, pale yellow, extremely juicy. Eye, small, open in a shallow uneven basin. Stem, medium to short, very stout, inserted at an angle. Growth, remarkably upright, stout shoots ; fertility great. Leaf, large, round oval, shallow serrate, turns vermilion, falls rather early. Origin, raised by M. Marrillat, a nurseryman of Craponne, near Lyons. First exhibited in 1872. A very fine fruit of second quality in flavour, but a favourite for market use and a prodigious cropper. It does not rot at the core as do so many autumnal pears.

MARIE BENOIST. *Her. Pom.*, II., 68. Dessert, February, large, 3¼ by 4, round conical, uneven, usually lop sided. Skin, a little rough. Colour, greenish yellow marked with thick patches of dark russet. Flesh, white, melting, a little gritty, very juicy, and of fair flavour. Eye, small, open in a wide and deep basin. Stem, stout and woody, usually inserted at an angle. Growth, strong; fertility fair. Leaf, down held, nearly flat, entire or shallowly irregularly serrate, turns medium red, hangs mid. Origin, raised by M. Auguste Benoist, of Brissac, France, and dedicated to his daughter Marie. It first fruited in 1863. As usually grown this is rather a coarse fruit, but in France it is of good quality. It probably requires a wall to bring out its best qualities.

MARIE LOUISE. *Her. Pom.*, II., 55. (Marie Louise Delcourt, Princess de Parme.) Dessert, October to November, medium, 3 by 4, long oval, a little uneven. Skin, smooth. Colour, pale green to yellow, with thin patches of fine russet, especially around the eye. Flesh, very pale, juicy, a little gritty, of a distinct and refined flavour. Eye, large, open, nearly on the surface of the fruit. Stem, rather long, woody, generally a little curved, often in a slight cavity. Growth, makes a spreading, straggling tree; fertility good. Leaf, narrow oval, held open, nearly entire, turns black. Origin, raised by the Abbe Duquesne of Mons in 1809, and named after Napoleon's second wife, the Archduchess of Austria. This is now one of the best known of the pears. It does well as a standard on suitable soils. On dry soils it comes rather more russeted and keeps rather longer.

Marie Louise Delcourt : *see Marie Louise.*

MARIE LOUISE D'UCCLE. *Her. Pom.*, II., 55. G. Uccle's Marie Louise. Dessert, October, fairly large, 3¼ by 4, oval, pyriform. Skin, a little rough. Colour, golden yellow, almost covered with fawn russet dots and patches. Flesh, palest yellow, very juicy, deliciously flavoured. Eye, medium, closed in a deep and narrow basin. Stem, stout, woody, rather long, generally at an angle. Growth, rather slender; fertility very good. Leaf, rather large, down curved, upfolded, boldly serrate, turns dull yellow red to black. Origin, raised by M. Gambier, of Rhode, near St. Genese, near Brussels, from a seed of Marie Louise. A fine pear, not quite justly appreciated. It is unfortunately very subject to scab. It makes a compact tree, but with a lot of whippy shoots.

Medaille : *see Napoleon.*

MICHAELMAS. (Michaelmas Nelis.) Dessert, mid to end September, medium, 2¼ by 2½, round, slightly conical. Skin, slightly rough. Colour, yellowish green. almost covered with cinnamon dots and nettings. Flesh, melting, yellow, of excellent flavour, remarkably juicy and sweet. Eye, open in a shallow, even basin. Stem, stout, ¾ in., in a deep cavity. Growth, upright spreading, making a well spurred tree. Leaf, very down curved, held nearly flat, serrate, turning a beautiful scarlet. Origin, raised in a cottage garden near Gravesend from a seed of Winter Nelis, and introduced by Messrs. Bunyard & Co. in 1900. A most excellent fruit in best condition before it turns yellow. This was originally called Michaelmas Nelis.

Michaelmas Nelis : *see Michaelmas.*

MONARCH. *Her. Pom.,* I., 4. F. Monarque de Knight. Dessert, January to February, small to medium, round conical, even. Skin, rough. Colour, yellow-green, covered with brown russet. Flesh, yellow, melting and delicious flavour. Eye, open in a shallow basin. Stem, rather short, stout. Growth, rather spreading, making a round headed tree; fertility good. Leaf, small, roundish, dark, a little upfolded, shallow crenate, turns orange red. Origin, raised by T. A. Knight, probably from a seed of the Autumn Bergamotte in 1830, and named in honour of William IV. It can be easily recognised in winter by its very large oval buds, which stand out like those of a red currant.

MONCHALLARD. *Decaisne*, V., 17. (Epine d'Eté, Epine Rose.) Dessert, August to September, fairly large, 2¼ by 3¼, pyriform, even. Skin, smooth. Colour, bright yellow with slight flush and strewn with numerous greenish dots. Flesh, very white, juicy, melting, flavour very delicious. Eye, open in a shallow basin. Stem, long, moderately stout, in a shallow cavity. Growth, vigorous, upright; fertility very good. Leaf, long oval, upfolded, down hanging, shallow serrate. Origin, found in a wood at Valeuil (Dordogne), about 1810, by M. Monchallard. According to a writer in the *Revue Horticole* (1863, 179), the fruit was first named Monsallard. A very delicious early fruit, now rather overlooked.

NAPOLEON. *Her. Pom.*, II., 38. (Medaille, Liart, etc.) Dessert, October to November, large 3 by 3¼, pyriform. Skin, smooth. Colour, yellowish-green with numerous russet dots and russet patches around eye and stem. Flesh, white, fine grained, a little gritty, extraordinarily juicy, sweet, and briskly flavoured. Eye, closed in a very deep narrow basin. Stem, short and stout in a rather deep and irregular cavity. Growth, moderate; fertility good. Leaf, rather large, little upfolded, down curved, turns orange red, falls early. Origin, raised by M. Liart, a gardener at Mons, in 1808. The tree was purchased by l'Abbe Duquesne for 33 francs, and by him named Napoleon. There is a pear also named Napoleon III., equally distinct as were the two Emperors. Its numerous synonyms, such as Roi de Rome, Gloire de l'Empereur and Captif de St. Helene, tell their story of Imperial ambitions and their result. A valuable fruit, hardly strong enough on Quince for most soils.

NEC PLUS MEURIS. *Her. Pom.*, II., 68. Dessert February to March, small, 2 by 2, round oval, very uneven. Skin, a little rough. Colour, greenish yellow nearly covered with rough brown russet and occasionally with a slight brown-red flush. Flesh, pale yellow, melting and deliciously perfumed. Eye, large open in a small basin. Stem, very short and stout, continued. Growth, upright; fertility excellent. Origin, this pear is not the Nec Plus Meuris of France, or Van Mons, which is our Beurré d'Anjou. The figure in the Herefordshire Pomona is correct but the origin given is wrong. I have not been able to find the correct name of this variety, and it is very probably French or Belgian.

NOUVEAU POITEAU. *Her. Pom.*, II., 55. G. Neue Poiteau. (Retour de Rome, Choix de l'Amateur.) Dessert, November, rather large, 3¾ by 4, oval pyriform, uneven. Skin, rough. Colour, pale greenish yellow, nearly covered with reddish russet and slight flush. Flesh, white, slightly green under the skin, very melting, sweet and quite first class. Eye, closed or slightly open, rather small, in a large uneven basin. Stem, stout, rather long, generally at an angle. Growth, upright spreading, making an angle of 45°; fertility good. Leaf, rather large, slightly upfolded, regularly and finely crenate. Origin, raised by Van Mons and first fruited in 1843. It was dedicated to the great pomologist Poiteau, but as there already existed a variety bearing this name the adjective was added.

NOUVELLE FULVIE. *Fl. and Pom.*, 1863, 64. G. Neue Fulvie. (Fulvie Gregoire, Belle de Jarnac.) Dessert, November to December, 2½ by 3½, pyriform, a little uneven. Skin smooth, covered with fine cinnamon russet. Colour, golden brown, Flesh, pale yellow, very juicy, a little firm, moderately good flavour. Eye, open in a wide, shallow, slightly ribbed basin. Stem, rather long, generally at an angle, continued. Growth, rather spreading, branches arching; fertility good. Leaf, small, narrow, upfolded, very finely crenate, light green, turning bright orange, falling rather early. Origin, raised by M. Gregoire Nelis, of

Joidoigne, Belgium, in 1854. A useful fruit, keeping sometimes till January. It makes a good cordon, but requires a wall in the North.

OIGNON. Culinary, October, medium, 3 by 3, flattened round, inclining to Bergamotte shape. Skin, rough. Colour, dull yellow, almost covered with patches of rough russet. Flesh, coarse grained, breaking, suitable only for cooking. Eye, large, open in a shallow basin. Stem, long and woody in a deep cavity. Growth, extremely vigorous; fertility extraordinary. Leaf, large, round, held flat, irregularly serrate. Origin, uncertain. It is described by André Leroy only so far as I have discovered. It may be, as he suggests, the Oignon d'Eté de Bretagne, mentioned by Le Lectier in 1628. This is grown for market purposes around Maidstone, and is perhaps the most fertile pear grown, branches breaking down through the weight of the fruit. In growth and leaf it is very distinct.

OLIVIER DE SERRES. *Her. Pom.*, II., 40. Dessert, February to April, medium, 2¼ by 2½, round much flattened, apple-like, uneven. Skin, rough. Colour, olive green, covered with rough russet. Flesh, white, half melting, with a brisk musky flavour. Eye, a little open in a deep basin. Stem, medium, stout, woody, in a deep cavity. Growth, rather weak and dwarf; fertility irregular. Leaf, long, narrow, much upfolded, neatly and markedly serrate, turns yellow-brown, occasionally a little red. Origin, raised by M. Boisbunel of Rouen from a seed of Forunée d'Angers, first fruited in 1861. It was named after Olivier de Serres the great French Agronome whose " *Théatre d'Agriculture* " was first published in 1600 and to whose birthplace Arthur Young made a pious pilgrimage. One of the best of late varieties deserving a wall to bring it to perfection. The illustration in the *Herefordshire Pomona* shows the fruit too yellow in colour. It is more greenish brown in reality.

Orpheline d'Enghien : *see Beurré d'Arenberg.*

191

PASSE COLMAR. *Verger* I., 59. G., Regentin. Dessert, medium, 2½ by 3½, pyriform, nearly even. Pale green, smooth, changing to pale yellow, often with thin russet patches and dots. Flesh, yellowish-white, melting, sweet and perfumed, extremely juicy. Eye, open in a fairly deep basin. Stem, medium, stiff and woody, inserted on level or in a slight cavity. Growth, moderate, a little spreading, leaves small, oval, held out on a long pedicel, regularly serrate. Origin, raised by the Abbé Hardenpont at Mons about 1760. There are several Pears named Passe Colmar, with and without a distinguishing adjective, Santa Claus being one (*q.v.*). This, however, is the variety described by Leroy and long known under this name in England.

PASSE CRASANNE. *Verger,* I., 38. G. Edel Crasanne. Dessert, March to April, large 3 by 3½, round oval, uneven and bossed on surface. Skin, rough. Colour, dull yellow brown, almost covered with rough russet Flesh, pale yellow-white, fine grained, very sweet and juicy, nearly first class. Eye, large closed, in a wide uneven basin. Stem, medium, stout and woody, in a narrow cavity. Growth, compact and bushy; fertility fair. Leaf, large, elliptical, tapering equally to each end, upfolded, undulating, hanging very late, almost entire, turning pale yellow. Origin, raised by M. Boisbunel, of Rouen, and first fruited in 1855. Makes a dense bushy tree, well spurred. A very fine fruit when well grown and ripened. A good wall with plenty of water during the growing season are desirable.

PETITE MARGUERITE. *Lauche,* II., 87. G. Kleine Margarethe. Dessert, end August, 2½ by 2, flat conical, uneven. Skin, fairly smooth. Colour, greenish yellow brown, red flush and broad stripes. Flesh, soft, a little mealy, pale, flavour very good, extremely juicy. Eye, nearly closed in a shallow basin. Stem, short and stout in a slight cavity. Growth, moderate, rather upright; fertility remarkable. Leaf, rather large, long oval, finely but irregularly serrate, turning orange red. Origin, raised by André Leroy at Angers about 1862. A very valuable early fruit, making an excellent standard and ripening just before Williams.

Phillipe Goes : *see Baronne de Mello.*

Piquery : *see Urbaniste.*

PITMASTON DUCHESS. *Her. Pom.*, I., 13. F. Williams' Duchess. G. Pitmaston's Herzogin. Exhibition or dessert, October to November, very large, $3\frac{1}{4}$ by $4\frac{1}{4}$, long pyriform. Skin, slightly rough. Colour, pale yellow, marbled with brown russet, especially around the stem. Flesh, pale yellow melting, very juicy and pleasantly flavoured in a good season. Eye, open in a rather deep basin. Stem, long and woody, generally at an angle. Growth, upright spreading, very strong, making a good open tree ; fertility good. Leaf, very large, round oval, dark, held nearly flat, irregularly serrate, turns dark red. Origin, raised by Mr. Williams, of Pitmaston about 1865, from Duchess d'Angoulême × Glou Morceau. A very popular fruit though decried by some, but of good quality when well finished. The figure referred to is rather smaller than the average.

Poire d'Esperen : *see Bergamotte d'Esperen.*

Poire de Juillet : *see Doyenné d'Eté.*

Poire de Pentecote : *see Easter Beurré.*

PRESIDENT BARABE. Dessert, till March, rather small, $2\frac{1}{4}$ by 3, round conical, uneven. Skin, rough. Colour, dull greenish yellow russet. Flesh, white, half melting, little acid with a delicious flavour. Eye, open almost on level. Stem, rather stout, fleshy, in a slight cavity. Growth, upright, but weak and apt to weep when older ; fertility moderate. Leaf, rather small, narrow oval, sharply pointed, undulating, finely serrate or entire, turns dull brown, falls early. Origin, raised by M. Sannier, of Rouen, from a seed of Bergamotte Esperen; first fruited in 1870. Introduced in 1877. This is a useful late variety, the flavour being more refreshing than most pears of its season.

PRESIDENT D'OSMONVILLE. Dessert, October, medium, oval tapering to stem, much bossed. Skin, rough. Colour, yellow, with russet veins expecially round stem. Flesh, white, melting, a little gritty, flavour very good, slightly musky. Eye, closed in a shallow wrinkled basin. Stem, rather long and thin. Growth, very strong, rather straggling; fertility moderate. Leaf, very large, round, little undulating, very boldly curved serrate, turns yellow brown, falls early. Origin, obtained in 1834 by Leon Leclerc, at Laval, and named after the President of the Horticultural Society of Mayenne.

PRESIDENT DROUARD. *Bull d'Arb*, 1886, 11. Dessert, till March, medium, 3½ by 4½, oblong pyriform, uneven. Skin, rough. Colour, palest yellow green, thickly covered with russet dots. Flesh, fine grained, white, very melting, sweet, richly perfumed. Eye, open in a rather deep even basin. Stem, rather short, stout, and woody in a slight irregular cavity. Growth, vigorous, upright; fertility good. Leaf, oval, upfolded, sharply serrate. Origin, raised by M. Olivier-Perroquet, from a seed of B. Napoleon in 1885. This pear is grown for market in France. Its chief fault is a slight tendency to scab.

PRINCESS. Dessert, November to December, medium, 2½ by 4, long conical, even. Skin, smooth, pale yellow with red brown flush, much like Louise Bonne, Flesh, melting and juicy sweet and refreshing. Leaf, almost exactly like Louise Bonne. Growth, upright, pyramidal. Raised by Messrs. Rivers from a seed of Louise Bonne. A good and free cropping pear.

Princess de Parme : *see Marie Louise.*

RAMILIES. Culinary, December to February, large, 3 by 3¼, oval pyriform, uneven. Skin, rough. Colour, yellow green with conspicuous russet dots and patches. Flesh, white, very firm, dry in texture. Eye, open in a small uneven basin. Stem, stout and fleshy at the end of the fruit. Growth, vigorous, straggling; fertility good. Leaf, rather large, held flat, little undulating, finely serrate. Origin, I have been unable to find the origin of this pear. It has a most unpleasant flavour when cooked and quite unworthy of cultivation.

Red Achan : *see Achan.*

Retour de Rome : *see Nouveau Poiteau.*

ROOSEVELT. Exhibition and dessert, October to November, very large, 3¾ by 4, oval, even. Skin, very smooth. Colour, pale creamy yellow, with brilliant red flush and conspicuous dots. Flesh, white, little breaking, juicy, flavour moderately good to good according to season. Eye, open in a shallow, slightly uneven basin. Stem, stout, rather long, fleshy in a slightly uneven cavity. Growth, stout and compact, upright; fertility very good. Leaf, medium, long, oval, sharply serrate. Origin, introduced by Messrs. Baltet, of Troyes, France, about 1906. This is one of the largest pears grown, and though I have not found the fruit of more than fair quality, I am told that in some districts it is considered better than this.

ROUSE LENCH. *Her. Pom.,* II., 51. (Rousse Lench.) Dessert, January to February, rather large, 2½ by 3¼, long oval, uneven. Skin, a little rough. Colour, pale yellow green with thin russet nearly covering fruit, but ground colour shows through in patches. Flesh, pale yellow, a little firm, juicy, of fair flavour. Eye, open in a shallow basin, around which are several bosses. Stem, very long, woody, generally curved and inserted without depression. Growth, moderate, rather drooping when aged; fertility extreme. Leaf, medium, oval, upfolded, down hanging, deeply serrate.

195

Origin, raised by T. A. Knight, and named after the estate of Rouse Lench, near Evesham, then occupied by Sir W. Rouse Broughton, his son-in-law. It first fruited in 1820. A fruit of moderate merit, not coming up to Hogg's description in my experience.

Rousse Lench : *see Rouse Lench.*

ROUSSELET DE RHEIMS. *Verger*, II., 64. G. Rousselet von Rheims. (Giroflé.) Culinary or dessert, September, small, 2 by 2½, oval conical, even. Skin, smooth. Colour, greenish yellow with brown red flush and conspicuous dots. Flesh, yellowish white, half melting, juicy with distinct flavour, common to the Rousselets. Eye, large, open on level. Stem, long and slender, woody, inserted at apex of fruit. Growth, good, making a good standard : fertility excellent. Origin, a very old variety which was mentioned by Le Lectier in 1628. It is occasionally found in old orchards in this country. The Gros Rousselet is often grown also under the name " de Rheims," but is quite a distinct variety. An excellent cooking pear and quite acceptable for dessert uses.

ST. GERMAIN. *Decaisne*, IV., 4. Culinary, December to January, medium, 4 by 3, long conical or calebasse, uneven, one side rather swollen. Skin, smooth. Colour, grass green changing to pale greenish yellow, covered with minute russet dots and a little russet round stem Flesh, whitish, fairly fine grained, extra juicy, very richly perfumed. Eye, open in a very shallow basin. Stem, 1 in., woody, generally at an angle, on surface. Growth, vigorous, hardy ; fertility moderate. Leaf, long oval, a little upfolded, finely serrate, held up. Origin, this was found growing wild in the banks of the river Fare at St. Germain-d'Arca, and was known to writers in the seventeenth century. This pear has been somewhat abused, but when grown on light soil it is of good quality and still worth trying.

St. Michel : *see Doyenné Blanc.*

ST. SWITHIN. Dessert, July to August, medium, pyriform. Skin, smooth, pale green, almost covered with fine russet and fairly red on one side. Flesh, greenish white, melting, sweet and refreshing. Eye, closed in a very shallow basin. Stem, stout, one inch long. A nice fruit, valued for its earliness, but there are better at this season. Raised by Messrs. Rivers from a seed of Calebasse Tougard, and introduced before 1884.

SANGUINOLE. *Her. Pom.*, II., 34. (De Sauge, Grenarde.) Culinary, August to September, small, 2 by 1¾, round conical, even. Skin, rough. Colour, bronzed russet with slight red cheek. Flesh, firm, wine red, gritty, slightly sweet. Eye, wide open on a level. Stem, very long, slender, in a slight cavity. Growth, vigorous, little spreading; fertility great. Leaf, long oval, finely serrate, held nearly flat, undulating. Origin, this has been known for several centuries and is still occasionally met with in orchards of cider fruit. There are several varieties of pears with this curious beetroot coloured flesh, of which drawings may be seen in Decaisne's " *Jardin Fruitier,*" vol. VI., plates 13 and 14.

SANTA CLAUS. Dessert, December, medium, conical, slightly pyriform, fairly even. Skin, slightly rough. Colour, dull brown red, practically covered with russet. Flesh, pale yellowish, melting, and deliciously flavoured. Eye, a little open in an even basin. Stem, long and slender, 1 in. to 1¼ in. Growth, vigorous, upright; fertility moderate. Leaf, large, broad oval, upfolded, down hanging, irregularly shallow serrate, turning rich claret red. Origin, this was introduced from France by Col. Brymer, of Dorchester, and is probably the French Passe Colmar, but not the Passe Colmar of Hardenpont. A very delicious fruit, which deserves the attention of all pear lovers.

SECKLE. *Her. Pom.*, I., 28. G. Seckle's Birne. Dessert, October to November, small, round oval, even. Skin, rough, Colour, dark brown red with conspicuous white dots. Flesh, yellow, tender, remarkably sweet and rich. Eye, open on a level. Stem, short and stout. Growth, rather upright, rather weak; fertility good. Leaf, medium, round, oval, sharply pointed, boldly curved serrate, turns crimson brown. Origin, found in a wood near Philadelphia by a trapper called Dutch Jacob, and named after Mr. Seckle, a later cultivator of the land on which it stood. Introduced to England in 1819. A most delicious fruit of the sweetmeat order and the favourite pear of Walt Whitman. It does best on Pear stock as it is a little too dwarfed on Quince.

SOLDAT LABOUREUR. *Her. Pom.*, I., 24. G. Blumenbach's Butterbirne. Dessert, November to December, medium, 3 by 3½, round pyriform, uneven. Colour, pale yellow, nearly covered with cinnamon russet in patches and dots. Flesh, pale yellow slightly melting, very juicy and vinous, a little gritty. Eye, open on a level. Stem, short and stout in a very slight uneven cavity. Growth, strong, inclined to be upright; fertility excellent. Leaf, long oval; upfolded, widely serrate. Origin, the first seedling raised by Major Esperen (about 1820) and named by him in reference to his career. An excellent fruit much cultivated on the Continent, deserving more attention in this country.

SOUVENIR DE CONGRES. *Her. Pom.*, I., 28. Dessert, September, large, calebasse form much flattened at eye, rather uneven. Colour, bright yellow, with scarlet cheek and cinnamon striped russet. Flesh, yellowish, tender, very sweet, musky flavour. Eye, open in a rather deep uneven basin. Stem, rather long, stout. Growth, upright spreading, spurring well, rather compact; fertility good. Leaf, large, roundish oval, dark green, upfolded, neatly and regularly crenate, turns fine crimson red. Origin, raised by M. Morel, a nurseryman of Lyon-Vaise, France, and first fruited in 1863. A very valuable fruit for autumnal use. The figure in the *Herefordshire Pomona* is rather too small.

SUCREE DE MONTLUCON. *Decaisne*, VI., 27. G. Susse von Montluçon. (Sucrée Vert.) Dessert,

October, medium, 3 by 3¾, oval conical, uneven. Skin, smooth. Colour, lemon yellow, very rarely russeted in patches. Flesh, palest yellow, transparent, extremly juicy and well flavoured. Eye, large and closed in a narrow shallow basin. Stem, medium, rather stout and woody. Growth, vigorous and hardy; fertility good. Leaf, rather large, upfolded, very neatly serrate. Origin, found in a hedge at Montluçon, France about 1812, by M. Rochet. A very delicious fruit, worthy of cultivation.

Sucrée Vert : *see Sucreé de Montluçon.*

SUMMER BEURRE D'ARENBERG. *Her. Pom.,* I., 26. F. Beurré d'Arenberg d'Eté. Dessert, September, rather small, 2 by 2¼, short conical, even. Skin, rough. Colour, pale green with thin russet. Flesh, yellow, very melting and juicy, richly flavoured. Eye, open in a rather deep basin. Stem, long, rather slender, inserted obliquely, curved. Growth, upright spreading; fertility good. Leaf, flat, roundish, finely serrate. Origin, raised by Mr. Rivers and first fruited in 1863. It makes a weak tree on Quince, and should be on pear or double grafted.

Summer Doyenné : *see Doyenné d'Eté.*

SUMMER ROSE. *Lind. Pom. Brit.,* III., 102. F. Caillot Rosa. G. Duhamel's Rosenbirne. (Caillot Rosat, Epine Rose.) Dessert, August, small to medium, 2¼ by 2, flattened round quite apple-like, even. Skin, a little rough. Colour, pale yellow, nearly covered with a strong red flush and large conspicuous dots. Flesh, white, crisp, juicy and sweet, always rather gritty. Eye, open in a shallow basin. Stem, long and woody in a deep and uneven cavity. Growth, very strong; fertility great. Leaf, oval, nearly flat, coarsely shallow serrate. Origin, a very old fruit, quite possibly the " Cailleau " mentioned in the " Roman de la Rose " of Jehan de Meung (1310).

The name Cailleau is said to be derived from (a) the stony concretions of the fruit, (b) the quail-like spottings of the fruit. This is the Caillot Rosat of France, but our English variety is quite distinct.

SWAN'S EGG. *Her. Pom.*, II., 34. F. Oeuf de Cygne. G. Schwaner Eierbirne. Dessert, October, small, 2¼ by 2¼, round, a little conical. Skin, rough. Colour, greenish yellow almost covered with thick brown russet, occasionally with dull brown flush. Flesh, white, rather firm, fairly juicy and a little musky. Eye, open almost on surface. Stem, very long and slender, woody. Growth, slender, very upright ; fertility great. Leaf, fairly large, oval, almost entire. Origin, this has been known for some years, and was first described by Batty Langley in 1729.

THOMPSON'S. *Her. Pom.*, II., 34. G. Die Thompsons. (Van Mons, Vlesembeek.) Dessert, October to November, fairly large, 3½ by 4, oval pyriform, very uneven and bossed. Skin, rough. Colour, pale golden yellow with much russet marbling. Flesh, white, very melting and buttery, very delicious. Eye, open in a fairly deep basin. Stem, short, and stout, generally with a fleshy fold at insertion. Growth, upright spreading ; fertility moderate. Leaf, narrow oval, little undulating, sharply serrate, turns pale claret red. Origin, raised by Van Mons and sent to England about 1820 without a name. Sabine, then secretary of the Royal Horticultural Society, named it after Robert Thompson, then fruit foreman at Chiswick. This delicious fruit should be in all collections and worthily commemorates the name of our greatest pomologist. It does best on the pear stock.

De Tongre : *see Durondeau.*

TRIOMPHE DE JODOIGNE. *Her. Pom.*, I., 22. Dessert, December to January, large, 3½ by 4, oval pyriform, tapering markedly to stem, uneven. Skin, smooth. Colour, clear green changing to lemon yellow, marbled with russet. Flesh, white, half melting, very juicy and sweet, sometimes a little astringent. Eye, small, open, in a shallow bossed basin. Stem, long, stout and woody, on level. Growth, vigorous, straggling; fertility good. Leaf, large, oval, nearly flat, undulating, almost entire. Origin, raised by Simon Bouvier, of Joidoigne, in 1830, first fruited in 1843. Rather a variable fruit; in some soils it is quite good.

TRIOMPHE DE VIENNE. Dessert, September, medium, 3½ by 2½, pyriform oval, uneven. Skin, smooth. Flesh, nearly white, melting, very juicy and of delicate flavour. Eye, open in a shallow basin. Stem, 1½ in., surrounded by stronger russet. Growth, moderate on Quince; fertility very good. Leaf, medium rounded oval, entire or faintly crenate, turns brilliant crimson red. Origin, raised by M. Collaud, gardener at Montagnon, in 1864, and put into commerce by M. Claude Blanchet, of Vienne, France. A valuable fruit which will be appreciated by those who find Williams too strongly scented. A little gritty; it is rather weak on Quince, and does best on pear for most soils.

URBANISTE. *Her. Pom.*, II., 48. F. des Urbanistes. G. Colomas Herbst Butterbirne. (Piquery, Beurré Drapiez, Coloma, etc.) Dessert, October, medium, 2¾ by 3½, roundish oval, variable, even. Skin, smooth, almost greasy. Colour, bright, yellow, dotted and marbled with greyish russet. Flesh, white, fine grained, very melting and buttery, very juicy and of an agreeable sub-acid perfumed flavour. Eye, open in a shallow basin. Stem, short and stout, often fleshy. Growth, moderate at first, later becoming quite vigorous; fertility good. Leaf, oval, upfolded, nearly entire. Origin, unknown. An excellent fruit not much grown now. It has submitted as Leroy says, to many "surprenant baptêmes," and has a long list of synonyms. It does well on Quince. Urbaniste Seedling is a distinct variety.

UVEDALES ST. GERMAIN. *Her. Pom.*, I., 15.
F. Belle Angevine. (Belle Angevine.) Culinary, till
March, enormous, 3¼ by 5½, very long, pyriform or calebasse, uneven. Skin, smooth. Colour, grass green
changing to pale yellow, covered with sharp black
dots and a ring of russet around eye. Flesh, white
firm, gritty. Eye, closed, much twisted, surrounded by
uneven bosses. Stem, very long and stout, fleshy,
inserted at end of fruit with a few uneven bosses around
it. Growth, extra vigorous; fertility moderate. Leaf,
large, pointed oval, upfolded, pale, regularly and finely
serrate, turns deep crimson. Origin, uncertain. It was
named Belle Angevine by M. Audusson, a nurseryman
at Angers, about 1820, but it is probably much older.
It was named after Dr. Uvedale, who lived at Enfield about
1690. Belle Angevine is therefore a later name. Too
gritty for stewing and quite valueless for any purpose
except to "epater les bourgeois." As Leroy says,
" elle paie de mine, voila tout ! "

Van Mons : *see Thompson's.*

VAN MONS LEON LE CLERC. *Fl. and Pom.*,
1866, 89. G. Van Mons Butterbirne. Dessert, end
October to November, large, 3¼ by 4¼, oval, slightly
pyriform, even. Skin, smooth, becoming almost greasy
when ripe. Colour, straw yellow, with many touches
of grey russet specially marked around stem. Flesh,
greenish white, fine melting, very juicy, with delicious
Bergamot flavour. Eye, small open almost on level.
Stem, medium, fairly stout, level with surface. Growth,
upright, slightly spreading; fertility moderate. Leaf,
long oval, pale, nearly flat, turns pinkish orange. Origin,
raised at Laval before 1828, by M. Leon le Clerc, and
dedicated to Van Mons. It is rather delicate on Quince,
and is best double grafted. It often keeps till nearly
Christmas in colder situations, but should be gathered
fairly early and very carefully handled.

VERULAM. (Black Beurré.) Culinary, till March,
fairly large, 3 by 3¼, round conical, uneven. Skin,

rough, entirely covered with yellowish brown russet. Flesh, greenish white, coarse, and slightly sweet, turning a fine red when cooked. Stem, stout and woody, 1 in. long. Eye, open, almost on level with surface. Fertility good. Leaf fairly large, oval and faintly serrate. Origin, there are so many conflicting accounts, of the origin of this fruit that I cannot feel sure of the exact history. A rather inferior fruit, seldom better than cooking quality.

VICAR OF WINKFIELD. *Her. Pom.*, II., 66. F. Curé. G. Pastorenbirn. Culinary, December to January, very large, 3¾ by 4½, long calebasse, uneven. Skin, smooth. Colour, grass green fading to pale yellow. Flesh, pale yellow, rather firm, dry and woolly. Eye, large and clove like, wide open in a shallow narrow basin. Stem, long and woody, generally inserted at an angle. Growth, very vigorous; fertility good. Leaf, round, sharply pointed, a little uncupped, held out, regularly and finely serrate. Origin, discovered in a wood near Villiers-en-Brenne, France, about 1760, by M. Leroy, curé of the parish. It was introduced to England by the Rev. W. L. Rham, of Winkfield, Berkshire, to which circumstance it owes its English name. This variety grows very vigorously and makes a good standard or pyramid. Some authors have stated that in a warm year it attains dessert quality but I have not found this so.

Vlesembeek : *see Thompson's.*

White Doyenné : *see Doyenné Blanc.*

Wiehelmine : *see Beurré d'Amanlis.*

WILLIAMS BON CHRETIEN. *Her. Pom.*, I., 9. G. Williams Christbirn. (Bartlett.) Dessert, September, fairly large, 3¾ by 4½, oval pyriform, uneven. Skin, nearly smooth. Colour, golden yellow with russet dots and marbling and faint red stripes. Flesh, white, transparent, very juicy and sweet, with a strong musky flavour. Eye, open, in shallow irregular basin. Stem, short, rather stout, generally at an angle. Growth, moderate; fertility good. Leaf, medium, round, finely and regularly serrate, hangs late, turns rich crimson red. Origin, raised by a schoolmaster named Stair, of Aldermaston, about 1770. In that county it is still called "Stair's Pear." It took its name "Williams" from its distributor, a nurseryman of Turnham Green; on its introduction to America it was again named after its importer, Mr. Bartlett. This is quite the best of early Pears, and should be gathered when still green and ripened in the fruit-room. The musky flavour is less pronounced when grown on a North wall. It makes a good standard.

WINDSOR. F. Madame. G. Windsor Birn. (Halle-mine.) Dessert, August, medium, 2½ by 3¼, oval pyriform. Skin, very smooth, Colour, palest lemon yellow. Flesh, crisp, white, slightly acid, no particular flavour. Eye, open on level with prominent ribs around. Stem, long, fairly stout, inserted without depression. Growth, vigorous; fertility good. Leaf, large, round, held flat, sharply serrate. Origin, according to Leroy this was raised by an amateur in Holland from a seed of the Bonne Chretien d'Eté, not far from the village of Hallemine. First described by Knoop in 1771, under the name Hallum Bonne. This is often called Cuisse Madame in England, but in error. It makes a large, upright standard, but keeps for so short a period that it is not worth growing.

Winter Achan : *see Achan.*

WINTER NELIS. *Her. Pom.*, II., 38. F. Nelis d'Hiver. G. Coloma d'Hiver. (Bonne de Malines.) Dessert, November to January, medium, 2½ by 2½, round conical, a little uneven. Skin, rough. Colour, greenish yellow nearly covered with thin dark brown russet, increasing round eye. Flesh, greenish white, transparent, very juicy and sweet, delicately perfumed. Eye, open in a shallow even basin. Stem, rather long, woody in a narrow uneven cavity. Growth, weak; fertility good. Leaf, rather small, narrow oval, held flat, shallow serrate or entire. Origin, raised at Malines by Jean Charles Nelis, and imported into this country in 1818. This is one of the most valuable winter pears. It ripens slowly and successively, but is ready to be eaten before the green has changed much. It is best grafted on pear, and makes a nice standard.

WINTER WINDSOR. Culinary, November, medium 2¼ by 3, conical pyriform, even. Skin, smooth. Colour, greenish yellow with light red brown flush. Flesh, white, firm, tasteless. Eye, open in a very wide shallow basin. Stem, 1 in., fleshy at insertion, continued. Growth, vigorous; fertility very good. Leaf, long oval, held down, nearly flat, shallow serrate. Origin, an old English variety mentioned by Parkinson. Hogg gives Petworth as a synonym, but Parkinson enumerates this separately. Quite worthless, as it rapidly rots at the core in November.

ZEPHIRIN GREGOIRE. *Her. Pom.*, II., 38. G. Zephirin Butterbirn. Dessert, November to January, small, 2¼ by 2¼, round conical. Skin smooth. Colour, green fading to pale yellow green with irregular patches of fine cinnamon russet and numerous small dots. Flesh, pale yellow, very tender, flavour very sweet and highly perfumed. Eye, rather small, open in a shallow even basin. Stem, rather short, very stout and woody, on level. Growth, very dwarf; fertility good. Leaf, rather small, round oval, upfolded, undulated, generally entire, turns dark claret red. Origin, raised by M. Gregoire at Joidoigne, supposedly from seeds of Passe Colmar. First fruited in 1843. This valuable fruit shares with Josephine de Malines the quality of keeping over a long season in the fruit room and is one of the most reliable of its season. It should be worked on pear.

Vivish & Baker, Printers, Maidstone.

Lightning Source UK Ltd.
Milton Keynes UK
172123UK00005B/51/P